Improving Patient Safety

Improving Patient Safety
Tools and Strategies for Quality Improvement

Edited by
Raghav Govindarajan, MD
Harleen Kaur, MD
Anudeep Yelam, MD

Routledge
Taylor & Francis Group

A PRODUCTIVITY PRESS BOOK

First edition published in 2019
by Routledge/Productivity Press
605 Third Avenue, New York, NY 10017
4 Park Square, Milton Park, Abingdon, Oxon OX14 4RN

First issued in paperback 2022

© 2019 by Taylor & Francis Group, LLC
Routledge/Productivity Press is an imprint of Taylor & Francis Group, an Informa business

No claim to original U.S. Government works

ISBN 13: 978-1-03-247577-6 (pbk)
ISBN 13: 978-1-4987-8502-0 (hbk)

Publisher's Note
The publisher has gone to great lengths to ensure the quality of this reprint but points out that some imperfections in the original copies may be apparent.

Visit the Taylor & Francis Web site at
http://www.taylorandfrancis.com

and the Productivity Press site at
www.ProductivityPress.com

Contents

Preface

Medical errors are considered as one of the major factors affecting patient safety in the healthcare system. They are the eighth leading cause of mortality in the United States, resulting in approximately 44,000 preventable deaths annually. Nearly one in five Americans reports having experienced medical errors of some kind affecting them or their family members. These rising numbers show that medical errors are a growing epidemic in the United States.

With this book, we aim to draw the attention of the readers on some of the common medical errors and patient safety/quality improvement issues faced in the healthcare system today through clinically relevant, vignette-based descriptions of patient safety issues. The vignettes are derived from the editor's (Raghav Govindarajan's) own experience as a clinician, educator, and administrator.

Each chapter highlights a particular aspect of patient safety in a nonpunitive, non-accusatory tone along with a brief review of pertinent literature. The spectrum of medical errors discussed in this book includes system-based errors, diagnostic errors, errors due to communication failure, and physician-related errors. Further, each chapter provides a comprehensive, clinically relevant review of literature with easy-to-understand tables, flowcharts, and figures.

This book also serves as an outline for medical schools, nursing schools, medical residencies, and any other educational courses to develop their own patient safety and quality improvement curriculum.

While the book is written with the intention of educating healthcare providers and any personnel who are involved in patient care either directly or indirectly (of all stages and at all levels), the clinical vignettes and material discussed in the book will be a great read even for the general audience and will provide an insight into some of the pressing issues affecting our healthcare system today.

Editors

Raghav Govindarajan, MD, is a board-certified neurologist and neuro-muscular physician with a deep and personal interest in patient safety and medical errors. He was a victim of a medication error which caused long-term complications affecting his liver, consequences he still faces today. With this personal experience as well as that of his patients, he has a strong passion for patient safety with particular interest in avoiding communication errors.

He is currently an assistant professor and an associate clerkship director of neurology at the University of Missouri, Columbia. In his current position, he has close interaction with medical students and residents with whom he constantly shares patient safety stories and lessons learned from it.

Dr. Govindarajan has a strong background in teaching, having won ten teaching and mentorship awards. He has also been awarded the "Golden Doc" award by the Arnold P. Gold Foundation for providing compassionate and patient-centered care, in addition to the compassionate care award by the Schwartz Foundation. He is the founding member and advisor of Gold Humanism Honor Society at the University of Missouri.

Dr. Govindarajan has strong leadership experience, having been elected as president-elect of his county medical society, and serves as the director of Clinical Quality Improvement and Outcomes, physician leader of the Clinical Quality Improvement Workgroup, and physician leader of the committee.

He is the author of numerous articles and case reports in peer-reviewed journals.

Harleen Kaur, MD, is a clinical researcher in the Department of Neurology at the University of Missouri, Columbia. She has a strong passion for patient safety and quality improvement which was triggered after experiencing a personal tragic event that affected the care of one of her loved ones.

In addition to multiple publications and presentations, she has a strong passion for patient-centered care.

Anudeep Yelam, MD, is a clinical researcher in the Department of Neurology at the University of Missouri, Columbia. He has a significant experience in working as a volunteer physician in multiple rural hospitals providing care to the underserved population. This experience in rural medicine has prompted his interest in developing system-based care and use of technology to improve the quality of care in rural settings.

List of Contributors

Ahmer Asif
University of Missouri
Columbia, Missouri

Emily Bailey
Truman State University
Kirksville, Missouri

Tripti Chopade
University of Missouri
Columbia, Missouri

Nakul Katyal
University of Missouri
Columbia, Missouri

Danish Kherani
University of Missouri
Columbia, Missouri

Nidhi Shankar Kikkeri
University of Missouri
Columbia, Missouri

Keerthana K. Kumar
University of Missouri
Columbia, Missouri

Sireesha Murala
NTR University of Health Science
Vijayawada, Andhra Pradesh,
    India

Shivaraj Nagalli
Yuma Regional Medical Center
Yuma, Arizona

Laura Qi
University of Missouri
Columbia, Missouri

Suganiya Srikanthan
Saint James School of Medicine
University of Toronto
Toronto, Ontario

Chapter 1

Introduction to Patient Safety and Medical Errors

Nakul Katyal
University of Missouri

Introduction

Patient safety and healthcare-related errors have now become an important healthcare issue worldwide. In recent years, there have been improvements in regard to improving the patient safety, and many quantifiable problems have been addressed such as medication errors, healthcare-associated infections, and postsurgical complications. Comparatively, diagnostic errors have received less attention, even though landmark patient safety studies have consistently found that diagnostic errors are widely prevalent. Many recent studies have reported on the incidence, scope, and cost of adverse events related to healthcare errors. In a Harvard Medical Practice Study, diagnostic errors accounted for 17% of preventable errors in hospitalized patients. In a medical chart review of 30,121 patients admitted to 51 acute care hospitals in New York State, in 1984, Brennan et al. reported that preventable adverse events occurred in 3.7% of admissions. Medication errors and adverse drug events have been extensively investigated because they are both relevant and preventable. In a study carried out by Bates et al. in two teaching hospitals in Boston, 1% of the events were noted to be fatal, 12% were life-threatening, 30% were serious, and 57% were significant. Of the adverse events, 42% classified as life-threatening or serious were preventable. The medication errors were associated with the use of analgesics, antibiotics, sedatives, chemotherapeutic agents, cardiovascular drugs, and anticoagulants.[1] In a 2004 review of 25 years of malpractice claims, diagnostic errors were the leading cause of a claim (28.6%) and resulted in the highest proportion of total payments (35.2%). Further, diagnostic errors more often resulted in death than other causes (40.9% versus 23.9%) and were responsible for payments of US$38.8 billion.

Source of Errors in Healthcare

The literature identified two broad sources of error: human error and systemic error. Human error is further divided into random/personal error and systematic error. Random errors are those isolated personal errors that cannot be explained by underlying causes, external forces, or preceding events, and are due to personal behavior in a particular situation. Systematic errors, on the other hand, are those human errors that are not isolated but occur regularly due to some underlying undetected causes such as software or transfer errors. Figure 1.1 shows the sources and causes of errors in healthcare.[2]

Types of Medical Errors

The most widely used classification in regards to medical errors is by the Institute of Medicine (IOM). Table 1.1 represents different types of medical errors as per the IOM approach.

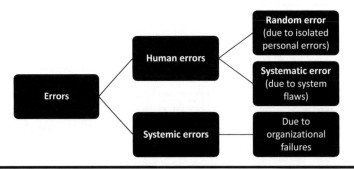

Figure 1.1   Sources and causes of errors in healthcare.

Table 1.1   Type of Medical Errors Following IOM Approach

Diagnostic
Error or delay in diagnosis Failure to employ indicated tests Use of outmoded test or therapy Failure to act on results of monitoring or testing
Treatment
Errors in the performance of a procedure or a test Errors in administering treatment Error in the dose or method of using a drug Avoidable delay in the treatment Inappropriate care
Preventive
Failure to provide prophylactic treatment Inadequate monitoring or follow-up of a treatment
Others
Failure of communication Equipment failure Other system failures

Terminologies in Patient Safety

The Hospital Survey on Patient Safety Culture, released in November 2004, was designed to assess hospital staff opinions about patient safety issues, medical errors, and event reporting. The survey includes 42 items that measure 12 areas, or composites, of patient safety culture.[3] Each of the 12 patient safety culture composites is listed and defined in Table 1.2.

Healthcare Statistics

The first comparative database report, released in 2007, included data from 382 U.S. hospitals. The survey was designed to assess hospital staff opinions about patient safety issues, medical errors, and event reporting. The survey also included two questions that ask respondents to provide an overall grade on patient safety for their work area/unit and to indicate the number of events they reported over the past 12 months. The 2016 user comparative database report included data from 680 hospitals and 447,584 hospital staff

Table 1.2   Patient Safety Culture Composites and Definitions

Patient Safety Culture Composites	Definitions
1. Communication openness	Staff can freely voice their opinion if they see something that may negatively affect patient care and should be able to question those with more authority freely.
2. Feedback and communication about error	Staff are informed about errors that happen, are given feedback about changes implemented, and discuss the ways to prevent errors from happening again.
3. Frequency of events reported	A log of errors/events should be recorded and categorized as follows: • Mistakes caught and corrected before affecting the patient • Mistakes with no potential to harm the patient • Mistakes that could harm the patient but do not
4. Handoffs and transitions	Important patient care information should be made available across the hospital units and during shift changes.
5. Management support for patient safety	Hospital management should provide a work environment that promotes patient safety and shows that patient safety is a top priority.
6. Nonpunitive response to error	Staff should feel that their mistakes and event reports are not held against them and that mistakes are not kept in their personnel file.
7. Organizational learning—continuous improvement	Mistakes have led to positive changes, and changes are evaluated for effectiveness.
8. Overall perceptions of patient safety	Procedures and systems are good at preventing errors, and there is a lack of patient safety problems.
9. Staffing	There should be enough staff to handle the workload, and work hours are appropriate to provide the best care for patients.
10. Supervisor/manager expectations and actions promoting safety	Supervisors/managers consider staff suggestions for improving patient safety, praise staff for following patient safety procedures, and do not overlook patient safety problems.

(Continued)

Table 1.2 (*Continued*)   Patient Safety Culture Composites and Definitions

Patient Safety Culture Composites	Definitions
11. Teamwork across units	Hospital units cooperate and coordinate with one another to provide the best care for patients.
12. Teamwork within units	Staff support each other, treat each other with respect, and work together as a team.

respondents. The average hospital response rate was 55%, with an average of 658 completed surveys per hospital.[3]

Table 1.3 shows the average percent positive response for each of the 12 patient safety culture composites across hospitals in the 2016 database.

The areas of strength or the composites with the highest average percent positive responses were as follows: teamwork within units (82% positive), supervisor/manager expectations and actions promoting patient safety (78% positive), and organizational learning—continuous improvement (73% positive).

Table 1.3   Composite-Level Average Percent Positive Response—2016 Database Hospitals

Patient Safety Composites	Positive Response (%)
Teamwork within units	82
Supervisor/manager expectations and actions promoting safety	78
Organizational learning—continuous improvement	73
Management support for patient safety	72
Feedback and communication about error	68
Frequency of events reported	67
Overall perceptions of patient safety	66
Communication openness	64
Teamwork across units	61
Staffing	54
Handoffs and transitions	48
Nonpunitive response to error	45

The areas with potential for improvement or the composites with the lowest average percent positive responses were as follows: nonpunitive response to error (45% positive), handoffs and transitions (48% positive), and staffing (54% positive).

References

1. La Pietra, L., et al., Medical errors and clinical risk management: State of the art. *Acta Otorhinolaryngol Ital*, 2005. **25**(6): pp. 339–346.
2. Maamoun, J., An introduction to patient safety. *J Med Imaging Radiat Sci*, 2009. **40**(3): pp. 123–133.
3. Study. Available at: www.ahrq.gov/professionals/quality-patient-safety/index.html. Accessed on July 25, 2018.

Chapter 2

Developing an Outline for Patient Safety Curriculum

Nakul Katyal
University of Missouri

ACGME Standards for Quality Improvement and Patient Safety Curriculum

The past decade has seen remarkable changes in healthcare system with an extensive focus on the need for quality improvement and patient safety (QI/PS).[1] This focus has resulted in the introduction of newer innovations in QI/PS education among U.S. medical schools and teaching hospitals. Resident participation is critical in quality improvement projects as they have the firsthand knowledge of the areas that need improvement.[1] Moreover, educational quality improvement projects can teach them core improvement and implementation skills.[1] In 2014, Accreditation Council for Graduate Medical Education (ACGME) introduced guidelines for all accredited institutions on resident involvement in quality and safety improvement.[1] As per the ACGME institutional standards, accredited institutions must provide opportunities to residents and fellows on QI/PS (Table 2.1).[1]

The ACGME has proposed different models for resident involvement in quality improvement projects (Table 2.2).[1]

The ACGME has defined core competencies in QI/PS that serve as basic curricular and assessment building blocks.[2]

Table 2.1 ACGME Standards for Patient Safety and Quality Improvement

Patient Safety	Quality Improvement
• Residents are required to report errors, adverse events, unsafe conditions, and near misses in a protected manner that is free from reprisal. • Residents must contribute to interprofessional root cause analysis and other similar risk reduction strategies.	• Residents must receive training on usage of data to improve the system of care, reduce healthcare disparities, and improve patient outcomes. • Residents must participate in interprofessional QI initiatives.

Table 2.2 Model for Resident Involvement in Quality Improvement Projects

Bottom-Up	Top-Down	Emerging Hybrid Models
• Resident identifies an area of weakness. • Often done as an elective. • Limitations include scope, scale, and time constraints.	• Residents are involved in working institutional quality improvement projects. • Limitations include time constraints.	• Longitudinal involvement of residents in institutional quality improvement projects. • Sequential group projects allow more time for implementation and tracking.

■ **Patient care:** It is compassionate, appropriate, and effective for the treatment of health problems and the promotion of health.

■ **Medical knowledge:** This includes knowledge about established and evolving biomedical, clinical, and cognate (e.g., epidemiological and social–behavioral) sciences and the application of this knowledge to patient care.

■ **Practice-based learning and improvement:** This involves investigation and evaluation of their own patient care, appraisal and assimilation of scientific evidence, and improvements in patient care.

■ **Interpersonal and communication skills:** This results in effective information exchange and teaming with patients, their families, and other health professionals.

■ **Professionalism:** It is manifested through a commitment to carrying out professional responsibilities, adherence to ethical principles, and sensitivity to a diverse patient population.

■ **Systems-based practice:** It is manifested by actions that demonstrate an awareness of and responsiveness to the larger context and system of healthcare, and the ability to effectively call on system resources to provide care that is of optimal value.

The Association of American Medical Colleges (AAMC) issued a special report on integrating quality improvement and patient safety across the Continuum of Medical Education with a goal to ensure that every medical school and teaching hospital in the United States has access to a critical mass of faculty that are ready, able, and willing to engage in, role model, and lead education in QI/PS and in the reduction of excess healthcare costs.[2] This report proposed three core recommendations with several sub-recommendations (Table 2.3).[2]

Table 2.3   AAMC Core Recommendations and Sub-Recommendations

Recommendation 1	Sub-Recommendations
In order to achieve QI/PS goals for education and practice, the medical schools, teaching hospitals, accreditation bodies, examination organizations, and specialty bodies should ensure the integration of QI/PS concepts into meaningful learning experiences across the continuum of physician professional development and the summative evaluations used for professional certification and licensure.	1.1 It is essential that education and clinical leaders integrate QI/PS concepts and competencies into meaningful educational experiences across the continuum of physician professional development. 1.2 As they create learning experiences and assess QI/PS competencies, medical education leaders should partner with other health professions. 1.3 State, regional, and national accrediting licensing and (re)certifying bodies need to align their requirements for QI/PS across the continuum of physician professional development from undergraduate to continuing medical education. 1.4 The application of QI/PS competency assessment that measures across the continuum of physician professional development is necessary for the purposes of formative and summative feedback. 1.5 In order to assess progress toward the achievement of QI/PS competencies, national examination bodies should incorporate QI/PS elements into summative evaluations and provide feedback to both individual learners and educational programs.

(Continued)

Table 2.3 (*Continued*)   AAMC Core Recommendations and Sub-Recommendations

Recommendation 2	Sub-Recommendations
In order to improve the processes and outcomes of care, medical schools and teaching hospitals should expect all clinical faculty to be proficient in QI/PS competencies and be able to identify, develop, and support a critical mass of faculty as expert educators to create, implement, and evaluate training and education in QI/PS for students, residents, and colleagues.	2.1 Given the size and scope of the need to train faculty in QI/PS, the collaboration of national organizations with interest in this area is essential to the successful achievement of the vision and goal articulated in this report. 2.2 In accordance with the importance of improving healthcare quality and patient safety, faculty should be recognized for their clinical, educational, and scholarly contributions in QI/PS, in concert with other institutional policies and guidelines regarding promotion and tenure.
Recommendation 3	**Sub-Recommendations**
Academic and clinical leadership should share a common commitment to QI/PS and demonstrate a concrete alignment of the academic and clinical enterprises in a manner that produces excellent health outcomes valued by healthcare professionals and the public.	3.1 To achieve sustained improvements in care, it is critical to align and coordinate the efforts of senior clinical and educational leaders. 3.2 By ensuring the necessary infrastructure and resources, clinical and academic leaders can create a future in which QI/PS supports the clinical education and research missions of medical schools and teaching hospitals. 3.3 In order to develop and assess the effect of appropriate educational interventions, it is necessary for educators to have access to clinical data, moderated by Health Insurance Portability and Accountability Act (HIPAA) concerns and other confidentiality protections. 3.4 To augment current efforts to recognize clinical achievements in QI/PS, national bodies should establish criteria by which individuals and institutions can be recognized for QI/PS efforts in education and research.

Table 2.4 Outline of Patient Safety Curriculum Meeting ACGME Standards for QI/PS

Knowledge	Skill	Attitude	Evaluation
Understand system errors, human factors engineering, communication issues, diagnostic errors, and electronic medical record	Understand Plan, Do, Study, Act (PDSA), fishbone diagram, root cause analysis	Understand the culture of patient safety	Capstone project evaluation

The six aims of quality in healthcare (safe, timely, efficient, effective, equitable, and patient centered) present core concepts to be incorporated by all physicians across the continuum of learning, from the beginning of undergraduate training to the final phase of a career in medicine.[3] For this to occur, QI/PS must be seen as a key component of the scientific foundations of medicine. Like other competencies, successful performance in QI/PS demands proficiency in four major parameters: skill, knowledge, attitude, and evaluation.

■ **Knowledge:** Learners must know how to evaluate, synthesize, and incorporate the data, reports, and anecdotes that form the substrate upon which improvement activities occur.
■ **Skill:** Learners must understand the context in which the medical care is delivered, analyze processes to identify sensitive levers for change, work with appropriate partners to implement change, and assess if their strategies have been successful.
■ **Attitude:** Learners need to be able to communicate the results of their work to broaden the impact and increase institutional learning.
■ **Evaluation:** Evaluation is necessary to identify the key elements of QI/PS performance and to provide accurate global assessments (Table 2.4).

References

1. Philibert I, Weiss K, Rey DG. Research and Quality Improvement Skills for Residents—Implications for CLER. Clinical Learning Environment Review. *AAMC Webinar* March 24, 2014.

2. Headrick LA, Baron RB, Pingleton SK, Skeff KM, Sklar DP, Varkey P, et al. Teaching for Quality—Integrating Quality Improvement and Patient Safety Across the Continuum of Medical Education: Report of an Expert Panel. Association of American Medical Colleges. January 2013.

3. Committee of Quality of Care in America, Institute of Medicine. *Crossing the Quality Chasm: A New Health System for the 21st Century.* Washington, DC: National Academy Press. 2001.

Chapter 3

Understanding System Errors

Traditionally medicine has treated errors as failings of individuals due to a lack of knowledge or skill. System approach, by contrast, looks at the failings of individuals in the context of poorly designed systems. Such an approach helps in identifying the factors responsible for human errors and change/modify the underlying systems to reduce the occurrence of the same errors or minimize their impact on the patients.

In this chapter, we will explore and understand different types of system errors. We will also try to explain the different ways applied to reduce these errors using human factors engineering. We will further emphasize the communication issues, ways to develop culture of patient safety, and finally conclude with proper use of electronic medical records to improve patient safety.

Section 1: Human Factors Engineering

Clinical Vignette 1: Every Sound Alarms

Danish Kherani
University of Missouri

Clinical vignette discusses a case where alarm fatigue resulted in critical events being missed resulting in the death of a patient. We will also discuss human factors engineering (HFE) and its relevance to medical errors and the role of alarms in the hospital setting.

THE CASE

Elsa is a 55-year-old woman with a past history of diabetes, hypertension, and chronic kidney disease. She was admitted to the hospital for chest pain for the past 5 h. Electrocardiogram (EKG) along with cardiac troponins were ordered. EKG showed no evidence of significant ischemia, but troponins were slightly elevated. She was admitted to the floor for observation and was placed on a cardiac monitor and was being managed as having a non-ST segment elevation myocardial infarction.

Overnight, the patient's cardiac monitor kept constantly alarming with warnings of "low voltage" and "ventricular fibrillation." The nurse initially responded to these alarms; she checked on her continuously whenever the alarms went off and found her well. The resident physician was also paged about the alarms, who came and checked on the patient only to find her sleeping well. The nurse and the resident felt that the alarms were misreading, and so they silenced all the telemetry alarms.

The next morning when the nurse went to perform morning vitals, the patient was found to be unresponsive and cold with no palpable pulse. Code blue was called, and the team began to perform cardiopulmonary resuscitation. Despite the resuscitative efforts, the patient could not be revived. The cause of death was unclear but was thought that she might have likely had a fatal arrhythmia after the monitors were disconnected.

COMMENTS

In the abovementioned vignette, silencing all telemetry alarms led to the patient's death. The patient in the vignette was at high risk for developing arrhythmias due to her underlying myocardial ischemia, which is evident by her elevations in cardiac biomarkers and her comorbidities such as diabetes, hypertension, and chronic kidney disease. Had the alarms not been turned off, the arrhythmia would have triggered an appropriate alert, and the patient would have survived. This case clearly demonstrates the hazards associated with hospital alarms. It also provides an opportunity to evaluate and understand why such harms exist and how to mitigate them.

Healthcare professionals find the constant notifications bothersome and tend to silence or completely disable them. Warnings have been issued about deaths due to silencing alarms on patient monitoring devices. Moreover, several federal agencies and national organizations have disseminated alerts about alarm fatigue.

DISCUSSION

The purpose of clinical alarms is to enhance patient safety by alerting the healthcare providers and staff to deviations from a predetermined normal status. The alarms alert clinicians when

1. A patient's condition is deteriorating or
2. When a device is faulty.

By design, alarms are highly sensitive so that they do not miss an important event. However, this high sensitivity is achieved at the expense of specificity. Various devices, including beds, infusion pumps, cardiac monitors, ventilators, mechanical vital sign machines, sequential compression stockings, and many others, have audible alarms competing for caregivers' attention. Unless designed properly to alert the clinicians to only important details, these could distract and frustrate the caregivers and sometimes may put patients at risk.

ALARM FATIGUE

Alarm fatigue is defined in the literature as the desensitization of a clinician to an alarm stimulus that results from sensory overload causing the response of an alarm to be delayed or missed.[1] It can lead to clinician's environmental distractions and also interferes with the ability of a caregiver to perform critical patient care responsibilities resulting in patient safety issues. It has become a critical problem that The Joint Commission (TJC) issued a sentinel event alert on alarms in April 2013[2] and made alarm management a National Patient Safety Goal starting in 2014. The Emergency Care Research Institute, an independent nonprofit organization that addresses patient safety, has also named alarm hazards as number one of the "Top 10 Health Technology Hazards" for both 2012 and 2013.[3,4]

The development of alarm fatigue is not surprising—in a study by Drew et al., there were nearly 190 audible alarms each day for each patient.[5] If only 10% of these were true alarms, then the nurse would be responding to more than 170 audible false alarms each day, more than 7 per hour. Consequently, rather than alerting that something is wrong, the alerts become a "background noise" that clinicians perceive as part of their typical working environment. As a result, caregivers become desensitized and simply tend to ignore the alarms.

PREVALENCE AND SEVERITY OF ALARM FATIGUE

Alarm fatigue is a national problem.[3,4,6] From 2005 through 2008, the U.S. Food and Drug Administration Manufacturer and User Facility Device Experience (MAUDE) database received 566 reports of patient deaths related to monitoring device alarms. A 4-month review of the MAUDE database between March 1, 2010, and June 30, 2010, revealed 73 alarm-related deaths with 33 attributed to physiologic monitors.[7] Due to these concerning findings, studies related to alarm fatigue are crucial; when the phenomenon is evidenced, attention is directed to alarm-related problems, and data are provided for minimizing these problems during the intensive care unit routines.[7]

CAUSES AND CONTRIBUTING FACTORS TO ALARM FATIGUE

In its sentinel event alert, TJC identified the following factors that contributed to alarm fatigue[2]:

- Alarm parameter thresholds set too tight
- Alarm settings not adjusted to the individual patient
- Poor EKG electrode practices resulting in frequent false signals
- The inability of staff to hear alarms or detect where an alert is coming from

- Inadequate staff training on monitors and alarms
- Inadequate staff response to alarms
- Malfunctioning alarms

HFE TO DEAL WITH THE PROBLEM OF ALARM FATIGUE

HFE is the study of how humans interact with each other, with equipment, and with the environment. It complements existing patient safety efforts by specifically taking into consideration that, as humans, frontline staff will inevitably make mistakes. Therefore, the systems with which they interact should be designed for the anticipation and mitigation of human errors. The goal of HFE is to optimize the interaction of humans with their work environment and technical equipment to maximize safety and efficiency. Special safeguards include usability testing, standardization of processes, and use of checklists and forcing functions.[8] The HFE process is described in Table 1 below.

Table 1   HFE Process

Concept phase	Perform studies and analyses
Design input	Develop requirements
Design output	Develop specifications
Verification	Test output against input
Validation	Test against patient and user need

To improve patient safety, it is necessary to understand the human condition, why we make mistakes, and the steps that an organization can take to change the conditions under which people make mistakes. First, there needs to be an acknowledgment of the issue from senior leadership in the organization with the result that it is seen as a priority and appropriate resources allocated.

Second, a system approach involving a multidisciplinary team that is representative of senior leadership, clinical nurse specialists, biomedical personnel, information technology specialists, physicians, and quality and risk management specialists is required to develop and implement a strategy that is effective and evidence based. The team is responsible for investigating the current alarm management status in monitored units throughout the organization and examining the technology that may need to be reconfigured as part of the overall alarm fatigue reduction strategy.

There are several ways to help diminish the din of alarms throughout the hospital, improve patient safety, and boost clinician satisfaction (Table 2):

Table 2   Ways to Reduce the Noise of Alarms

Ways to Reduce the Noise of Alarms	*Comments*
Monitoring the equipment	• Cleaning, replacing the parts, and ensuring that the unit is working as desired • Establishing a routine to inspect, clean, and maintain the equipment. This helps to reduce the alerts due to technical malfunctions • Timely replacement of aging monitors with newer available technology. This ensures that the sounding alarm is a clinically relevant one.
Decreasing clinically irrelevant alerts	For example, changing the monitor's thresholds from "warning" to "crisis." It meant that the alert was clinically consequential and significantly needed attention, prompting nurses to react to any
Funnel alerts to the right people	By bypassing the nurse station and notifying the alerts to the right on-duty clinicians preferred device (pager, smartphone, etc.)
Triage alerts with a software	Triaging alarms using software by incorporating the facility's current priority levels and using a built-in logic to pass along the highest levels of alerts first
Silencing the noise	By tracking the events that are truly meaningful to staff and alerting intelligently with automated settings for events with lower acuity
Tailoring alerts to patient characteristics	Device parameters can be adjusted for individual patients depending on their specific condition
Stopping false alarms	"False alarm" refers to an instance when monitoring equipment indicates a physiologic event when no actual event occurs. Research shows that 85%–95% of alarms are false.[9–12]

About 85%–95%[9–12] of the alarms are false positives, which require no intervention. It is also important to understand that not all the alarms are false. Assuming so could lead to delay in response to deliver appropriate care, thus resulting in patient's harm and medicolegal issue.

It is vital to fix our alarm alert systems to achieve the highest levels of both sensitivity and specificity. The goal is to eliminate alarm fatigue and provide a safer healthcare environment. One way of addressing the alarm fatigue is by increasing the value of information of each alarm rather than adding more alarms. This can be achieved by decreasing the number of false and clinically irrelevant alarms. Ultimately, educating both the staff and the patients brings in successful changes and improves the quality of care.

REFERENCES

1. McCartney, P.R., Clinical alarm management. *MCN*, 2012. **37**(3): p. 202.
2. The Joint Commission, Sentinel Event Alert Issue 50: Medical Device Alarm Safety in Hospitals. 2013; Available from: www.joint-commission.org/sea_issue_50/.
3. Top 10 technology hazards for 2012. The risks that should be at the top of your prevention list. *Health Devices*, 2011. **40**(11): pp. 358–373.
4. Top 10 health technology hazards for 2013. *Health Devices*, 2012. **41**(11): pp. 342–365.
5. Drew, B.J., et al., Insights into the problem of alarm fatigue with physiologic monitor devices: A comprehensive observational study of consecutive intensive care unit patients. *PLoS One*, 2014. **9**(10): p. e110274.
6. Top 10 health technology hazards for 2014. *Health Devices*, 2013. **42**(11): pp. 354–380.
7. Cvach, M., Monitor alarm fatigue: An integrative review. *Biomedical Instrumentation Technology*, 2012. **46**(4): pp. 268–277.
8. Siewert, B. and M.G. Hochman, Improving safety through human factors engineering. *Radiographics*, 2015. **35**(6): pp. 1694–1705.
9. Atzema, C., et al., ALARMED: Adverse events in low-risk patients with chest pain receiving continuous electrocardiographic monitoring in the emergency department. A pilot study. *American Journal of Emergency Medicine*, 2006. **24**(1): pp. 62–67.
10. Lawless, S.T., Crying wolf: False alarms in a pediatric intensive care unit. *Critical Care Medicine*, 1994. **22**(6): pp. 981–985.
11. Siebig, S., et al., Intensive care unit alarms—How many do we need? *Critical Care Medicine*, 2010. **38**(2): pp. 451–456.
12. Tsien, C.L. and J.C. Fackler, Poor prognosis for existing monitors in the intensive care unit. *Critical Care Medicine*, 1997. **25**(4): pp. 614–619.

Clinical Vignette 2: Man and His Machine

Ahmer Asif
University of Missouri

Clinical vignette discusses medical complication arising from a faulty glucometer and subsequent complication whereby patient goes into a hypoglycemic coma. We will also discuss how human factors (HF) engineering (HFE) can be applied to reduce errors.

THE CASE

Ms. Tiffany, a 42-year-old female, was admitted to the hospital for the management of hypertension and chronic renal failure. She had a past medical history of Type-1 diabetes mellitus with associated nephropathy. On admission, she was started on insulin and orders were placed to repeat blood glucose finger stick testing four times a day. She was also put on labetalol for the control of her blood pressure. According to her electronic health record notes, the patient had a history of experiencing hypoglycemia when taking labetalol, so a note was added in the medical records to watch for any signs of hypoglycemia closely. She was doing fine on insulin administration and labetalol till the second day of her admission. The finger sticks were clearly documented by the nursing staff every 4 h, which were in normal range.

On the third day of admission, after the evening nursing shift change, a recently recruited nurse took over the charge and started monitoring the patient. The evening and night finger-stick glucose levels came out to be 102 and 127, and she administered the insulin accordingly. Two hours later, the patient was found to be unresponsive during which the nurse checked the blood glucose level and it was 97. Medical specialists were called to evaluate the patient and found her to be unresponsive with decerebrate posturing, right gaze deviation, and a questionable seizure activity. They suspected hypoglycemic coma and asked the nurse to repeat the blood glucose level again with a different glucometer, and it came out to be 34 this time, pointing toward a faulty glucometer being used for previous readings. The patient was immediately intubated and stabilized. She was then transferred to the medical intensive care unit where she remained comatose for over a week. Over the following 2-month period, she had a gradual recovery but continued to have difficulty with writing names and identifying objects. After a week, she was discharged to a rehabilitation facility for intensive neurological therapy.

COMMENTS

This clinical scenario explains a *medical error* in the shape of a faulty glucometer resulting in the development of a severe clinical complication in a patient otherwise stable enough to get discharged from the hospital. If the glucometer was calibrated and had undergone validity testing before use, this patient would have avoided the hypoglycemic coma leading to a disability. It also emphasizes on the fact that medical equipment needs to be improved and standardized in order to prevent the unexpected patient sufferings. We can do this by engaging the HFE during the design of medical devices/equipment to make them more user adherent, cost-effective, and practically safe.

DISCUSSION

Medical error is an inadvertent act (of either commission or omission) or one that does not achieve its envisioned outcome.[1] It is the failure of a planned action to be completed as anticipated (an error of execution), the use of an erroneous plan to achieve an objective (an error of planning),[2] or a deviation from the process of care that may or may not cause harm to the patient.[3] Patient harm from medical error can occur at the individual or system level. While many errors are nonconsequential, an error can end the life of someone with a long-life probability or fast-track an imminent death, something quite similar to what we discussed in the aforementioned clinical vignette due to a faulty glucometer. The nomenclature of errors is mounting to better categorize preventable factors and events.[4] They are a staid problem of public health and a leading cause of death in the United States. It is a difficult problem as it is thought provoking to reveal a consistent cause of errors and, even if found, to provide a consistent viable explanation that minimizes the chances of a recurrent event. By recognizing unfortunate events occur, learning from them, and working toward preventing them, patient safety can be improved.[5] There are two major types of errors:

1. Errors of commission occur because of the wrong action taken. Examples include administering a medicine to which a patient has a known allergy or checking the blood sugar level with a faulty glucometer with the patient developing hypoglycemic coma consequently.
2. Errors of omission occur because of actions not taken. Examples are not strapping a patient while sitting in a wheelchair or not stabilizing a stretcher prior to patient transfer.

The field of HFE, also called ergonomics, is the discipline that attempts to identify and address these medical errors. Its goal is to optimize the relationship between humans and systems.[6] The field takes into account human strengths and limitations in the design of interactive systems that involve people, tools, and technology, and work environments to ensure protection, efficiency, and ease of use. HF engineers' job is to study a peculiar activity in terms of its component tasks and then assess the physical/skill demands, psychological workload, team dynamics, features of the work setting, and device design required to complete the task optimally. They work on real human beings at control and try to design systems that improve safety and minimalize the risk of error in complex environments. Generally focusing on the human–machine interface, HF engineers have developed safety analysis tools and solutions in many complex systems including commercial airplanes and nuclear power plants.

ORIGIN OF HFE

HFE in medical informatics is apprehensive about the collaboration between humans and new technology. Roots of HFE can be found in the 1970s and 1980s when concerns about the safe use of intricate technology became apparent in industrial environments and aviation. How systems can be used safely depends upon the understanding of the interaction between humans and computers.[7] This is the point where human cognition comes into play and that cognitive psychology can provide a conceptual framework for a safe methodology in the development of systems. Some historical major disasters proved to be excellent cases to study the complex interplay between humans and technology. Perrow et al., in his analysis of the Three Mile Island nuclear power plant accident, in 1981, described that "normal" accidents are intrinsic to complex systems, and that they arise from its characteristics and cannot be prevented at times.[8]

Then, Weick et al. reiterated the same arguments in 1990, in a study of the 1977 Tenerife air disaster where two wide-body airplanes collided on the runway but emphasized that close consideration to human behavior can help alleviate such events.[9] Perrow especially stressed on the fact that humans have to operate in such complex environments to prevent these mishaps. He even makes a case that in order to reduce the risk of "normal" accidents, complicated technologies should be avoided as much as possible. From their studies, four strategies to reduce risks of accidents arise:

a. The first strategy is the better design of technology, especially of those parts that interact with people, such as displays, monitors, gauges, and handles.
b. The second is better workplace design that should be primarily focused on routine tasks in order to free attention for difficult ones and exceptional or unexpected events.
c. The third is to introduce guidelines and protocols for tasks that need to be executed, for example, by means of checklists that are common in aviation.
d. The fourth strategy is to design and execute educational programs for users to improve their performance. How effective such strategies are, especially education, remains open for debate.

WHY DO WE NEED HFE?

Medical equipment, devices, and computer systems when designed accurately and safely have the prospect to improve patient care and to make the practice of medicine more effective. It requires user-oriented system designs, which employ recognized usability testing methods. By doing so, these systems will have more anticipatable human–computer interaction properties and will help medical practitioners to practice safer and more effective healthcare. Furthermore, healthcare organizations are progressively implementing electronic systems. These are also being encouraged by governments such as the United States as they perceive the electronification of healthcare as a way to monitor the practice, institute pay for performance, and create more value for their healthcare dollars spent. All of these advantages rely solely on systems that need to be error-free, that fit into the workflow of healthcare, and that proficiently assist the increasingly busy clinicians trying to provide the very best care for their patients.

CLASSIFICATION OF HF METHODS

HF methods as discussed in multiple books[10,11] can be classified into six different methods, which are as follows:

1. General methods (e.g., direct surveillance of work)
2. Assortment of information about people (e.g., physical measurement of anthropometric proportions)
3. Analysis and design (e.g., task analysis, time study)
4. Assessment of human–machine system performance (e.g., usability, performance measures, error analysis, accident reporting)
5. Organization and implementation of ergonomics (e.g., participative methods)
6. Evaluation of demands on people (e.g., psychological workload)

This demonstrates how diverse HF methods are that we can use to sort out multiple patient safety problems. Here we discussed the selected HF methods to evaluate faulty equipment, devices, and processes.

ERRORS AND RISKS ASSOCIATED WITH THE USE OF EQUIPMENT AND PROCESSES

With the use of HFE, it is documented that overlooked concerns in equipment design can lead to substantial safety hazards.[12] This can apply to large pieces of equipment or smaller devices. The most important fact that compounds the potential risk is that the operator typically assumes that the technology itself is trustworthy. Risks can also be increased when the guidelines or instructions are poor, the equipment design itself is deceptive or perplexing, or a device can be used for multiple, potentially contradictory actions.

To address usability problems with equipment or devices, we need to first identify the problems. To find out these problems in an efficient and reliable manner, experience from all users—across a division and across an institution—must be assembled and reviewed. The shared database can help facilitate the recognition of usability problems. Operators should be educated and encouraged to enter usability issues into the shared database.[13] In order to avoid missing important equipment-related inaccuracies that may pose a safety hazard to patients, the database should be checked repeatedly by employees who are responsible for a case review.

TENETS OF ERGONOMICS/HFE

These tenets illustrate what HFE uses as a base for beliefs (rather than the usual consideration of data alone) and how HFE goes about the change process.[14] In other words, they show what principles HF engineers follow while solving a patient safety problem. As such, they provide prescriptions of the generic interventions possible using HFE in any domain, including medical error and faulty devices. Table 1 presents the list of those tenets.[15]

EVALUATION OF TECHNOLOGIES USING HF

Technology is considered the driving force behind improvements in healthcare and when you look at the rate of change and recent innovations, many find it hard not to agree with that observation. Digital innovations have now made it possible for consumers to use portable devices to access their medical information, monitor their vital signs, take tests at home, and carry out a wide range of tasks. Technologies are introduced and presented as solutions to improve patient safety and prevent medical errors.[16] They can lead to enhancements in the patient safety only if they are designed, instigated, and used according to HF and systems engineering principles.[12,17]

The HF process in the medical device field takes a very risk-centric approach, generally referred to as a "prevention through design" strategy. The principal objective is to design out the characteristics of a system or device that could lead to human error. The HF process generally includes four primary phases: (1) preliminary analysis, (2) design modification and formative evaluation, (3) validation testing, and (4) implementation stage.

1. **Preliminary analysis:** The preliminary analysis starts prior to the design of the device or equipment. It is sought to better understand who the users are, what their needs are, what kind of setting they use the device in, what specific tasks they need to achieve, what their curbs are, and a risk analysis of those

Table 1   Tenets of Ergonomics/HFE

Assumptions

1. Mismatch of task demands to human capabilities gives rise to errors and stress.
2. In any complex system, initiate with human needs and system needs and assign functions to meet these needs.
3. Honor thy user: use different models and measurements to provide the detailed technical understanding of how people interact with systems.
4. It is usually preferable to change the system to fit the operator than changing the operator to fit the system. At least develop employees' criteria and training systems in parallel with the equipment, environment, and interface.
5. Design for a range of operators rather than an average; accommodate those beyond the design range by custom modifications to equipment.
6. Operators are typically trying to do a good job within the limitations of their equipment, environment, instructions, and interfaces. When errors occur, look beyond the operator for root causes.

Change Principles

1. Begin design with an analysis of the system and human needs using function and task analysis.
2. Use the task analyses to discover potential as well as existing human/system mismatches.
3. Operators have an essential role in designing their own jobs and equipment and are capable of contributing to the design process on equal terms with professional designers.
4. Optimize the job via equipment, environment, and procedure design before optimizing the operator through selection, placement, motivation, and training.
5. Use valid ergonomic techniques to measure human performance and well-being before and after the job change process.

Interventions

1. Prepare well for any technical change, especially at the organizational level.
2. Involve operators throughout the change process, even those in identical jobs and on other shifts.
3. Use teams comprising operators, managers, and HF engineers (at least) to implement the change process.

tasks as they are related to the device use. This phase also includes analysis of the user interface designs of the products already in use. The methodologies, study focus, and outcomes that occur during the preliminary analysis phase can help us to develop an early interface design.

2. **Design modification and formative evaluation (usability testing):** In this stage, multiple HF tools are available and can be used to ensure that technologies fit human characteristics and are usable.[18,19] It involves a full assessment of your device's interactive characteristics and measures project performance by objective means. The manufacturers and vendors of healthcare technologies are greatly using usability testing and evaluation methods. This phase of the process is accomplished via risk-based iterative usability testing. The main focus of this testing is on safety and usability of the product's design (Figure 1).

   A characteristic usability testing is relatively small which involves five to eight participants, where a researcher observes the actual users in a controlled environment. A set of task-based scenarios that are representative of real device use are formulated and the participants go through them. The researcher, on the other hand, observes each participant's

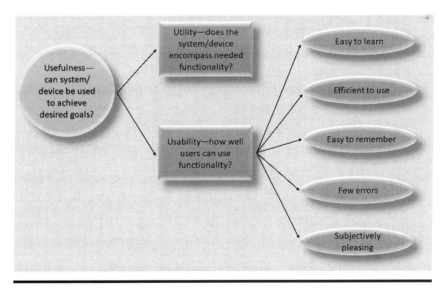

Figure 1 Some elements of usefulness. These depictions assist to accentuate the goals and challenges to the design of a well-formed system/device.

behavior as they are going through the tasks and records data on their interactions.[20,21] The data collected in the study are used to inform the next iteration of the design. Several of the early usability tests help us to reveal and improve multiple problems that the participants face during the testing.[22] They include a struggle with the data entry, navigation of the device, design faults in the home screen, and information retrieval tasks. Gosbee and Gosbee, in 2010, provided practical and comprehensive information about usability evaluation and testing at the stage of technology design.[23]

3. **Validation testing:** At the end of the development process and formative tests, an HFE validation test should be conducted to ascertain that the new technology is safe and effective for human use. The purpose of the validation study is to confirm whether representative users in the intended use environment could use the new technology safely and effectively or not. Study participants can include representative users, for example, healthcare providers or diabetic patients in our case, who are using multiple kinds of technologies in the past (e.g., glucometer). Participants are asked to perform a comprehensive, realistic set of basic and advanced task-based scenarios with the new technology. Data are collected via a software data log, participant journals, follow-up interviews, and video/audio tape recordings. The results can help us to mitigate potential errors and several events that occur using the new technology.

4. **Implementation stage:** After the design modification, usability, and validation testing, the next imperative step is the implementation of the new technology. For the anticipated future, the healthcare organizations will face pressures to implement technologies that have the potential to reduce medical errors and help the healthcare providers do their jobs better. It is indispensable to design technology implementation processes according to scientific principles if the patient safety potential of these technologies is to be realized.[24–26] Healthcare systems that ignore implementation design principles increase the risk that users (physicians, nurses, pharmacists) will discard the technologies that could ultimately make the patient safety better. Karsh et al., in 2004, highlighted the following principles for technology implementation to promote patient safety in his review of the literature[27]:

- Top management commitment to the change
- Responsibility and accountability structure for the change
- A structured approach to the change
- Training
- Pilot testing
- Communication
- Feedback
- Simulation
- End-user participation.

Once the new technology has been implemented, the job is not yet over. It is imperative to continue monitoring its use in the "real" context and to identify potential problems and work-arounds. These work-arounds may arise from a lack of fit between the context of use, the technology, and the representative user's task. Some of these interactions may not be foreseen at the stage of designing the technology and may be "visible" only after the technology is in use in the real context over a span of time. This emphasizes the need to adopt a "continuous" technology change approach that identifies problems associated with the technology's use.[26,28]

Engaging the HFE during the design of the medical devices has multiple benefits. Patient safety is the most important and useful benefit. This safety comes in the shape of decreased patient risk through a design that has been heavily tested with representative users in its envisioned use environment in order to extermi-nate design flaws. Another benefit of using the HFE for designing the medical devices may be representative user adherence. The evidence is there, indicating that a reduction in the complexity of medical devices may increase representative user adherence.[29,30] Reduced device complexity, in part, can be imitated from improved device usability. Ancillary benefits of a systematic HFE process may include reducing or eliminating the need for costly modification(s) after product launch, improving overall comfort of use (improved comfort of use is a byproduct of good HFE practices, not the sole outcome), reducing the probability of product recalls due to design imperfections, and enhancing the look and feel. Entire benefits resulting from the systematic implementation of a sound HFE process will converge to generate a medical product/ device that creates a patient experience that is safer, more efficient, and more satisfactory.

REFERENCES

1. Leape LL. Error in medicine. *JAMA*. 1994;272(23):1851–1857.
2. Reason J. *Human Error*. Cambridge: Cambridge University Press; 1990.
3. Reason J. Understanding adverse events: The human factor. In Vincent C, ed. *Clinical Risk Management: Enhancing Patient Safety*. London: BMJ Books; 2001, 9–30.
4. Grober ED, Bohnen JM. Defining medical error. *Canadian Journal of Surgery*. 2005;48(1):39–44.
5. Oyebode F. Clinical errors and medical negligence. *Medical Principles and Practice*. 2013;22(4):323–333.
6. Kantowitz BH, Sorkin RD. *Human Factors: Understanding People-System Relationships*. New York: Wiley; 1983.
7. Beuscart-Zéphir MC, Elkin P, Pelayo S, Beuscart R. The human factors engineering approach to biomedical informatics projects: State of the art, results, benefits and challenges. *Yearbook of Medical Informatics*. 2007;2(1):109–127.
8. Perrow C. Normal accident at three Mile Island. *Society*. 1981;18(5):17–26.
9. Weick KE. The vulnerable system: An analysis of the tenerife air disaster. *Journal of Management*. 1990;16(3):571–593.
10. Salas E, Wilson KA, Priest HA, Guthrie JW. Design, delivery, and evaluation of training systems. In: G. Salvendy, *Handbook of Human Factors and Ergonomics*, 3rd Edition. Hoboken: John Wiley & Sons, Inc.; 2006, 472–412.
11. Wilson JR, Corlett N. Methods in the understanding of human factors. *Evaluation of Human Work*, 3rd Edition. Boca Raton, FL: CRC Press; 2005, 16–46.
12. Salvendy G. *Handbook of Human Factors and Ergonomics*. Hoboken, NJ: John Wiley & Sons; 2012.
13. Kruskal JB, Yam CS, Sosna J, Hallett DT, Milliman YJ, Kressel HY. Implementation of online radiology quality assurance reporting system for performance improvement: Initial evaluation. *Radiology*. 2006;241(2):518–527.
14. Gawron VJ, Drury CG, Fairbanks RJ, Berger RC. Medical error and human factors engineering: Where are we now? *American Journal of Medical Quality*. 2006;21(1):57–67.
15. Drury CG. The ergonomics society the society's lecture 1996 ergonomics and the quality movement. *Ergonomics*. 1997;40(3):249–264.
16. Donaldson MS, Corrigan JM, Kohn LT. *To Err Is Human: Building a Safer Health System*. Washington, DC: National Academies Press; 2000.
17. Sage A, Rouse W, editors. *Handbook of Systems Engineering and Management*. New York: John Wiley & Sons; 1999.

18. Mayhew D. *The Usability Engineering Lifecycle*. San Francisco, CA: Morgan Kaufmann Publisher; 1999.
19. Nielsen J. *Usability Engineering*. Amsterdam: Morgan Kaufmann; 1993.
20. Albert W, Tullis T. *Measuring the User Experience: Collecting, Analyzing, and Presenting Usability Metrics*. Waltham, MA: Newnes; 2013.
21. Kuniavsky M. *Observing the User Experience: A Practitioner's Guide to User Research*. Waltham, MA: Elsevier; 2003.
22. Fairbanks RJ, Caplan S. Poor interface design and lack of usability testing facilitate medical error. *The Joint Commission Journal on Quality and Safety*. 2004;30(10):579–584.
23. Gosbee JW, Gosbee LL. *Using Human Factors Engineering to Improve Patient Safety*. Oakbrook Terrace, IL: Joint Commission Resources; 2010.
24. Korunka C, Carayon P. Continuous implementation of information technology: The development of an interview guide and a cross-national comparison of Austrian and American organizations. *Human Factors and Ergonomics in Manufacturing & Service Industries*. 1999;9(2):165–183.
25. Korunka C, Weiss A, Zauchner S. An interview study of 'continuous' implementations of information technology. *Behaviour & Information Technology*. 1997;16(1):3–16.
26. Weick KE, Quinn RE. Organizational change and development. *Annual Review of Psychology*. 1999;50(1):361–386.
27. Karsh B. Beyond usability: Designing effective technology implementation systems to promote patient safety. *BMJ Quality & Safety*. 2004;13(5):388–394.
28. Carayon P. Human factors of complex sociotechnical systems. *Applied Ergonomics*. 2006;37(4):525–535.
29. Rakow PL. Perspective on contact lenses. Increasing compliance by reducing complexity. *Journal of Ophthalmic Nursing & Technology*. 1994;13(5):244–245.
30. Rau JL. Determinants of patient adherence to an aerosol regimen. *Respiratory Care*. 2005;50(10):1346–1356; discussion 57–9.

Clinical Vignette 3: Expensive Gift

Anudeep Yelam
University of Missouri

Clinical vignette discusses how a patient's condition is missed due to an error in the sign-out board which was recently bought and installed at a huge expense. In addition, we will discuss ways to improve sign-out process using human factors engineering (HFE).

THE CASE

Jane is a 40-year-old woman with a known history of migraine. She was admitted to the inpatient neurology consult for an episode of headache for 2 days along with nausea and vomiting. Headache is 9/10 on pain assessment chart. She had six episodes of vomiting in the last 24 h. Her examination was unremarkable. She was apprehensive to the lights in the room and requested to dim them.

She was started on dihydroergotamine infusion and metoclopramide and have noticed a subjective improvement in her headache as well as nausea and vomiting 10 h after initiating the treatment. The resident signed out the patient to a night call resident and had updated him over the phone about her condition.

During the night, the patient alerted the nurse that she was having chest pain and bad headache. The resident was paged regarding her complaints who called the nurse and asked for her vitals while he was on his way to attend the patient. Her vitals were as follows:

Blood pressure	170/100 mmHg
Pulse	110 beats/min
Respiratory rate	15 breaths/min

The resident asked the nurse to stop the infusion immediately and ordered to start her on intravenous labetalol which controlled her blood pressure and chest pain. He reviewed the electronic health record and sign-out board that has been recently installed. It did not have any preexisting condition listed. On calling the resident who signed out the patient, he admitted that he forgot to mention that she had preexisting uncontrolled hypertension.

COMMENTS

This case provides an opportunity to discuss about the importance of sign-out process. Had the resident took enough time to discuss face to face with the incoming night shift resident about the patient instead of over the phone, the chance of missing the history of hypertension would have been less and the events leading to hypertensive urgency would have been prevented.

DISCUSSION

Communication problems between healthcare providers are the most common cause of death and preventable inhospital disability and death. Sign-out is the transfer of care from one set of healthcare providers to another. It includes transfer of information regarding patient's state and plan of care.[1]

Despite sign-outs being the most important component of care, most organizations and hospitals have an informal and unstructured process with no universal standardization. This could lead to miscommunication, treatment delays, prolonged hospital stays, and concern for patient safety. Joint Commission requires all healthcare providers to implement a standard approach to sign-out communications.[2] However, the evidence is lacking on to which interventions are effective.

It is essential to understand the barriers and the ways to overcome them for effective sign-out process.[1] We discuss briefly about them in Table 1.

HOW DOES HFE SOLVE THE SIGN-OUT PROCESS?

HFE focuses on the design and analysis of interactive systems that involve people, technical equipment, and work environment.[3] It takes into consideration that humans will inevitably make mistakes and that the systems with which they interact should be designed to help anticipate, mitigate, and counteract human errors.[3] HFE has long been used to improve patient safety in aviation and nuclear plants. It was first introduced to medicine in the 1980s in the practice of anesthesia which resulted in decline of injury and death in the operating room.[3]

HFE uses checklists as a solution to address the sign-out process. In one study, implementation of checklist was associated with a reduction in the rates of deaths and inpatient complications. The number of deaths was reduced to 1.5% versus 0.8% after the implementation of checklists. Inpatient complications were also

Table 1 Four Barriers and Ways to Overcome Them with Regard to the Sign-Out Process

Barriers in Sign-Out Process	
Physical setting	The environment in which sign-out process takes place is important. It has to be • Private—patient confidentiality should be respected. • Quiet—little to no background noise and fewer interruptions from the staff and patients. • Appropriate lighting with enough writing space to take notes.
Social setting	• This is important so that the healthcare providers involved in the patient care are comfortable about discussing the treatment options. • Sign-out process takes place between residents, attending physicians, residents of other disciplines, fellows, and nurses. Each has a high potential for reinforcing differences in status and power of those involved in handoffs.
Language barrier	• Only accepted abbreviations should be used in both written and verbal presentation. • Repeating verbal order entries ensures that the receiver has heard and understood the order and also allows for any corrections by the speaker.
Medium of communication	Direct communication (face-to-face) handoffs are preferred over mediated communications (email, phone, pager, electronic records). In-person handoffs allow for effective exchange of information and provide a better opportunity for any concerns or questions as they arise.

reduced to 7% from 11% in patients who underwent noncardiac surgeries.[4]

Checklists can be developed for any process that is repeatedly performed and for which accuracy is required, such as sign-out process.[3] It can improve team communication and consistency,

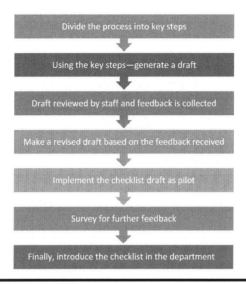

Figure 1 captions:

Figure 1   Steps to develop an effective checklist to improve patient safety.

and also ensures that the steps for the sign-out process are performed in the correct order as intended, thus ensuring no vital information is missed.[5]

The key steps in developing a checklist to improve patient safety are provided in (Figure 1).[3]

More studies are required to come up with the standardized guidelines of sign-out process. Till then, effective systems have to be put in place as to maximize the workflow and improve patient care.

Few guidelines to establish a safe and effective sign-out process are described in Table 2.[6]

Table 2   Ten Steps to Establish a Safe and Effective Sign-Out Process

Time	It is important to ensure ample time for adequate sign-out process. Each patient's sign-out process includes a discussion of a brief history of present illness, comorbidities, important events in the past 24 h, tasks for each patient, and plan of care.
Active	Signing out should be an active process. The person taking over should be able to ask for any questions they might have, and also, they should have a complete understanding and knowledge about each patient and task.

(Continued)

Table 2 (*Continued*)   Ten Steps to Establish a Safe and Effective Sign-Out Process

Sick	It is important to emphasize on sick patients with the management plan and threshold to transfer to a higher level of care clearly outlined. Residents on call should be encouraged to see sick patients before they can take care of other patients or tasks.
Senior	Know who is the senior resident or attending on call and contact them before beginning the call night.
One list	Make sure to use one standard list or form for each service with an emphasis on confidentiality and proper methods to dispose when finished.
Details	List should include date of admission, important medications, and general plan.
Outstanding tasks	Use an updated, accurate list of outstanding tasks to be performed and information that the on-call resident needs to gather outlined in bold.
Outstanding labs	Sign out all pending laboratory tests, studies, consults, and what the chief physician needs to be told.
Admissions	Any expected admissions should be explained to the on-call resident, making pertinent history and exact purpose for admission understood so that the on-call resident can fill out admission orders correctly and in a timely fashion once the patient arrives at the hospital.
Morning updates	The list should be updated in the morning and enough time is given for pre-rounds sign-out, emphasizing major events and patients whose course deviated from the expected.

REFERENCES

1. Solet, D.J., et al., Lost in translation: Challenges and opportunities in physician-to-physician communication during patient handoffs. *Acad Med*, 2005. **80**(12): pp. 1094–1099.
2. Handoffs and Signouts. Patient Safety Primer June 2017; Available from: https://psnet.ahrq.gov/primers/primer/9/handoffs-and-signouts.
3. Siewert, B. and M.G. Hochman, Improving safety through human factors engineering. *Radiographics*, 2015. **35**(6): pp. 1694–1705.

4. Haynes, A.B., et al., A surgical safety checklist to reduce morbidity and mortality in a global population. *N Engl J Med*, 2009. **360**(5): pp. 491–499.

5. Gawande, A., *The Checklist Manifesto: How to Get Things Right* (New York: Henry Holt and Company), 2009.

6. Kemp, C.D., et al., The top 10 list for a safe and effective sign-out. *Arch Surg*, 2008. **143**(10): pp. 1008–1010.

Section 2: Communication Issues

Clinical Vignette 1: Doctors Are from Mars and Nurses Are from Venus!

Tripti Chopade
University of Missouri

Clinical vignette discusses the communication failure between nurse and physician leading to severe allergic reaction to the patient. Various barriers leading to nurse–physician miscommunication and strategies to resolve this issue are discussed in detail.

THE CASE

SCENARIO 1: OUTPATIENT CLINIC OF ORANGE COUNTY COMMUNITY HOSPITAL

Mr. Smith, a 78-year-old Caucasian man with the medical history of hypertension and chronic bronchial asthma for the last 25 years, recently visited a very busy outpatient clinic of Dr. House, a primary care physician working in an overcrowded Orange County Community Hospital. Mr. Smith had recently moved to the town to live close to his daughter and had newly established outpatient care with Dr. House. During his visit, he complained of a recurrent nasal block, persistent nasal discharge progressively worsening since the last 4 months. His asthma was well controlled with budesonide inhaler and intermittent use of Albuterol nebulizer. His vitals were stable during the visit with blood pressure—142/90 mmHg, heart rate—76/min, and respiratory rate—24/min.

On thorough physical examination, Dr. House noticed bilateral nasal polyp formation. On chest auscultation, he heard mild wheezing and rhonchi, consistent with his history of chronic bronchial asthma. Correlating the history of chronic bronchial asthma with bilateral nasal polyps, Dr. House thought the possibility of aspirin sensitivity in Mr. Smith and enquired further about any allergy to aspirin or prior intake of aspirin. Dr. House did not have access to Mr. Smith's previous medical records yet. Mr. Smith denied any known drug allergies other than seasonal allergies, and he was unsure if he had ever taken aspirin-containing tablets before. He mentioned his increasing forgetfulness over the last couple of years. Dr. House decided to continue the same medications for his asthma, hypertension, and advised otolaryngology appointment for evaluation of nasal polyps and neurology appointment for his memory issues. He briefly added to his note about the possibility of aspirin sensitivity and cautioned Mr. Smith regarding avoidance of aspirin whenever possible due to a risk of exacerbation of asthma and severe allergic reactions. Dr. House's schedule was packed till evening, and he was stressed out with the overflow of patients in his clinic as usual. As he left to see his next patient thinking about Mr. Smith and his memory issues, he thought to tell his nurse to inform Mr. Smith's daughter regarding the cautious use of aspirin and wanted her to add the same in his medical record in the drug allergy section. The nurse, Ms. Black, was busy on phone answering to other patients. Dr. House was in rush and he couldn't wait as the next patient was already in the room. He quickly left a handwritten note on a table where the nurse, Ms. Black, sits. A few days later, Dr. House was having another hectic day in his office, his nurse, Ms. Black, received a call from daughter of Mr. Smith requesting her to confirm with Dr. House whether Mr. Smith can take over the counter pain medicine for his recent headaches as he doesn't want to visit doctor's office for such a trivial issue. Ms. Black, the nurse, who was aware of how busy Dr. House was that day and was intimidated to bother him as he always preferred not being bothered for trivial things whenever he is busy with patients. The nurse, Ms. Black, quickly pulled the medical record of Mr. Smith and confirmed whether Mr. Smith had any known allergies to any medication by double checking with a daughter who had no clue about any such allergies of her father. Mr. Smith's daughter mentioned the nurse about her concerns regarding her father's progressively worsening memory as he couldn't even tell the details of his last visit to her. Ms. Black, who was an experienced nurse working in the hospital for more than 15 years, thought that it was just a minor headache and Mr. Smith would feel better with any of the over-the-counter analgesic drug. She advised the same to Mr. Smith's daughter and asked her to visit the office if he won't feel any better or symptoms worsen. A few hours later, when Dr. House enquired the nurse about any phone calls for him, she told him that she had taken care of most of them. Dr. Smith moved ahead to see his next patient!

Scenario 2: The Emergency Room of Orange County Community Hospital

A few hours later, Mr. Smith became unresponsive and collapsed on the floor suddenly. He was brought to the emergency room by the emergency medical team called by his daughter. Unfortunately, Mr. Smith had developed cardiopulmonary arrest. He was resuscitated and transferred to the ICU but remained comatose for few days and died. On further evaluation and inquiries, it was found that Mr. Smith due to his forgetfulness had accidentally taken two tablets each containing 325 mg of aspirin, for his headaches after which he collapsed. The reason for his death was considered due to idiosyncratic reaction to aspirin leading to anaphylactic shock.

COMMENTS

Clear communication between the physician and the nurse conveying the accurate patient information in a timely manner to the daughter of this patient might have prevented such catastrophic event. The physician either could have added aspirin caution in electronic medical record (EMR) chart by himself or could have confirmed the same with the nurse verbally and checked back. He assumed that nurse will take care of it by simply leaving a note placed on the table in a busy office. Unfortunately, he failed to verbally communicate with the nurse about his concerns with regard to Mr. Smith's possible aspirin sensitivity and memory issues. The nurse, on the other hand, could have been assertive to ask patient's daughter to call again later or to ask Dr. House as the patient has requested his opinion. Being the first line of contact, the nurse should have been more cautious while dealing with any medical advice to the patient without informing the physician and without checking the medical records. Assuming things without clearly communicating can lead to dangerous consequences/harm to the patient as in this vignette. Continuous inflow of outpatients, stress, busy schedule, inadequate perceptions of each other's role, the hesitation of speaking up/questioning, and so on are some of the factors contributing to communication failure.

This vignette emphasizes the importance of implementation of "closed-loop communication" and building a trustworthy relationship between nurses and physicians to initiate an open and effective communication.

DISCUSSION

INTRODUCTION

Interpersonal communication is a very important factor in healthcare where several lives are dependent on a collaborative teamwork of various healthcare providers including physicians, nurses, trainee physician, case managers, pharmacists, and physician assistants. The Joint Commission on Accreditation of Healthcare Organizations has found that communication errors are the third highest of the root causes behind the sentinel events in healthcare and account for two-thirds of serious medical errors.[1] There are several barriers that lead to communication failure among healthcare providers. These challenges are unique not only to every practice and subspecialty but also to different settings and shifts (e.g., weekday vs. weekend and daytime vs. night). Members of the healthcare community need to anticipate, explore these challenges, and implement appropriate solutions as per the work areas and requirements. An efficient and accurate clinical communication plays a key role in the transmission of information and providing high-quality healthcare to the patients.

In a retrospective review of 16,000 in-hospital deaths, communication errors were found to be the leading cause, twice as frequent as errors due to inadequate clinical skill.[2]

In a review of litigated surgical outcomes, communication failures between the medical staff accounted for 87% of the system failures that led to an indemnity payment.[3] In this chapter, we will focus on barriers in nurse–physician communication and how to overcome them.

NURSE–PHYSICIAN COMMUNICATION

Being vanguard of a healthcare, communication between nurses and physicians, is a vital element of the patient care. Nurse–physician communication has a huge impact on patient safety and outcome. Evidence suggests that lack of collaboration between doctors and nurses leads to suboptimal patient care, additional cost burden due to unnecessary admissions, prolonged hospital stays, delay in care, unnecessary investigations, and inadvertent health damage. This ultimately creates less work satisfaction and more stress among healthcare providers. Effective communication is a building block to a good work relationship and subsequently and to a good collaboration between physicians and nurses.

An Irish playwright George Bernard Shaw has aptly written, "A single biggest problem in a communication is the illusion that it has happened."

Failure of physicians to communicate effectively with nurses regarding their plans and rationale behind the plans may lead to serious harm to lives of patients. Even trivial errors due to breakdowns or delays in communications between medical staff can be catastrophic to lives of patients, as witnessed in our clinical vignette.

Barriers in nurse–physician communication are as follows (Figure 1):

1. **Busy schedule/stressful work environment**: Lack of time is one of the major factors in communication failure. Because nurses and physicians can be independently busy in their respective roles, finding time to communicate properly becomes difficult.[4] Stressful work environment due to a high number of patients and a shortage of staff at the workplace contribute to lapses in communication and interprofessional disconnect.

2. **A continuous flow of interruptions and multiple patient handoffs**: It affects the ability of nurses and physicians to

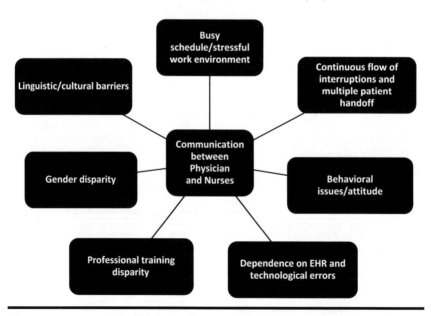

Figure 1   Several studies have been conducted to address the issues of communication between nurses and physicians globally. There are multiple barriers that hinder the communication between physicians and nurses.

connect effectively and establish a trusting and collegial relationship.[5] Different healthcare professionals from multiple disciplines of medicines might be involved in a patient care at different times and even at different locations. This limits the opportunity of face-to-face or other synchronous communication (phone call/video conference, etc.).

3. **Gender and role status disparity**: Gender disparity among healthcare team members can create a barrier to effective communication.[6] Males tend to prefer clear, quick, fact-based communication, whereas females prefer a more in-depth discussion style that attempts to understand the reason for occurrences.[7] Longstanding hierarchical communication practices related to role status and gender may result in fragmented nurse–physician communication. Nurses tend to hesitate in questioning the authority.[8] The status-based communication styles and lack of team-centered communication among the nurses and physicians hinder the optimal patient outcome.[9]

4. **Professional education and training disparities**: Due to a difference in the training, perception and views about the well-being are divergent among the physicians and nurses. Physicians are familiar with the precise medical terminologies as a part of their medical training, whereas nurses are used to relating the information in narratives.[10] The Joint Commission (2009) noted that the fact that both these professionals are trained differently can cause friction leading to nurse–physician disconnect.

5. **Attitude/behavioral factors**: Lack of mutual respect, misbehavior, condescending behavior, and intimidating or disruptive behavior of physicians lead to poor communication between physicians and nurses. This has been responsible for poor work satisfaction and lack of autonomy in nurses.[11] Similarly, inadequate communication with nurses, failure of nurses in following orders, not responding in a timely manner, unpreparedness, or inadequate information about patient can lead to dissatisfaction and frustration among physicians.[12] This leads to a poor interpersonal relationship and stressful work environment. All these factors ultimately hamper the quality and safety of patient care.

6. **Dependence on electronic systems and technological errors**: Electronic information systems were implemented to increase

quality and efficiency. However, it has reduced the frequency of face-to-face communication between nurses and physicians. Most often, the problems with electronic records occur when critical issues are not addressed at a time due to lack of additional verbal communication emphasizing the urgency.

According to Robinson and colleagues, nurses and physicians express a desire to follow up on urgent orders or electronic messages with some form of verbal contact.[13]

Communication modalities, such as text pagers, patient inbox messaging, and electronic ordering systems, can contribute to increased errors and are not always effective in conveying the urgency of the situation. Technological errors or inefficiency of users (e.g., malfunctioning of computers or pagers or poor connectivity) can lead to failure of effective communication.

7. **Linguistic/cultural barriers**: Due to diversity in healthcare, it is not uncommon to work with professionals with many foreign languages and diverse cultural upbringing. Misunderstandings between nurses and physicians due to language and cultural barriers can be harmful to patient safety as well as healthy work environment.

Addressing these barriers to effective communication and factors contributing to communication failure is essential to prevent inadvertent health effects on patients to achieve optimal patient safety. It is important to understand that the problem of communication is not to be finger pointed as either "nurses' problem" or "physicians' problem." Instead, it needs to be considered as a communal problem, and institutions/organizations need to be equally accountable for the same.[14]

UNDERSTANDING THE PRINCIPLES OF EFFECTIVE CLINICAL COMMUNICATION

Effective clinical communication is a clear, direct, explicit, and respectful exchange of information between the members of healthcare team. When possible, the communication should be fact-based and short. It is useful to note down the important points during the meeting. In a lengthy conversation, it is easy to forget or overlook initial critical points. It is more likely to occur in the supportive and safe environment. Excellent listening skills, effectively conveying and clarifying the rationale behind certain action plans, assertiveness, and openness to each other's suggestions beyond the traditional hierarchy and professional stereotypes are some of the key elements of such effective communication. It has been an observed tendency of nurses to sidestep to avoid the conflicts with physicians.[15] Both nurses and physicians should understand that clinical conflicts are unavoidable facts of clinical practice. Open and respectful team environment should be encouraged to build trust in nurses and physicians to address such conflicts in a timely manner. In a polite and friendly manner, a physician needs to confirm that his/her message is properly conveyed to the nurses/ technologists. Communication is a two-way street, where both or multiple parties should be given a chance to talk, remembering every individual talk as per his/her pace, style, and accent. One should not be forced to oblige; at the same time it's necessary that the conversation should not be digressing (Table 1).

Based on various studies done to improve the patient safety and quality of healthcare, we will review some of the evidence-based solutions to facilitate the effective nurse–physician communication.

3 E's of effective communication include:

1. **Establishing organizational culture:** Creating a cultural change in the organization by fostering a patient-centered, safety-focused, open environment supporting the teamwork and

Table 1   Principles of Effective Nurse–Physician Communication and Collaboration[16]

Effective communication techniques
Organization of information to be relayed
Communicate with confidence, clarity, and mutual respect
Active listening
Giving feedback constructively
Respectful language
Recognition of individual's uniqueness/contributions
Importance and impact of teamwork
Continuous improvement of one's communication skills
Contributes own professional perspective in discussions with the interprofessional teamwork.

mutual respect among the healthcare providers is the foremost step to improve nurse–physician communication.

Establishing strong administrative support to encourage such communications beyond the perceived barriers of traditional hierarchy and professional stereotyping is crucial to building trust and confidence between nurses and physicians. Administrative leaders play a major role in supporting the open communication and teamwork between nurses and physicians. Based on several studies on nurse–physician communication and the Joint Commission reports, following are some of the proven interventions to foster nurse–physician communication and patient safety through organizational culture change:

– **Creating adequate policies** to address disruptive behavior, a major barrier to nurse–physician communication.
– **Encouraging patient-centered approach by flattening the traditional hierarchy within the organization and cultivating respect** among the various disciplines (nurses, physicians, etc.) providing patient care as a collaborative team.
– **Interdisciplinary education**: Regular teaching experiences provided by nurses for physicians and vice versa can help to personalize the nurse–physician relationship.[17] A disparity in communication styles of nurses and physicians can be addressed by interdisciplinary simulation training and shadowing.[18]
– **Nurturing the culture of active listening by authoritative figures**: Those at the authoritative positions/leaders need to develop and nurture active listening skills and be more patient to answer any questions from nurses. This encourages open discussion, strengthens the teamwork, and ultimately helps to resolve any conflicts in the planning of patient care.
– **Empowerment of nurses**: Leaders can support nurses in communicating confidently and assertively with physicians in several ways, such as encouraging them to participate in multidisciplinary committees, interdisciplinary simulation training facilitating continuing education, a pursuit of specialty certification to gain new skills, and by providing focused communication training. Organizational leaders should consider pursuing Magnet designation as a means for improving the work environment for nurses.

A detailed review of six research studies based on essentials of magnetism, by Schmalenberg and Kramer in 2009, has suggested that nurses who work in hospitals that have achieved Magnet designation report higher quality relationships with physicians than peers who work in hospitals without Magnet status.[19] In addition, specifically addressing the conflict between nurses and physicians can help prevent negative interpersonal dynamics (Joint Commission, 2009).

– **Generating adequate workforce and allocating the responsibilities** appropriately, creating a healthy stress-free environment for physicians to work and communicate effectively.

– **Implementing interprofessional communication training** as part of an undergraduate curriculum for medical and nursing students.

– Language training and cultural exchange programs for non-native nurses and physicians.

2. **Encouraging face-to-face or direct verbal communication**: In the modern era of widespread use of EMRs where information can be instantly uploaded, updated, and shared with the team, face-to-face communication between nurses and physicians is being compromised to a varying extent. Unfortunately, few studies have found that use of the EMR significantly decreased face-to-face communication between nurses and physicians contributing to medical errors affecting patient safety and interprofessional relationships.[20] Updating critical information, adding prescription, or ordering investigations on EMR should not be assumed to be read, understood, or taken care of by nurses or physicians as expected. In order to understand a perspectives/rationale behind any intervention or care plan, to clarify any doubts, and to emphasize any urgency, additional verbal or preferably a face-to-face communication between nurses and physicians should be encouraged as a part of organizational culture. There are several opportunities to encourage nurse–physician communications, such as **bedside rounds** or **interdisciplinary meetings** with participation of both physicians and nurses. In a study conducted in two 30-bed teaching units of a tertiary hospital in the United States, O'Leary et al. found increased ratings on

the quality of nurse–physician communication after introducing **daily structured interdisciplinary rounds**.[21] As advocated by Joint Commission (2009), **creating interdisciplinary patient care team with designated team manager** may set a platform for all health providers to communicate effectively. Such designated team leader will be accountable for fostering the effective communication at a right time. This is thought to be effective in mitigating several issues related to poor communication as well as building a "teamwork" between nurses and physicians.

3. **Exchange of information via communication tools/ checklists**: To mitigate the issue of insufficient information or inadequate knowledge, exchange of information can be achieved utilizing effective tools of communication between nurses and physicians. Agency of Healthcare Research and Quality and Joint Commission for accreditation (2009) developed a program known as Team STEPPS. It is a teamwork training program that focuses on the development of four core competencies, which are leadership, situation monitoring, mutual support, and communication. It includes training nurses and physicians about the utilization of communication tools, such as Situation-Background-Assessment-Recommendation (SBAR), callouts (communicating verbally to other staff important decisions so they can anticipate next steps), and huddles (a brief face-to-face communication between care providers in which information is exchanged and the care plan is clarified).

STRUCTURED COMMUNICATION TRAINING

The SBAR is a structured communication tool that provides a framework for communication between members of the healthcare team about a patient's condition.

S = Situation (a concise statement of the problem)
B = Background (pertinent and brief information related to the situation)
A = Assessment (analysis and considerations of options—what you found/think)
R = Recommendation (action requested/recommended—what you want)

Being easy to remember and utilize, SBAR helps nurses for framing any conversation, especially critical ones, requiring physician's immediate attention and action.[22]

It allows for an easy and focused way to set expectations for what will be communicated and how between the members of the team, which is essential for developing teamwork and fostering a culture of patient safety.

Structured communication training of nurses to gain adequate patient information and increased preparedness before contacting physicians give confidence and knowledge which facilitate a smooth exchange of patient information.

Daily goals worksheet: Simply recording the details of patient management, such as planned procedures, medications, investigations, consults, and family meetings, on a worksheet as a part of daily multidisciplinary rounds can help both physician and nurses aware of the ongoing status of patient care. Such recorded worksheets can be made accessible to all the team members, easing the process of handoff.

A study done at medical ICU in Beth Israel Hospital, New York[23] has found that using a simple tool such as a "**daily goals worksheet**" has proven to be effective in bridging the communication gap between busy nurses and physicians by significantly improving the understanding of patient care goals among them resulting in shortened ICU stays.

Documentation during handoff: As a single team manages many patients and many teams are consulted to manage a complicated case at one time, it is vital for the primary team to make sure the management is aligned and there is no discrepancy in the different recommendations by different teams. If a discrepancy arises, it should be dealt with in a timely fashion. In a verbal handoff, it is easy to mix up one medication or order to another patient. All handoffs must be written and acknowledged. It's a common occurrence in a medical world when an overnight on-call team doesn't know why the particular medication or investigation is in place. A rationale behind management needs to be documented, so if the condition of the patient changes, on-call healthcare providers should be able to take an informed decision rather than just following orders.

Recent guidelines for enhancing teamwork in healthcare recommend a **closed-loop communication (CLC) protocol**, which

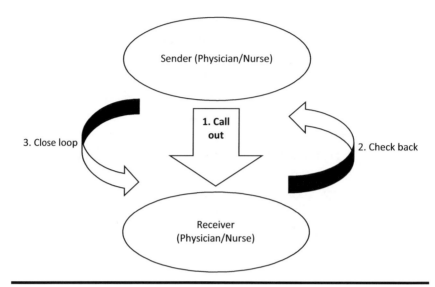

Figure 2 CLC: (1) Sender calls out the receiver to send a message; (2) receiver checks back with the sender to acknowledge the receipt of a message; (3) sender closes the loop by confirming whether the receiver has interpreted the message correctly.

means ensuring that information sent was received and interpreted correctly, to support effective clinical communication among healthcare team (Figure 2).[24]

CLC has been assumed to be a necessary component to ensure and facilitate safe team communication to prevent errors in healthcare.[24,25] Although there are guidelines suggesting the effectiveness of such measures in reducing errors due to communication failure, there is a strong need for validated training models to implement these tools in interdisciplinary practice.[26]

Access to reliable and efficient communication tools is a must to have effective communication between nurses and physicians. Along with emails, pagers, and electronic health records (EHRs), utilization of smartphones has allowed two-way synchronous information exchange and opportunities for clarification; it eliminated the wait time for physicians to respond to pages, reduced work interruptions, and nurses' time away from their patients.[27] These communication tools must be run on a secure network to be following Health Insurance Portability and Accountability Act privacy regulations. To avoid technical errors and for safety purpose, these tools need to pair with system-wide, software-based platform.

Although there are several interventions that have been undertaken to improve nurse–physician communication, the strategies invented are of limited utility and studies on larger scales need to be conducted. Also, there is limited evidence of interventions for minimizing communication breakdown due to stress, overflow of patients, or the inadequate workforce. Nurse–physician communication improvement still needs significant attention by exploring effective measures against aforementioned barriers.

Ultimately, it is essential to understand that trusting relationship that fosters effective communication between nurses and physicians, the frontiers of patient safety, is the only way to improve coordination of healthcare and eventually patient safety.

REFERENCES

1. The Joint Commission. Sentinel Event Data; Root Causes by Event Type. Retrieved from www.jointcommission.org/assets/1/18/Root_Causes_Event_Type_2004-2Q_2015.pdf.
2. Wilson RM, Runciman WB, Gibberd RW, Harrison BT, Newby L, Hamilton JD. The quality in Australian health care study. *Med J Aust*. 1995; 163(9):458–471.
3. Morris JA Jr, Carrillo Y, Jenkins JM, Smith PW, Bledsoe S, Pichert J, White A. Surgical adverse events, risk management, and malpractice outcome: morbidity and mortality review is not enough. *Ann Surg*. 2003; 237(6):844–851; discussion 851–852.
4. Rosenstein AH, O'Daniel M. Disruptive behavior and clinical outcomes: perceptions of nurses and physicians. *Am J Nurs*. 2005; 105(1):54–64; quiz 64–65.
5. Tschannen D, Keenan G, Aebersold M, Kocan MJ, Lundy F, Averhart V. Implications of nurse-physician relations: report of a successful intervention. *Nurs Econ*. 2011; 29(3):127–135.
6. Fernandez R, Tran DT, Johnson M, Jones S. Interdisciplinary communication in general medical and surgical wards using two different models of nursing care delivery. *J Nurs Manag*. 2010; 18(3):265–274. doi:10.1111/j.1365-2834.2010.01058.x.
7. McCaffrey RG, Hayes R, Stuart W, Cassel A, Farrell C, Miller-Reyes S, Donaldson A. An educational program to promote positive communication and collaboration between nurses and medical staff. *J Nurses Staff Dev*. 2011; 27(3):121–127. doi:10.1097/NND.0b013e318217b3ce. PubMed PMID: 21602629.
8. Seago JA. Professional communication. In RG Hughes (Ed.), *Patient Safety and Quality: An Evidence-Based Handbook for Nurses* (pp. 1–23) (2008), Rockville: Agency for Healthcare Research and Quality.

9. Matzke B, Houston S, Fischer U, Bradshaw MJ. Using a team-centered approach to evaluate effectiveness of nurse-physician communications. *J Obstet Gynecol Neonatal Nurs.* 2014; 43(6):684–694. doi:10.1111/1552-6909.12486. Epub 2014 Aug 26.

10. Arford PH. Nurse-physician communication: an organizational accountability. *Nurs Econ.* 2005; 23(2):72–77, 55. Review.

11. Saber DA. Frontline registered nurse job satisfaction and predictors over three decades: a meta-analysis from 1980 to 2009. *Nurs Outlook.* 2014; 62(6):402–414. doi:10.1016/j.outlook.2014.05.004. Epub 2014 May 28.

12. Burns K. Nurse-physician rounds: a collaborative approach to improving communication, efficiencies, and perception of care. *Medsurg Nurs.* 2011; 20(4):194–199. PubMed PMID: 21941931.

13. Robinson FP, Gorman G, Slimmer LW, Yudkowsky R. Perceptions of effective and ineffective nurse-physician communication in hospitals. *Nurs Forum.* 2010; 45(3):206–216. doi:10.1111/j.1744-6198.2010.00182.x.

14. Lyndon A, Zlatnik MG, Wachter RM. Effective physician-nurse communication: a patient safety essential for labor and delivery. *Am J Obstet Gynecol.* 2011; 205(2):91–96. doi:10.1016/j.ajog.2011.04.021. Epub 2011 Apr 16. Review.

15. Corser WD. The contemporary nurse-physician relationship: insights from scholars outside the two professions. *Nurs Outlook.* 2000; 48(6):263–268. Review.

16. Missi P. Enhancing Nurse-Physician Communication and Collaboration, 2016, NE-BC Bellarmine University, doctoral project.

17. Bujak JS, Bartholomew K. Transforming physician-nurse communication. Deteriorating relationships must be reversed for the benefit of patients, staff and the organization. *Healthc Exec.* 2011; 26(4):56, 58–59.

18. Liaw SY, Siau C, Zhou WT, Lau TC. Interprofessional simulation-based education program: a promising approach for changing stereotypes and improving attitudes toward nurse-physician collaboration. *Appl Nurs Res.* 2014; 27(4):258–260. doi:10.1016/j.apnr.2014.03.005. Epub 2014 Apr 18.

19. Schmalenberg C, Kramer M. Nurse-physician relationships in hospitals: 20,000 nurses tell their story. *Crit Care Nurse.* 2009; 29(1):74–83. doi:10.4037/ccn2009436. Review.

20. Taylor SP, Ledford R, Palmer V, Abel E. We need to talk: an observational study of the impact of electronic medical record implementation on hospital communication. *BMJ Qual Saf.* 2014; 23(7):584–588. doi:10.1136/bmjqs-2013-002436. Epub 2014 Feb 6.

21. O'Leary KJ, Haviley C, Slade ME, Shah HM, Lee J, Williams MV. Improving teamwork: impact of structured interdisciplinary rounds on a hospitalist unit. *J Hosp Med*. 2011; 6(2):88–93. doi:10.1002/jhm.714. PubMed PMID: 20629015.
22. http://www.ihi.org/resources/Pages/Tools/SBARToolkit.aspx
23. Narasimhan M, Eisen LA, Mahoney CD, Acerra FL, Rosen MJ. Improving nurse-physician communication and satisfaction in the intensive care unit with a daily goals worksheet. *Am J Crit Care*. 2006; 15(2):217–222. PubMed PMID: 16501141.
24. Salas E, Wilson KA, Murphy CE, King H, Salisbury M. Communicating, coordinating, and cooperating when lives depend on it: tips for teamwork. *Jt Comm J Qual Patient Saf*. 2008; 34(6):333–341.
25. Salas E, Sims DE, Burke CS. Is there a "big five" in teamwork? *Small Group Res*. 2005; 36:555–599.
26. Härgestam M, Lindkvist M, Brulin C, Jacobsson M, Hultin M. Communication in interdisciplinary teams: exploring closed-loop communication during in situ trauma team training. *BMJ Open*. 2013; 3(10):e003525. doi:10.1136/bmjopen–2013–00352.
27. Whitlow ML, Drake E, Tullmann D, Hoke G, Barth D. Bringing technology to the bedside: using smartphones to improve interprofessional communication. *Comput Inform Nurs*. 2014; 32(7):305–311. doi:10.1097/CIN.0000000000000063.

Clinical Vignette 2: Different Paths Yet the Same Goal

Tripti Chopade
University of Missouri

Clinical vignette discusses the medication error which resulted in the patient being hospitalized due to a communication error between patient and physician coming from different cultural backgrounds. We will establish cultural awareness as a foundation of patient safety.

THE CASE

Ms. Rubina Sayed, a 65-year-old female from a conservative Muslim family, recently visited Dr. Strange's busy outpatient clinic for a follow-up health visit, accompanied by her son. Ms. Sayed immigrated to the United States from Qatar with her son before 2 years. During her last few visits, Dr. Strange noticed her consistently high blood pressure with systolic 140 mmHg and diastolic 100 mmHg. At her last visit 6 months back, Dr. Strange advised lifestyle modification and close monitoring of blood pressure at home. Dr. Strange and his office nurse surprisingly noticed that during every encounter, Ms. Sayed preferred to remain quiet and her son always spoke on her behalf. Dr. Strange used to hardly comprehend her language due to her non-native accent and lack of English proficiency. He totally relied on her son who was relatively more proficient in the English language. During this visit, Dr. Strange asked few questions to the son inquiring about her general well-being. Her present blood pressure was 142/98 mmHg despite salt restriction and increased physical activities as confirmed by the patient's son. Her other vitals were within normal limits and she seemed to have no acute symptoms or concerns. Previously done routine diagnostic workup was normal as well. Dr. Strange was finishing his hectic clinic day before rushing for the departmental meeting. He overheard the incomprehensible conversation between the mother and son. With a bit of amusement, Dr. Strange asked her son about their wish to start a medication for her newly diagnosed hypertension. Her son simply nodded in agreement, while Ms. Sayed avoided the direct eye contact in anguish. Dr. Strange decided to start her on antihypertensive medicine and ordered a diuretic tablet Furosemide 40 mg twice a day. He briefly gave instructions regarding how to take pills to Ms. Sayed's son and asked to return to his clinic in 3 months. The son was concerned about the side effects of the drug and was curious to discuss if she can be able to tolerate it as they were planning to have Ramadan celebration for a month, a ritual in his community. Dr. Strange assured him not to worry as it was one of the safe and very commonly used first-line drug for hypertension. Dr. Strange emphasized compliance to the medication and concluded his visit as he rushed for the meeting. A few weeks later, Ms. Sayed was admitted to hospital due to generalized weakness, lethargy, persistent dizziness, and sudden collapse on the floor hurting her head. On arrival, she was pale and severely dehydrated with dry oral and eye mucous membranes, and lost skin turgor. Her blood pressure was 70/50 mmHg, heart rate 100/min, and her laboratory reports showed significant electrolyte abnormalities with severe hypokalemia and hypernatremia. On further inquiry to the son, he mentioned about his mother's recent fasting where she has restricted water intake due to fasting during the holy month of Ramadan. She had practiced fasting throughout her entire life without any difficulty. This time her recently started diuretic medication exacerbated her dehydration further leading to severe electrolyte imbalance and hypotension.

COMMENTS

As seen in this clinical vignette, the physician failed to connect directly or communicate effectively with the patient due to language barrier as well as due to lack of cultural awareness. Spending more time to understand the patient's religious beliefs and to address the nonverbal clues of concerns could have opened the door to effective communication. If only physician would have frankly enquired about what Ramadan (a holy month of Islamic year during which strict fasting is observed from sunrise to sunset) is all about and how it may raise the health concern for the patient, he either would have emphasized the importance of maintenance of hydration while being on diuretic or would have chosen an alternative medication for treating her hypertension. Apart from cultural unawareness, the assumption of the patient or her son's understanding of the treatment plan, lack of empathy, and curiosity to know the patient better or to understanding cultural context related to patient's health condition has led to unforeseen health complication of dehydration in this patient.

DISCUSSION

CULTURAL COMPETENCE AS A FOUNDATION OF PATIENT SAFETY

"The good physician treats disease but a great physician treats the patient." – William Osler

To provide a wholesome care to patients, it is of utmost importance for every physician to understand a patient as a human being and several aspects of being a unique individual, such as varying perspectives, religious/nonreligious beliefs, rituals, languages, and cultural upbringing.

In today's era of globalization, physicians from different parts of the world deal with culturally and ethnically diverse population. There is a huge cultural diversification in healthcare. Intercultural communications between doctors and patients have a huge impact on the quality of healthcare. The demographic profiles of the United States illustrate a nation rich in cultural and racial diversity. Approximately 29% of the population are minorities, and demographic projections indicate an increase to 50% by the year 2050.[1] Broadening the cultural understanding to establish clear communication between physicians and patients is the need of time!

Let's understand the basic concept of culture and culture competence and why it is important to address the same.

Culture is a system of beliefs, values, rules, and customs that are shared by a group and is used to interpret experiences and direct patterns of behavior. Culture plays a large role in shaping each individual's health-related values, beliefs, and behaviors, and it clearly impacts clinical care.[2]

Effective communication—the exchange of messages in which the meaning is mutually understood—between the provider and the patient is pivotal for patient satisfaction, adherence, and safety. Failure to effectively communicate during the cross-cultural interaction between physicians and patients from different cultures and ethnicity increases the possibility of medical errors.

Nearly 50% of U.S. physicians perceive languages and cultural diversity as a major obstacle in providing a high-quality care to patients.[3] The single biggest barrier to the advancement of the highest standards of health worldwide is the systemic neglect of culture in health and healthcare.[4] A growing number of health organizations, such as the Joint Commission and National

Committee for Quality Assurance, are determined to embrace the cultural diversity in healthcare by investing in leadership and resources for the same.

The concept of cultural competence in healthcare has emerged in recent decades. Although global, cultural competence is widely practiced in the United States and being embedded in the medical education curriculum. Cultural competence in healthcare entails the ability to provide care to patients with diverse values, beliefs, and behaviors as well as tailoring healthcare delivery to meet patients' social, cultural, and linguistic needs. The goal is to create an environment of safety in which there is mutual respect, openness, and willingness to listen, and there is shared understanding and acknowledgment of the unique identity of others.

Cultural awareness simply entails specific skills such as recognizing and knowing one's own and other people's cultural identities and beliefs.

Cultural competency enables providers to work effectively with others, such as colleagues and patients, in cross-cultural situations.[5]

Becoming culturally competent involves developing and acquiring the skills needed to identify and assist patients from diverse cultures. To quickly identify the services required by a patient, thereby increasing positive health outcomes, physicians (healthcare providers) must acquire the necessary skills and mindset. Cultural competence is considered the core ability needed during cross-cultural physician–patient communication.[6] The disparity of care arising from cultural and linguistic incompetence in healthcare practice could result in noncompliance, poor patient satisfaction, misunderstanding, suboptimal patient safety, and poor doctor–patient relationship.

Accept and Adapt to Cultural Diversity

Most immigrants and physicians have received little or no formal training in intercultural relations.[7] Physicians do not learn about theories of intercultural or cross-cultural communication and intercultural communication competence developed by social scientists. It is of critical importance for medical professionals to understand the role of culture while creating the treatment and recovery plan for an individual. Key determinants of patient satisfaction, such as trust, empathy, respect, and curiosity, need to be implemented by physicians for a sound intercultural communication in a daily practice.

Cultural competence is a process built upon by asking questions about the patient and the family but also about yourself.[8] In order to develop the culturally competent force of clinicians, it is very essential to understand that the intercultural communication skills can be acquired and practiced. Cultural awareness and cross-cultural communication skills are as important as medical skills.[9] Being self-aware is the first step toward achieving the skills of cultural competence. When physicians are completely aware of their beliefs, attitudes, biases, and behaviors, they can effectively handle the situation of dealing with patients from different cultural background, for example, a physician who is against the use of birth control medicines or abortion due to cultural/religious beliefs can explain that directly to patients and hand over the care to someone who is more comfortable in doing so.

Factors contributing to culture-related miscommunication and strategies to mitigate this issue are discussed in details in this chapter.

The Patient-Based Approach to Improve Cultural Competency

The patient-based cross-cultural curriculum developed by J. Emillo Carillo and colleague is helpful for healthcare providers at all levels to establish an excellent cross-cultural relationship with the patients by overcoming the sociocultural barriers. By adopting a patient-centered approach to understand, communicate with, and care for patients from a diverse cultural background, it is possible to avoid the cultural generalization by physicians.[10] We will explore in detail the four essential components (Figure 1) of patient-based approach to developing cultural competence among phsicians.[10]

1. **Accessing core cross-cultural issues:** Physicians today get exposed to a vast number of patient populations from a different ethnic and cultural backgrounds. It is practically impossible for the physicians to understand every culture while holding one's unique cultural values. Physicians need to be aware of certain common and recurring cross-cultural issues

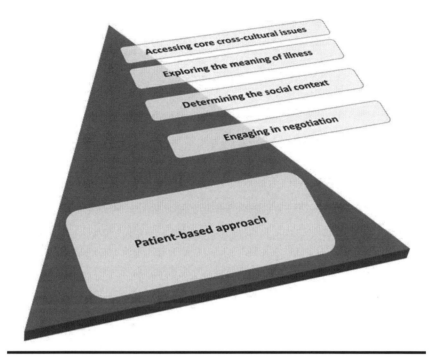

Figure 1   Patient-based approach to cultural competence.

among particular cultures to facilitate the effective clinical communication. Due to the varying degree of acculturation, it is necessary for physicians to look at each patient's situation in a unique manner. Recognizing various core issues of cross-cultural communication by asking direct questions can bridge the communication gap and help to build a trustworthy relationship between physicians and patients during any cross-cultural encounters (Figure 2).[10]

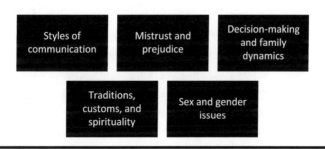

Figure 2   Core cross-cultural issues/"hot-button" issues in cross-cultural communication.

Styles of communication: Miscommunication and misunderstanding tend to occur due to differences in the style of communication including verbal as well as nonverbal (e.g., eye contact, body language, facial expressions, touch, etc.) communication during a cross-cultural clinical encounter. Some patients are culturally less assertive while making a healthcare decision. In such events, physicians should encourage the inputs from patients and remain open to listen and address his/her fears patiently. Physicians can to be observant to the preferences of patients such as eye contact and touch, and learn by experience what makes a patient more comfortable during the clinical encounter. Any assumptions regarding the patient's acceptance or denial of the plan should be directly communicated and confronted with patients in a polite way. It is essential for physicians to know how patients prefer to hear their health information, such as diagnostic results and prognosis, especially while delivering critical health issues-related news to patients and their families. Flexibility is the key for physicians to adopt culturally diverse communication styles.

Linguistic barriers/inadequate communication skills: Many doctors feel incompetent to communicate and relate to patients from different ethnic backgrounds due to a lack of adequate communication skills or language barrier. On reviewing a number of U.S. studies on language barriers among Latino and Asian patients, Ramirez found that linguistic barriers can lead to a number of negative consequences, such as an increased chance of noncompliance, feelings of fear and despair, and problems in achieving rapport.[11]

Moreover, the inability of patients to understand and speak the language of their physician may be an important obstacle in seeking appropriate care. Although it is beyond doubt that poor language proficiency will hinder adequate doctor–patient communication, it's important to note that several other studies have found that despite language barrier, patient satisfaction was based on doctor's kind attitude, mutual understanding, and so on.[12]

Overcoming language barrier: Centers for Medicare & Medicaid Services Office of Minority Health (OMH) has developed culturally and linguistically appropriate services to combat disparities in healthcare quality among ethnic minorities and people with low English proficiency. Physicians need to be aware of such services and should take advantage of the same as needed. Avoiding medical jargons, repeating patient's words, and utilizing body language to show empathy and to build trust are some of the ways in which physicians can communicate with patients despite the language barrier.

Mistrust and prejudices: Trust is a vital component of physician–patient relationship. Physicians should communicate clearly, understand the patient's perspectives, and address any concerns or mistrust upfront. Active listening, building a partnership by creating a sense of involvement in decision-making within the patients, open-ended questioning, and so on are some of the ways physicians can build the trust within patients.[13]

Racial disparity/perceptual biases: Physicians' generalized assumptions or prejudices against certain ethnic/culturally diverse population result in discrimination and inequality in healthcare. Multiple factors contribute to racial disparity in healthcare, including barriers to effective clinician–patient interactions (e.g., language and literacy issues and different cultural beliefs), systems barriers (e.g., lack of interpreter services or ethnically diverse clinicians), and clinician biases.[14] It has been observed that minority patients, especially those not proficient in English and are from different ethnic backgrounds, are less likely to get empathy and attention from physicians.

Sexual and gender issues: Gender and sexuality also affect the concept of the health and disease in several communities. In many parts of the world, including the Middle East, Africa, and South Asia, gender roles are strictly defined and enforced. The male role is commonly seen as that of protector and spokesperson for the family.[15] Patients from traditional or conservative community hesitate to share their sexual or personal issues with physicians of the opposite gender. To build a trust within a patient, a physician needs to ask the patient's preferences, discuss the concerns, and whenever possible, arrange the services accordingly.

Differences in cultural value, traditions, and religious/ spiritual beliefs: The differences in beliefs about health and illness as well as differences in cultural values are associated with gaps in doctor–patient communication.[16] Spirituality, religiosity, and personal beliefs are important components of the social determinants that affect patients' health behaviors and adherence to treatments.[17] Religious/spiritual beliefs play an important and powerful role in recovery.

Addressing the difference in cultural beliefs/traditions and accepting cultural diversity: Physicians need to accept the fact of dealing with culturally diverse population and have an open mind about the health beliefs of people from multicultural backgrounds. If patients' cultural beliefs are coming in the way of health, a physician should convey the rationale behind the medical advice. Whenever feasible, a physician may provide alternative treatments that are within cultural norms of patients. Physicians need to acknowledge the feelings and emotional issues, such as loneliness, adjustment, and cultural shock, among the immigrant population. By being an empathetic and patient listener, physicians can help to develop confidence in patients.

Decision-making and family dynamics: Unlike most of the patients in Western culture, patients form non-Western cultures rarely exhibit autonomy in making health-related decisions and many of them rely on a family decision. In ethnic minority patients, doctor's interaction with their family members matters more and doctor's curiosity about a family's well-being is appreciated. Understanding the dynamics within ethnically diverse patients' families is an important component in providing culturally sensitive communication.[18] Most of the doctors from Western culture are used to direct their communication to the individual patient rather than a family.[19] For patients, their illnesses may be connected to their community context and family; relations, culture, and values are inseparable. A family may play a significant role in decision-making despite intact decision-making capacity of an individual. When doctors and patients have different perceptions of the role of the family especially in very sensitive issues, such as an end of the life care, chances of miscommunication increase hampering the physician–patient and physician–family relationship. Therefore, knowledge about expectations and habits of patients and their family is considered as a specific skill for acquiring a cultural competency.[20,21] Physicians must learn tact and techniques to negotiate with family members as per the patient's preferences. Open communication and legal documentation should be considered whenever applicable (e.g., waiving a right of patients if a family wants to withhold some information to be delivered).

2. **Exploring the meaning of illness:** Kleinman[22] in his theory of explanatory models proposed that individuals from different cultures have totally different perception, experience, and ways of coping with diseases and maintaining health. Explanatory models are "notions about an episode of sickness and its treatment that are employed by those engaged in the clinical process." Physician's explanatory models of illness are traditionally emphasizing the biological and physical aspects of disease etiology (biomedical models). Although culture is the main determinant of patient's explanatory models, other factors such as socioeconomic status and education level play role in building such models. A holistic concept of health and spiritual aspect of disease causation are commonly found in patients who are from eastern (e.g., Southeast Asian) cultures. It is important to educate the physicians to incorporate psychosocial, behavioral aspects of illness into their biomedical explanatory models. During a cross-cultural encounter, respectful questioning and reassurance by physicians help to elicit the exact meaning of illness for a patient, fears or doubts in their minds, expectations, and any other barriers in diagnosing and treating their illnesses.

   Do Not Assume, Just Ask! Kleinman et al.[23] have developed a set of questions to elicit the patient's explanatory model (Table 1). These questions can be practiced by physicians during the cross-cultural encounters to explore the patient's perspectives as well as to understand the expectations, agenda, and tailor the management accordingly.

Table 1   Exploring the Meaning of Illness

Explanatory model: What do you think has caused your problem? What do you call it? Why do you think it started when it did? How does it affect your life? How severe is it? What worries you the most? What kind of treatment do you think would work?
The patient's agenda: How can I be most helpful to you? What is most important for you?
Illness behavior: Have you seen anyone else about this problem besides a physician? Have you used nonmedical remedies or treatments for your problem? Who advises you about your health?

3. **Determining the social context of patient:** Social factors play major role in disease processes.[24] Socioeconomic status, education/literacy, migration/environmental changes, social stressors, and support system formulate a social context for an individual's illness. Physicians can learn the practical techniques to identify the social context by asking focused questions as in a review of systems during the clinical encounter (Table 2). Only after determination of social issues of the patients, a physician can discuss the strategies, available resources, and solutions to deal with these issues.

4. **Negotiating across the culture:** Physicians being an expert in dealing with particular illnesses and a patient being uniquely experiencing the disease can differ in their perspectives about the illness irrespective of sociocultural background. Sociocultural diversity further increases the discrepancy in the perception of disease, need of treatment, concerns, expectation, and so on. Facilitation of cross-culture negotiation is used to address the explanatory models and management options.

   Six phases of reaching mutually acceptable agreement between physician and patient from the different sociocultural background are relationship building, agenda setting, assessment, problem clarification, management, and closure.[25] The

Table 2 Social Context "Review of Systems"

Control over the environment: Is money a big problem in your life? Are you ever short of food or clothing? How do you keep track of appointments? Are you more concerned about how your health affects you right now or how it might affect you in the future?
Change in the environment: Where are you from? What made you decide to come to this country (city, town)? When did you come? How have you found life here compared to life in your country (city, town)? What was medical care like there compared with here?
Social stressors and support network: What is causing the most difficulty or stress in your life? How do you deal with this? Do you have friends or relatives that you can call on for help? Who are they? Do they live close to you? Are you very involved in a religious or social group? Do you feel that God (or a higher power) provides a strong source of support in your life?
Literacy and language: Do you have trouble reading your medication bottles or appointment?

six phases are integrated with the strategies of Katon and Kleinman[26] to provide a framework for cross-cultural negotiation.

Negotiating explanatory models: Physicians should be trained to describe the biomedical explanatory model in simple and understandable terms, using the patient's terminology and conceptualization. Physicians need to simplify the management plans to the patients and their families. Also, there is a need to double check the understanding and acceptance of the treatment plan by the patient. When there is a conflict, a physician must reevaluate core cultural issues and social context (e.g., bring in family members or maximize interpretation.)

To ensure the patient's safety and optimal outcome for culturally diverse patient population, Seibert et al. (2002) have created a ten-point checklist that facilitates cultural awareness and cultural sensitivity among the healthcare providers (Table 3).

Table 3   Cultural Sensitivity and Awareness Checklist

Focus	Instruction
1. Communication method	Identify the patient's preferred method of communication. Make necessary arrangements if translators are needed.
2. Language barriers	Identify potential language barriers (verbal and nonverbal). List possible compensations.
3. Cultural identification	Identify the patient's culture. Contact your organization's culturally specific support team (CSST) for assistance.
4. Comprehension	Double-check: Does the patient and/or family comprehend the situation at hand?
5. Beliefs	Identify religious/spiritual beliefs. Make appropriate support contacts.
6. Trust	Double-check: Does the patient and/or family appear to trust the caregivers? Remember to watch for both verbal and nonverbal cues. If not, seek advice from the CSST.
7. Recovery	Double-check: Does the patient and/or family have misconceptions or unrealistic views about the caregivers, treatment, or recovery process? Make necessary adjustments.

(Continued)

Table 3 (*Continued*)   Cultural Sensitivity and Awareness Checklist

Focus	Instruction
8. Diet	Address culture-specific dietary considerations.
9. Assessments	Conduct assessments with cultural sensitivity in mind. Watch for inaccuracies.
10. Healthcare provider bias	Always remember, we all have biases and prejudices. Examine and recognize yours.

CULTURAL COMPETENCY STRUCTURED TRAINING IN THE UNITED STATES

There are several reports of racial and ethnic disparity in healthcare in the United States.[27] Despite decades of attention and awareness, healthcare disparities persist across the United States. Liaison Committee on Medical Education (LCME), the accrediting body for U.S. medical schools, took a great initiative to address and eliminate these disparities. LCME incorporated cultural competency training as a part of medical curriculum whereby medical students require to demonstrate a standard level of "cultural competence" upon graduation.[28]

Physician training in cultural competence not only reduces the provider bias but also improves the physician–patient communication.[29] Understanding patient's culture, educational, professional background, and biological differences helps physicians to make effective diagnosis and management of their overall health issues.

The American Medical Association has designed the program launched in June 2017[30] to train the residents (physicians in training) in cultural competency by providing the interactive, online tutorials and track their progress in fulfilling the core-competency requirements of the Accreditation Council for Graduate Medical Education. The cultural competency module falls under the umbrella of interpersonal and communication skills.

To aid in patient–physician interactions, the Graduate Medical Education Competency Education Program (GCEP) module touts the acronym LEARN, a communication framework designed by Dr. Berlin and Dr. Fowkes Jr.[31]

LEARN stands for

L: **Listen**, encouraging patients to explain their situation.
E: **Explain** clearly.

A: **Acknowledge** the differences between what patients understand and what you know.

R: **Recommend** a treatment plan that is consistent with your conversation with a patient.

N: **Negotiate** to get agreement from patients on a course of action.

The Association of American Medical Colleges has developed the Tool for Assessing Cultural Competence Training to assist medical schools in developing and evaluating cultural competence curricula to meet these requirements.

To equip healthcare professionals with the knowledge, skills, and awareness that will enable them to better respond to the needs of the increasingly diverse U.S. population, the U.S. Department of Health and Human Services OMH commissioned "A Physician's Practical Guide to Culturally Competent Care." This self-directed e-learning program is accredited for physicians, physician assistants, and nurse practitioners.

Incorporating diverse physician workforce: The American Medical Association has adopted several policies to promote the diverse physician workforce to improve cultural competency (2017 Annual meeting AMA). Delegates adopted the policy to encourage medical school admission offices to use "holistic assessments" of applicants, to take into consideration "the diversity of preparation and the variety of talents that applicants bring to their education."[32]

Role of Patient Education in Cultural Competency in Healthcare

Patient–physician communication is a two-way process. Educating patients to be culturally sensitive, utilizing language assistance or interpreter resources, and understanding the limits of physicians are equally important to assure the healthy doctor–patient relationship.

The flip side of the coin: It is also essential to address the reason behind reluctance or neutral approach of physicians to serve for culturally diverse patients. As revenues are directly linked to a number of patients (turnaround time), clinicians are often pressured to see more patients and many times may not have enough time to connect with the patient. With electronic health records, physicians often spend more time in filling the chart than with the patients. Medicare/Medicaid, hospitals, and insurance provider should come up with an incentive program, which will compensate physicians for their extra time and efforts.

Embracing the cultural competency is the only way to effective communication for optimal patient safety in the era of widespread cultural diversity.

REFERENCES

1. Seibert PS, Stridh-Igo P, Zimmerman CG. A checklist to facilitate cultural awareness and sensitivity. *J Med Ethics*. 2002; 28(3):143–146.
2. Joseph R, Betancourt, MD, Green AR, Carrillo E. Cross-cultural care and communication, UpToDate (June 2018).
3. Center for studying health system change, 2010.
4. Napier AD, Ancarno C, Butler B, Calabrese J, Chater A, Chatterjee H, Guesnet F, Horne R, Jacyna S, Volkmann AM, Walker T, Watson J, Williams AC, Willott C, Wilson J, Woolf K. Culture and health. *Lancet* 2014; 384(9954):1607–1639.
5. U.S. Department of Health and Human Services' Office of Minority [HHS OMH], 2013.
6. Vijver, FJR, Breugelmans, MS. Research foundations of cultural competency training. In H.D. Richard & R.A. James (Eds.), *Cultural Competency Training in a Global Society* (2008), New York; London: Springer, 117–133.
7. Ferguson WJ, Candib LM. Culture, language, and the doctor–patient relationship. *Fam Med*. 2002; 34: 353–361.
8. Kodjo C. Cultural competence in clinician communication. *Pediatr Rev*. 2009; 30(2):57–64. doi:10.1542/pir.30–2–57.
9. Schouten BC, Meeuwesen L. Cultural differences in medical communication: A review of the literature. *Patient Educ Couns*. 2006; 64(1–3):21–34. Epub 2006 Jan 20. Review.
10. Carrillo JE, Green AR, Betancourt JR. Cross-cultural primary care: A patient-based approach. *Ann Intern Med*. 1999; 130(10):829–834.
11. Ramirez AG. Consumer-provider communication research with special populations. *Patient Educ Couns*. 2003; 50:51–54.
12. Patel S. Intercultural consultations: Language is not the only barrier. *Brit Med J*. 1995; 310:194.
13. Petersen LA. Racial differences in trust: Reaping what we have sown? *Med Care*. 2002; 40(2):81.
14. Green AR, Carney DR, Pallin DJ, Ngo LH, Raymond KL, Iezzoni LI, Banaji MR. Implicit bias among physicians and its prediction of thrombolysis decisions for black and white patients. *J Gen Intern Med*. 2007; 22(9):1231. Epub 2007 Jun 27.
15. Tirodkar MA, Baker DW, Makoul GT, Khurana N, Paracha MW, Kandula NR. Explanatory models of health and disease among South Asian immigrants in Chicago. *J Immigr Minor Health*. 2011; 13(2):385–394. doi:10.1007/s10903-009-9304-1.

16. Cass A, Lowell A, Christie M, Snelling PL, Flack M, Marrnganyin B, Brown I. Sharing the true stories: Improving communication between Aboriginal patients and healthcare workers. *Med J Aust.* 2002; 176(10):466–470.

17. Kretchy I, Owusu-Daaku F, Danquah S. Spiritual and religious beliefs: Do they matter in the medication adherence behaviour of hypertensive patients? *Biopsychosoc Med.* 2013; 7(1):15.

18. Mitchison D, Butow P, Sze M, Aldridge L, Hui R, Vardy J, Eisenbruch M, Iedema R, Goldstein D. Prognostic communication preferences of migrant patients and their relatives. *Psychooncology.* 2012; 21(5):496–504. doi:10.1002/pon.1923. Epub 2011 Feb 23.

19. Gulati S, Watt L, Shaw N, Sung L, Poureslami IM, Klaassen R, Dix D, Klassen AF. Communication and language challenges experienced by Chinese and South Asian immigrant parents of children with cancer in Canada: Implications for health services delivery. *Pediatr Blood Cancer.* 2012; 58(4):572–578. doi:10.1002/pbc.23054. Epub 2011 Mar 2.

20. Lingard L, Tallett S, Rosenfield J. Culture and physician-patient communication: A qualitative exploration of residents' experiences and attitudes. *Ann R Coll Phys Surg Can.* 2002; 35:331–335.

21. Williams SW, Hanson LC, Boyd C, Green M, Goldmon M, Wright G, et al. Communication, decision making, and cancer: What African Americans want physicians to know. *J Palliat Med.* 2008; 11:1221–1226.

22. Shen WW. Patients and healers in the context of culture: An exploration of the borderland between anthropology, medicine, and psychiatry. *Am J Psych.* 1982; 139(2):252–253.

23. Kleinman A, Eisenberg L, Good B. Culture, illness, and care: Clinical lessons from anthropologic and cross-cultural research. *Ann Intern Med.* 1978; 88:251–258.

24. De La Cancela V, Guarnaccia PJ, Carrillo JE. Psychosocial distress among latinos: A critical analysis of ataques de nervios. *Humanity Soc.* 1986; 10:431–447.

25. Botelho RJ. A negotiation model for the doctor-patient relationship. *Fam Pract.* 1992; 9:210–218.

26. Katon W, Kleinman A. Doctor-patient negotiation and other social science strategies in patient care. In L. Eisenberg & A. Kleinman (Eds.), *The Relevance of Social Science for Medicine* (1980), Boston, MA: Riedel.

27. Mayberry RM, Mili F, Ofili E. Racial and ethnic differences in access to medical care. *Med Care Res Rev.* 2000; 57(Suppl 1):108–145.

28. Liaison Committee on Medical Education. Accreditation Standards. 8 June 2004 www.lcme.org/standard.htm (27 December 2004).

29. Beach MC, Price EG, Gary TL, Robinson KA, Gozu A, Palacio A, Smarth C, Jenckes MW, Feuerstein C, Bass EB, Powe NR, Cooper LA. Cultural competence: A systematic review of health care provider educational interventions. *Med Care.* 2005; 43(4):356–373.
30. https://wire.ama-assn.org/education/residents-cultural-competence-starts-strong-dose-humility
31. Berlin EA, Fowkes, WC Jr. A teaching framework for cross-cultural health care. *Western J Med.* 1983; 139:934–938.
32. https://wire.ama-assn.org/education/ama-aim-more-diverse-better-prepared-physician-workforce

Clinical Vignette 3: It Was Erik's Fault!

Tripti Chopade
University of Missouri

Clinical vignette discusses the miscommunication between residents during sign-out resulting in prolonged hospital stay. Various strategies to improve resident sign-outs are discussed here.

THE CASE

Mr. White, a 65-year-old man with a past medical history of hypertension, coronary artery disease, and epilepsy, was admitted to the intensive care unit (ICU) with an acute change in mental status, fever, and neck rigidity. His tests were significant for increased white blood cell (WBC) count of over 20,000 cells/μL. Blood cultures were positive for *Streptococcus pneumoniae*, and he was already started on empiric antibiotic therapy with suspicion of meningitis at admission. The patient responded well to the intravenous antibiotic therapy and his WBC count started to trend down. Four days later, he was afebrile, vitals were stable, and was communicating well with his family and the team of physicians in the ICU. He was also able to ambulate with minimal support due to generalized weakness.

Erik, a postgraduation year 2 (PGY-2) neurology resident taking care of Mr. White, was happy to see improvement of Mr. White. He had a hectic day with the admissions of four new critically ill patients. At the end of the day, he double-checked on Mr. White and briefly signed out his care to Chelsie, a night-float resident. He mentioned about Mr. White's improved condition and plan of continuation of antibiotics with eventual step down of care to the general ward after discussing with attending next day morning.

Mr. White was reportedly drowsier overnight and had a breakthrough seizure with vigorous shaking noted by a nurse on call who reported Chelsie immediately. He had a prolonged postictal confusion and disorientation. Not being familiar with Mr. White's baseline mental status and receiving incomplete information from Erik, Chelsie and the team couldn't figure out the exact reason behind his sudden convulsion. After discussing with seniors, Chelsie planned for magnetic resonance imaging (MRI) brain and basic metabolic panel to investigate the underlying cause of the breakthrough seizure. Since it was weekend, a new team was cross-covering the patient the next day and Erik was off duty. After a thorough evaluation of patient's history by revisiting the chart and double checking with patient's relative and nurses, the team came to know about recently withheld anti-seizure medication (valproate) due to the concern of drug-induced hepatotoxicity in view of recently raised hepatic enzymes. As per the family, before withholding the medication by ICU doctor, the patient was compliant to the treatment and was seizure free for almost a year since his outpatient neurologist increased the dose last year. There was no record of an addition of any new anti-seizure medication to replace valproate as well as no mention of any seizure precautions on the chart during sign-out. Although the team managed Mr. White's breakthrough seizure uneventfully, it led to unnecessary investigations and prolonged stay for evaluation of seizure. Chelsie was upset with Erik for omitting this critical piece of information as it could have prevented seizure which caused repetition of investigations to find out the underlying cause, prolongation of ICU stay of Mr. White, and time-consuming hassle for the cross-covering team to figure out what went wrong!

COMMENTS

This case emphasizes the importance of effective communication during sign-out/handoff between residents to deliver all essential updates with regard to patient management. The resident didn't document discontinuation of the medication (valproate) on electronic medical record (EMR) and couldn't think about the unforeseen consequences of the same, resulting in failure of replacing it with safer alternative antiepileptic medication. Also, he didn't update this crucial information to other team during sign-out. This communication failure during the handover of the patient care led to patient's breakthrough seizure, additional workup, and prolonged hospital stay with additional cost burden. Nonetheless, it resulted in impairment of patient safety and exhaustion of other residents.

DISCUSSION

"Miscommunication often is not about what's said, but about what's unsaid."

Medical errors are a third leading cause of death in the United States.[1] Among the several other factors, miscommunication among the physicians involved in a care of patients is the major stumbling block in providing a safe environment with optimal care to hospitalized patients. Seventy percent of sentinel events in accredited healthcare entities result from communication failure.[2] As evidenced by The Joint Commission report (August 2012), 80% of serious medical errors do occur due to communication failures among the caregivers during transfer or handover of patient care. In academic centers, house staff or residents play a central role in providing care of inpatients under different medical specialty services. Failure of communication among the residents is one of the major cause of adverse events related to patient health.[3]

Handover or transition of care, popularly known as sign-out or handoff in the United States, simply means handling the responsibility of patient care from one physician (or a team of providers) to another. The primary objective of sign-out is an accurate transfer of information about patient's current state and plan of care. This is ideally done with both verbal as well as a written form of communication between the teams or residents. A transition of patient care serves as a substantial source of medical errors leading to delayed or inadequate management ultimately causing harm to patients. Such handovers although unavoidable do increase chances of omission of information or providing inaccurate information damaging the health of patients. Achieving continuity of care by avoiding the information gaps is a challenge in busy academic as well as private hospitals.

Accreditation Council for Graduate Medical Education **(ACGME) work-hour reform and its impact on patient safety:** Recently, studies have shown detrimental effects of residents' workload on quality care and safety of patients.[4,5] Also, there is evidence that medical errors are minimal with fewer work hours and doctor–patient ratio. This has led to work-hour reform by ACGME. ACGME resident work-hour restriction has been effectively implemented to reduce the resident fatigue which was another important factor contributing adverse events in academic centers.[6] Duty-hour restrictions have become more stringent since 2011 when overnight shifts are banned for residents and 16-h work-hour limits were put in place. This has led to an increased number of handoffs/sign-outs associated with inpatient care. Since the implementation of work hour restrictions in 2003, there is a 40% increase in intern handoffs per month as per the survey that was done in 2006. According to the same survey, an intern during the inpatient service also signed-out approximately 15 times.[5] The resident and intern "cross-covering" has become the major source of communication breakdown and discontinuity of care. This has increased the frequency of preventable adverse events in hospitalized patients.[7] The disjointed care by different physicians or medical teams with unfamiliarity to patients intensifies dissatisfaction among patients and families. The commonwealth fund recently conducted a poll regarding the patients' concerns about the healthcare revealing the lack of continuity of care as one of the topmost concerns. Currently, 20% of malpractice claims against internal medicine residents are the result of miscommunication during patient care transfer.[8]

Multiple sign-outs leading to the issue of fragmentation of patient care is a rising concern in healthcare today. Potential lapses in communication during care handover lead to delivery of different and sometimes even contradictory information to patients and their families. This ultimately takes a toll on a physician–patient relationship.

Members of a healthcare team, such as interns/residents, hospitalists, nurses, nutritionists, and physical therapists, all do experience the transfer of patient care at each transition point. In this chapter, we will focus on how sign-outs between residents affect the safety of patients, general barriers in an effective sign-out process, and how to improve the coordination of care among the residents during the handoffs or sign-outs to address this alarming issue.

Current status of resident sign-out: There are limited resources available to residents and other caregivers to address and implement effective ways of sign-outs. Residents are not being uniformly trained or supervised in a transition of patient care during their residency training.[9] A national survey done in 2006 has noted that very few residency training programs assess the ability of residents to conduct effective sign-outs.[10] Interns and junior residents learn how to sign out by observing more senior residents give sign-out.

Several academic institutes, therefore, have taken the initiative to incorporate various strategies to improve handoffs as a part of residency training. The ACGME now has an increased focus on communication skills during handoffs. It has now become mandatory for all the academic centers (residency programs) to minimize transitions in patient care by carefully designing the clinical assignments. Traditional sign-outs being implemented at some centers are still highly variable, unsupervised, and nonstandardized. This fact has led to increased potential for medical errors and fragmented care due to adverse events, prolonged hospital stay, and unnecessary medical expenses raising cost burden. Several authors have emphasized on constructing an effective sign-out process to improve a smooth transition of patient care from one provider to another (Figure 1).[3,11,12]

Effective communication during sign-out: As we see, resident sign-out is a point of vulnerability for communication failure.[13] Failure of residents to communicate the patient information effectively to the next team of residents endangers patient safety. It leads to uncertainty in decisions on patient care due to inaccurate or inadequate information regarding patient management affecting further care by unnecessary repetition of tests, the omission of certain important steps in the management, and delay/incorrect management. This highlights the importance of encouraging effective communication between the residents during the sign-out process to maintain the patient safety as well as harmony among all healthcare providers involved in the patient care.

Communication failures are far more complex and relate to hierarchical differences, concerns with upward influence, conflicting roles and role ambiguity, teamwork failure, and interpersonal power and conflict.[3]

As reported in a critical analytic study based on interviewing the internal medicine interns on night-float service at the University

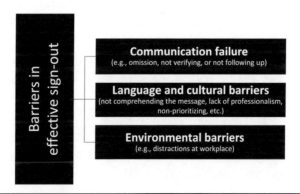

Figure 1   Illustrating barriers in an effective sign-out.

of Chicago, two categories of communication failures are found to be frequently encountered during sign-outs[14]:

1. **Content omission:** It includes omission of important information with regard to patient's active medication problems, medications and treatment plans, test results and consults, code status, baseline status, and so on.
2. **Failure-prone communication process:** It entails lack of face-to-face communication, illegible or unclear notes, and double sign-outs due to unfamiliarity with patient's status.

There is a profound variability in the ways handovers or sign-outs are being conducted in different hospitals and even in different departments in the same hospital. At some programs, providers prefer verbal communication, or written tools only, and others use electronic handoff tools. This further increases the variability in a process by which transition of care takes place across different teams in various academic centers.

The first and foremost step to address the communication failure during sign-outs is **standardizing the sign-out process** and **educating the residents to communicate effectively at the time of sign-outs**. In fact, the Joint Commission on Accreditation of Healthcare Organizations has suggested the implementation of standardization of the sign-out process as a National Patient Safety Goal (The Joint Commission 2007). The errors during sign-outs are preventable, and hospitals can improve and create a uniform process in which handover of care takes place to maintain the continuity of patient care.[15]

Improving the quality of care by improving the handovers (sign-outs): A standard, structured, and supervised handovers can improve the quality of care by reducing the errors associated with them.

The Joint Commission Center for Transforming Healthcare launched its newest project in the Targeted Solutions Tool (TST) suite: the Hand-off Communications TST. This new tool is designed to help healthcare organizations avoid communication-related miscues and errors during the handoffs.[16] Although currently there is limited evidence about the best and effective standardization approach, some of the strategies suggested by experts in the field of patient safety and quality care are discussed here.

Residents should take the sign-out as a learning opportunity where they can practice and improve their cognitive skills, such as detailed analysis of patient's condition, critical thinking, anticipation, recognizing the warning signs, planning management, interpersonal communication skills, teamwork, and collaboration with colleagues and hospital staff. Several studies have made recommendations and strategies for best practices to design safe and effective sign-out systems for residents.[4,16,17] These strategies may also be useful to hospitalists working in academic and community settings.

Using structured sign-out templates: A written template providing accurate, clear, relevant/pertinent, and updated information about a patient can minimize the content omission. Common themes to incorporate in the complete sign-out include identifying patient information, reasons for admission, code status, new events that have occurred, current medications, medications on hold (if any and reason), specific tasks to be completed, progress of illness, and anticipated events during the shift, along with a plan of action and rationale behind the plan. Whenever relevant (e.g., critically ill patient), information about advanced directive should be added to the sign-out.

Yale University researchers have developed a useful mnemonic to remember the criteria for an excellent sign-out named as **SIGNOUT** (Table 1).

The SIGNOUT mnemonic identifies criteria of comprehensive sign-out including relevant care to date, contingency plans for predictable overnight patient care events, and the importance of updated clinical information.

Table 1   Mnemonic to Remember for an Effective Sign-Out Process (SIGNOUT)

Sick or not sick, do not resuscitate orders?
Identifying patient information (name, MR #)
General hospital course (reason for admission)
New events of the day
Overall health status—getting better or worse
Upcoming possibilities with a plan, rationale
Tasks to complete overnight

Another mnemonic ANTICipate written by Vidyarthi et al.[4] is an excellent example to be used by academic centers as a guide to creating their own standard sign-out template. The ANTICipate mnemonic for written handoffs includes A—administrative data, N—new information (clinical update), T—tasks (what needs to be done), I—illness, and C—contingency planning/code status. One such standard template based on the elements of abovementioned mnemonics is created by researchers at the Ochsner health group (Table 2).[18]

Table 2   Effective and Safe Sign-Out by Using the Ochsner Handoff Template[18]

• **Demographics**
– Primary team
– Name, age, sex
– Medical record number
– Allergies
– Code status
– Body mass index
• **Illness level**
– Is the patient sick?
• **Reason for admission**
– Admitting diagnosis
– Chief complaint
• **Breif history of present illness**
– Details pertinent to current admission
– Pertinent past medical history
– Differential diagnosis
• **Hospital course**
– Current baseline status
– Updated, brief assessment by system or problem
– Recent procedures and significant events
• **Tasks**
– Advise of to-do items specific to this shift
– Advise of incoming information using if-then statements
• **Contingency plan**
– Anticipated special circumstances and plans
– Concerning family or psychosocial situations

The ultimate goal of such a structured template is to provide up-to-date and pertinent details of patient information to cross-covering residents for safe transition of care. To allow a closed loop feedback between the cross-covering residents, the sign-outs need to be edited daily.

Computer-based sign-out system (EMR handover tool): Currently, electronic sign-outs are replacing the most common and traditional sign-out methods involving the use of spreadsheets or handwritten notes. Wohlauer and colleagues demonstrated that this laborious process (handwritten sign-outs) required 51% of residents to spend 1–2 h every day transcribing data, and occasionally, this resulted in patients being completely missed on rounds.[19] With the huge patient turnover and limited staffing, it's hard for residents to spend their valuable time being spent in copying patient details from EMR on a regular basis.

Several authors have found the efficiency of computer-based sign-out as a mean of more accurate and efficient transition of patient care.[20,21]

Technological solutions can facilitate well-designed sign-out processes, but they cannot substitute for successful communication.[22] Effective verbal communication will almost certainly remain crucial to ensure proper transmission of essential clinical information and facilitate collaborative cross-checking.[23]

With the recent widespread use of computer-based sign-out systems, the issue of legible writing can be easily mitigated. Also, the standard fields used in computer-based sign-outs reduce the risk of content omission. Research suggests that the use of a computerized sign-out tool can save residents up to 45 min per day while also improving continuity of care. Seventy percent of the participating residents reported that the new tool helped them adhere to the 80-h workweek.[20,21] Automatic updating of crucial patient care information, such as medication history, vital signs, allergy information, and code status, reduces errors or omission of precarious information.

The computer-based sign-out is well designed and increases efficiency and satisfaction among the residents. However, total reliance on such electronic sign-outs without any verbal interactions increases the potential for miscommunication.

Encouraging face-to-face communication/verbal sign-outs: It's essential to understand that technology can never be a substitute for verbal or face-to-face communication where one can facilitate cross-checking of plans and collaborate with other members of a team. A skillful verbal communication delivering the accurate and essential patient information during sign-outs can be achieved using the standard language protocol. SBAR (Situation, Background, Assessment, and Recommendation) is one such tool being used to debrief the critical information about any patients during sign-outs. This model is originally based on the model used in the Navy to communicate the critical information. The SBAR process in healthcare involves first clarifying the situation, for example, identification of one's self, unit, patient, and room number. Then, pertinent background information related to the situation is communicated, which may include, but is not limited to, the admission diagnosis, list of current medications, and most recent vital signs. This is followed by an assessment of the situation and a recommendation of what to do. Whenever possible, face-to-face communications should be encouraged as telephonic conversations are usually inadequate, less effective, and more likely to be associated with errors.

The characteristics of effective verbal sign-out are pertinent, thorough, face-to-face, and one that entails the anticipation of events in order to be prepared to handle the patient care effectively and timely.

Other strategies such as interactive questioning and "read-back" techniques to confirm the understanding, keeping the information up to date, can be actively implemented by residents for effective and complete sign-outs. Remember each sign-out is the conversation, not a one-way communication like telegram.[24]

Minimizing distractions during sign-outs: Distractions in the form of phone/pager calls and interruptions by other physicians or team members can lead to communication-related errors hampering patient safety. Whenever possible, face-to-face verbal sign-outs should be arranged in a quiet place without any such distractions, allowing all the queries answered between cross-covering residents.

Residents and staff members should receive printouts of such written and verbal sign-out templates during formal training.

Evaluation and supervision of sign-outs by faculty: Recently, ACGME has mandated the careful evaluation of patient handoff process by faculty members. Such evaluations are necessary to pinpoint the deficiencies in accuracy as well as the competency of residents during sign-outs.[25] There are no validated tools available for evaluation of sign-outs, but some researchers have developed checklists which can be used by faculty to evaluate residents on the basis of sign-out and give them face-to-face feedback on a regular basis (e.g., twice a month). This has been found effective in improving the quality of residents' sign-outs as well as minimizing the adverse events affecting patient safety.[15] The goal of such evaluations and feedback from faculty is to develop insights about the significance of effective sign-out process and its role in patient safety.

Sign-out education as a part of a residency curriculum: Residents are trained formally to achieve the two of the core competency skills—communication and professionalism. These two skills are essential for the effective transition of care/handoffs. ACGME has mandated the focused handoffs (i.e., sign-out) training as a part of residency curriculum. Several studies have shown that teaching structured sign-outs helps to improve resident perceptions and performance of handoffs.[26,27] All ACGME-accredited residency programs are encouraged to facilitate sign-out education sessions to achieve competency among the residents during the transition of patient care.[28] The sign-out training is being conducted at several institutes via online modules and face-to-face interactive workshops. Researchers have found that online educational modules may provide an effective and time-efficient method for programs to teach a structured approach to patient handoffs. With the changing healthcare environment, achieving competency in conducting patient handoffs is clearly important for residents and may be efficiently assessed via an observed simulated handoff experience.[29]

Challenge of professionalism training in the context of discontinuity of care during sign-outs: Though medical students formally learn of professionalism during their preclinical years in the context of the doctor–patient relationship, this relationship of one doctor to one patient often breaks down during times of discontinuity at shift change/transition, which is often marked by unfamiliarity and lack of a prior knowledge of patients. In social sciences, this is referred to as shift-change mentality which can be correlated with "not my patient" type of attitude in residents. One of the goals of formal training of resident sign-out is to train residents to facilitate a smooth transition of patient care and optimize patient safety by developing a sense of shared responsibility and effective interpersonal communication skills during cross-covering.

In a nutshell, effective inter-physician communication is the foundation of patient safety and high-quality care. Residents being frontline care providers in academic centers, must acknowledge the inherent miscommunication in the healthcare. By notifying errors, understanding the reasons behind and implementing action plans to correct them in a timely manner and staying committed to standardized sign-outs, residents can proactively mitigate potential patient harm and improve quality of care.

REFERENCES

1. Makary MA, Daniel M. Medical error—The third leading cause of death in the US. *BMJ*. 2016; 353:i213.
2. https://www.jointcommission.org/assets/1/6/2006_Annual_Report. pdf
3. Sutcliffe KM, Lewton, E, Rosenthal MM. Communication failures: An insidious contributor to medical mishaps. *Acad Med*. 2004; 79(2):186–194.
4. Vidyarthi AR, Arora V, Schnipper JL, Wall SD, Wachter RM. Managing discontinuity in academic medical centers: Strategies for a safe and effective resident sign-out. *J Hosp Med*. 2006; 1(4):257–266. Review. PubMed PMID: 17219508.
5. Landrigan CP, Rothschild JM, Cronin JW, Kaushal R, Burdick E, Katz JT, et al. Effect of reducing interns' work hours on serious medical errors in intensive care units. *N Engl J Med*. 2004; 351:1838–1848.
6. Jamal MH, Rousseau MC, Hanna WC, Doi SA, Meterissian S, Snell L. Effect of the ACGME duty hours restrictions on surgical residents and faculty: a systematic review. *Acad Med*. 2011; 86(1):34–42. doi: 10.1097/ACM.0b013e3181ffb264. Review. PubMed PMID: 21099662.
7. Petersen LA, Brennan TA, O'Neil AC, Cook EF, Lee TH. Does house staff discontinuity of care increase the risk for preventable adverse events? *Ann Intern Med*. 1994; 121:866–872.
8. Singh H, Thomas EJ, Petersen LA, Studdert DM. Medical errors involving trainees: A study of closed malpractice claims from 5 insurers. *Arch Intern Med*. 2007; 167(19):2030–2036. PubMed PMID: 17954795.
9. Leatherman S, McCarthy D. Quality of health care in the United States: A chartbook, 2002—Focus on the patient, 2002: 99
10. Leora I, Horwitz, Harlan M, et al. Transfers of patient care between house staff on internal medicine wards: A national survey. *Arch Intern Med*. 2006; 166:1173–1177.

11. Riebschleger M, Philibert I. New standards for transitions of care: Discussion and justification. ACGME 2011 duty hour standards. www.acgme.org/acgmeweb/Portals/0/PDFs/jgme-11-00-57–59

12. Arora VM, Farnan JM. Care transitions for hospitalized patients. *Med Clin North Am.* 2008; 92(2):315–324.

13. Borowitz SM, Waggoner-Fountain LA, Bass EJ, Sledd RM. Adequacy of information transferred at resident sign-out (inhospital handover of care): A prospective survey. *Qual Saf Health Care.* 2008; 17(1):6–10.

14. Arora V, Johnson J, Lovinger D, Humphrey HJ, Meltzer DO. Communication failures in patient sign-out and suggestions for improvement: A critical incident analysis. *Qual Saf Health Care.* 2005; 14(6):401–407. PubMed PMID: 16326783; PubMed Central PMCID: PMC1744089.

15. Bump GM, Bost JE, Buranosky R, Elnicki M. Faculty member review and feedback using a sign-out checklist: Improving intern written sign-out. *Acad Med.* 2012; 87(8):1125–1131. doi:10.1097/ACM.0b013e31825d1215. PubMed PMID: 22722359.

16. Joint Commission Center for transforming healthcare releases targeted solutions tool for hand-off communications. *Jt Comm Perspect.* 2012; 32(8):1, 3.

17. Hill E, Cartabuke RH, Mehta N, Colbert C, Nowacki AS, Calabrese C, Mehdi A, Garber A, Mohmand M, Sinokrot O, Pile J. Resident-led handoffs training for interns: Online versus live instruction with subsequent skills assessment. *Am J Med.* 2017; 130(10):1225–1230. e6. doi:10.1016/j.amjmed.2017.06.003. Epub 2017 Jul 4. PubMed PMID: 28684343.

18. Breaux J, McLendon R, Stedman RB, Amedee RG, Piazza J, Wolterman R. Developing a standardized and sustainable resident sign-out process: An AIAMC national initiative IV project. *Ochsner J.* 2014; 14(4):563–568.

19. Wohlauer MV, Rove KO, Pshak TJ, Raeburn CD, Moore EE, Chenoweth C, Srivastava A, Pell J, Meacham RB, Nehler MR. The computerized rounding report: Implementation of a model system to support transitions of care. *J Surg Res.* 2012; 172(1):11–17. doi:10.1016/j.jss.2011.04.015. Epub 2011 May 5. PubMed PMID: 21777923.

20. Peterson LA, Orav EJ, Teich JM, et al. Using a computerized sign-out program to improve continuity of inpatient care and prevent adverse events. *J Qual Improv.* 1998; 24:77–87.

21. Van Eaton EG, Horvath KD, Lober WB, et al. A randomized trial evaluating the impact of a computerized rounding and sign-out system on continuity of care and resident work hours. *J Am Coll Surg.* 2005; 200:538–545.

22. Rosenblum ST, Grande J, Geissbuhler A, et al. Experience in implementing inpatient clinical note capture via a provider order entry system. *J Am Med Inform Assoc.* 2004; 11:310–316.
23. Patterson ES, Woods DD, Cook RI, et al. Collaborative cross-checking to enhance resilience. *Cogni Tech Work.* 2007; 9:155–162.
24. Cohen, MD, Hilligoss, B, Amaral, ACKB. A handoff is not a telegram: An understanding of the patient is co-constructed. *Crit Care.* 2012; 16:303.
25. Gakhar B, Spencer AL. Using direct observation, formal evaluation, and an interactive curriculum to improve the sign-out practices of internal medicine interns. *Acad Med.* 2010; 85(7):1182–1188.
26. Chu, ES, Reid, M, Schulz, T, et al. A structured handoff program for interns. *Acad Med.* 2009; 84:347–352.
27. Aboumatar, H, Allison, RD, Feldman, L, Woods, K, Thomas, P, Wiener, C. Focus on transitions of care. *Am J Med Qual.* 2014; 29:522–529.
28. Accreditation Council for Graduate Medical Education. 2013. Common program requirements. Section VI.B. Available at www. acgme.org/acgmeweb/Portals/0/PFAssets/ProgramRequirements/ CPRs2013.pdf. Accessed October 3, 2013.
29. Patterson ES, Roth EM, Woods DD, et al. Handoff strategies in settings with high consequences for failure: Lessons for health care operations. *Int J Qual Health Care.* 2004; 16:125–132.

Clinical Vignette 4: You Are Not Alone!

Tripti Chopade
University of Missouri

Clinical vignette discusses the miscommunication between nurses which resulted in patient fall and prolonged hospitalization. We will discuss the detrimental effects of workplace violence (nurse-to-nurse) on patient safety and evidence-based strategies to mitigate this issue.

THE CASE

Katie, a newly joined registered nurse (RN), was posted in a surgical ward in the large academic center 2 months back. Recently, she was taking care of Ms. X, a 45-year-old, morbidly obese female who had undergone laparoscopic cholecystectomy. Her surgery was uneventful, and she was recovering well in the surgical ward. Ms. Brown, a senior nurse, was supervising Katie and other junior nurses in the ward. Ms. Brown was quite intimidating due to her aggressive nature and condescending behavior toward the junior nurses. Late afternoon, Katie was busy reviewing physicians' orders when she heard the alarm bell from Ms. X room. She promptly went to attend Ms. X who wanted to get up and sit on the chair as she was tired of lying down on the bed all day long. It was Ms. X's post-surgery day 3 and she had an intravenous line, Foley's catheter in place. Katie was unsure if she alone can transfer Ms. X to the nearby chair. She quickly went to ask for help but couldn't find any of her junior colleagues at that time. Ms. X, the patient, was getting impatient. Katie saw her senior, Ms. Brown, working on a computer. Katie had a rough day as her morning began with Ms. Brown insulting her in front of other colleagues by accusing her of being dependent and inefficient. Being belittled by Ms. Brown earlier that day, Katie got intimidated to ask her for the help in assisting the transfer of the patient. She went back to the patient room and decided to try transferring the patient by herself. As she started supporting Ms. X while getting up from a bed, Ms. X couldn't control her balance and accidentally fell on the edge of chair hurting her forehead. Katie alone couldn't control the fall of Ms. X and regretted later. This prolonged her stay for additional management of forehead laceration.

COMMENTS

This vignette exemplifies the vertical violence/workplace bullying of new nurses/students by nurses in authoritative figure and its ultimate impact on patient safety. Katie, being a newly joined nurse in the practice, needed support and encouragement from the more experienced nurse who was supervising her. The senior nurse, on the other hand, was condescending and intimidating to her. The unprofessional behavior of senior nurse toward the junior one had affected the frank communication between the two. The collaborative workplace relationship was clearly lacking from both sides. Katie could have been more assertive to ask for the necessary assistance to prevent this fall without being intimidated.

DISCUSSION

> *"The ultimate tragedy is not the oppression and cruelty by the bad people but the silence over that by the good people."* – Martin Luther King, Jr

Communication between the members of a healthcare team is the key element in patient safety and quality care. Earlier, we have discussed how several forms of communication failure between healthcare providers (physician–nurse, physician–physician, physician–patient, etc.) and have also discussed some evidence-based strategies to overcome this issue. In this chapter, we will highlight the role of effective communication among the nurses, workplace bullying (oppression) in the nursing profession, and its impact on patient safety.

Nurses, being at the forefront of patient care, serve as a bridge to the physician–patient relationship by establishing and facilitating professional communication. Communication is in fact considered as the central task of nurses.[1,2] In an ever-evolving healthcare environment today, nurses play an equally important role in the diagnosis, management, and recovery of patients as the physicians.[3] During a hospital course, nurses are the one who spends maximum time beside the patients. As an RN to prevent unreasonable and foreseeable harm to a patient is the major responsibility of nurses despite any role or position. Nurses, therefore, may perceive themselves as "scapegoats" due to an undeniable need for establishing communication with others—health professionals, patients, and families.[4]

A collaborative working relationship is an essential element to improve the quality of nursing care and essentially patient safety. Traditionally, the nursing profession is known for the self-less and effortless service dedicated to the well-being of patients. Nurses are respected for their grace and compassion toward patients and their families during the critical periods of lives. The nursing profession is one of the highest ranked professions in the field of medicine for honesty and work ethics.[5]

Despite the astral reputation, unfortunately, the nursing field is plagued with the disruptive behaviors within the profession. As in several other professions, workplace bullying or oppression behavior is not uncommon in this profession. However, unlike other professions, workplace bullying or disruptive behaviors among nurses not only affect themselves or the workplace environment but also hamper patient safety and damage quality of healthcare. American Nurses Association has defined bullying as "Repeated, unwanted harmful actions intended to humiliate, offend and cause distress in the recipient."

Several types of bullying have been studied in the scientific literature such as intimidation, harassment, victimization, aggression, emotional abuse, and psychological harassment or mistreatment at a workplace, among others.[6] Bullying often involves the misuse of the power and injustice to those who are powerless. Researchers have used the term "horizontal (lateral)" and "vertical violence" which cover different types of harmful behaviors among the nurses including workplace bullying, aggression, and incivility.

Horizontal violence is a harmful behavior of one worker toward another who is of equal status within a hierarchy (such as staff nurses) that seeks to control the person by disregarding and diminishing his or her value as a human being. Nurse-to-nurse violence is a global truth. In a survey at a medical center, 65% of interviewed nurses reported nurse-to nurse violence has revealed the occurrence of nurse-to-nurse violence.[7] In an urban setting, 75% of nurses have found to be verbally abused by their nurse coworkers.[8]

Incivility is "one or more rude, discourteous, or disrespectful actions that may or may not have a negative intent behind them." It entails harmful behaviors such as gossiping; condescending the coworkers by calling them with demeaning names; using words, a tone of voice, or body language that humiliates or ridicules them;

belittling their concerns; profanities and pushing them or throwing things/hostile behavior; and noncooperation to coworker.[9,10]

DETRIMENTAL EFFECTS OF WORKPLACE VIOLENCE (NURSE-TO-NURSE) ON PATIENT SAFETY

A study done by Purpora et al. has reported the inverse relationship between horizontal violence and quality of care. It has been reported that as horizontal violence increased, the quality and safety of patient care decreased.[11] Vertical violence is another term coined by researchers to describe the harmful behavior of senior nurses (superior position) to the junior ones/subordinates.[12] As popularly quoted by the nursing professor Judith Meisner, "**Nurses eat their young**," abusive behavior of RN/educator toward student nurses or juniors is evidenced especially during the first years of their practice.[13] Young nurses do suffer from humiliation and stress due to such behavioral trend leading to low confidence, oppression of self, intimidation, and even quitting the jobs due to an unhealthy work environment. Repetitive abusive or hostile behavior from other nurses negatively impacts the mental and physical health of those who are victims of such behaviors.[14] This damaged work environment and a shortage of workforce due to the challenge of retention of nurses in a hospital ultimately takes a toll on quality of patient care and safety. As demonstrated in a study, there is a positive correlation between workplace bullying and medical errors attributed to the lower quality of nursing care due to personal effects and impaired functioning levels among the bullied nurses.[15] Sleep deprivation, depression, anxiety, poor concentration, and other psychophysical consequences among the practicing nurses are considered as the byproducts of workplace bullying impairing the quality of patient care and thus threatening the patient safety.

Organizational impact: Poor job satisfaction due to workplace violence leads to increased turnover of staff nurses, and nurses' retention is a huge challenge due to the increased tendency of bullied nurses to leave the jobs. The shortage of nurses is a growing concern at an organizational level as it not only lowers the productivity but causes additional financial burden in the form of expenses to recruit and train new employees (Figure 1).

Several different evidence-based strategies are proposed by nursing educational experts around the world as well as by

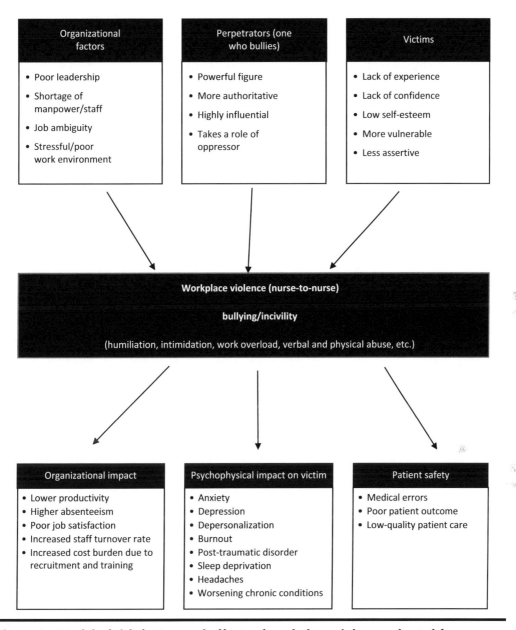

Figure 1 **Model of risk factors and effects of workplace violence adopted from a study by Moayed et al.**[16]

the American Nurses Association (ANA) to omit the workplace violence, bullying, and incivility are discussed here.

Break the silence—empowering the student nurses through the education: The first step to breaking the silence of nurses against lateral violence is to be aware of and understand the cycle of the disruptive behavior.[17] Young nurses prefer not to raise voice against such bullying or incivility at workplace due to fear and lack of knowledge. The issue of workplace violence among nurses is poorly recognized due to underreporting. By remaining silent despite experiencing or witnessing the workplace violence, one is perpetuating the cycle of the violence. Creating awareness of such potential horizontal/vertical violence among the nursing students earlier during their training and teaching them how to respond to the same earlier may help them be prepared and tackle the challenge. As recommended by experts, preventive approaches to workplace abuse are being added to the nursing education curriculum by ANA. Hidden oppression from the seniors or colleagues in the healthcare as well as suppression of anger and humiliation (self-oppression) affect the physical and psychosocial health of nurses. This cyclical pattern perpetuating unhealthy work atmosphere must be identified and interrupted. This can be addressed by educating nurses regarding the coping mechanisms such as exercising, journaling, meditation, and support groups. Student nurses need to be taught how to "speak up" for themselves. Also, they need to be assured of a support by nursing leaders against the disruptive behaviors at a workplace. Nursing educators must teach their students assertive techniques through simulations of a workplace scenario and prepare them for the inevitable. Some of the effective strategies to address the incivility in academic and practice settings, such as role playing, clinical simulation, and problem-based learning scenario, are worth being incorporated in the nursing educational curriculum.[18]

A model of education to increase the awareness of behavior and to use a technique of cognitive rehearsal of responses is considered as a powerful tool to combat disruptive behaviors among the nurses and to improve communication.[19] Nursing students must be educated to maintain an effective communication to deliver the patient-centered care. Understanding that any form of oppression/violence is unacceptable and should not be tolerated (zero tolerance) is crucial for self-protection. By integrating education into the post-clinical debriefing, effective communication strategies can be reinforced. There are online continuing education opportunities for nurses at all levels of practice to seek more information about the workplace violence prevention (NIOSH 2013). Through the preventive educational approach and resources, nurses will be more prepared to deal with the challenging situations at workplace.

Stress management among the nurses: To avoid the burnout and retain energy during the time of demand, nurses need to invest their time in self-care. The ANA has created an innovative program named Health Domains of the Healthy Nurse, Healthy Nation™ Grand Challenge including nutrition, physical activity, quality of life, rest, and safety.[20] Stress relieving strategies, such as meditation, prayers, reading, practicing forgiveness, and adopting spirituality or religious philosophies, can be utilized to cope up with the work-related stress which is the underlying factor of disruptive behaviors at workplaces.[21]

Creating codes of conduct: In one of the current literature review, it has been suggested that prelicensure nursing program must include the codes of conduct for student nurses beyond their academic dishonesty extending to social behaviors and communication policy.[22] Also, in a practice setting, nurses need to follow some code of ethics to maintain the culture of safety for colleagues and patients.

Be the change/role modeling: Students' behavior and communication are influenced by their role models during the training. Nursing educators and faculty can serve as role models and emphasize the professional behavior among the nurses through their own example. Uncivilized behavior from faculty, such as condescending, humiliating, noncooperating, and criticizing, create turmoil in students. Due to the hierarchical academic social structure, students feel powerless to raise their voice and respond against the uncivil behavior from the faculty. Anxious and confused with hypocritical behavior by mentors, students rather avoid opening up and self-sabotage themselves. Faculty members need to shoulder the responsibility of creating a stress-free, congenial academic environment among themselves as well. Such an environment is essential to retain the current faculty as well as recruit new faculty to avoid a shortage of nurse faculty. Importance of peer coaching and mentoring can be emphasized during the training.

Professional communication and collaboration training to create a culture of respect: Nurses at various levels and different roles need to develop effective communication skills to create a collaborative environment at a workplace. They can be taught how to effectively communicate with each other to resolve the conflicts and create a culture of respect by establishing a healthy interprofessional relationship. Agency for Healthcare Research and Quality's "Team Strategies and Tools to Enhance Performance and Patient Safety" (TeamSTEPPS) program (2013) is an evidence-based program developed to advance teamwork and communication among healthcare professionals.

Nursing leadership against the workplace violence: Nurses who are new in the practice need someone whom they can speak to regarding the disruptive behavior by senior nurses without any fear of retribution. Experienced nurses in a leadership role can take charge of the eradication of workplace violence among the nurses by creating and promoting **workplace violence prevention programs**. Such leaders can collaborate with the organizational administration to investigate and address the disruptive behaviors and workplace bullying by creating organizational policies against the same. The primary role of nurse leaders is to develop a code of conduct that defines acceptable behavior and behaviors that undermine a culture of safety. Nurse leaders contribute by their engagement in an evaluation and continuous improvement of the workplace violence prevention program as well as by proving counseling and support to those who are victims of such violence.

Nurses can overcome this challenge by remaining united to create a culture of respect and a sustainable professional environment centered on patient care and safety.

REFERENCES

1. Naish J. The route to effective nurse-patient communication. *Nurs Times*. 1995; 92:27–30.
2. Wallace PR. Improving palliative care through effective communication. *Int J Palliat Nurs*. 2001; 7:86–90. doi:10.12968/ijpn.2001.7.2.8919.
3. Van Niekerk LM, Martin F. The impact of the nurse-physician professional relationship on nurses' experience of ethical dilemmas in effective pain management. *J Prof Nurs*. 2002; 18:276–288. doi:10.1053/jpnu.2002.129223.
4. Ghiyasvandian, S, Zakerimoghadam, M, Peyravi, H. Nurse as a facilitator to professional communication: A Qualitative study. *Glob J Health Sci*. 2015; 7(2):294–303. doi:10.5539/gjhs.v7n2p294.

5. https://news.gallup.com/poll/224639/nurses-keep-healthy-lead-honest-ethical-profession.aspx?g_source=CATEGORY_SOCIAL_POLICY_ISSUES&g_medium=topic&g_campaign=tiles

6. Aquino K, Lamertz K. Relational model of workplace victimization: Social roles and patterns of victimization in dyadic relationships. *J Appl Psychol*. 2004; 89:1023–1034. doi:10.1037/0021-9010.89.6.1023.

7. Stanley KM, Martin MM, Nemeth LS, Michel Y, Welton JM. Examining lateral violence in the nursing workforce. *Issues Ment Health Nurs*. 2007; 28:1247–1265.

8. Rowe MM, Sherlock H. Stress and verbal abuse in nursing: Do burned out nurses eat their young? *J Nurs Manage*. 2005; 13:242–248.

9. Blanton, BA, Lybecker, C, Spring, NM. A horizontal violence position statement. Retrieved December 3, 2009, from http://proactivenurse.com/index.php?option=com_content&Itemid=22&id=83, 1998.

10. Cooper, JRM, Walker, J, Askew, R, Robinson, JC, McNair, M. Students' perceptions of bullying behaviors by nursing faculty. *Issues Educ Res*. 2011; 21:1–21.

11. Purpora, C. Horizontal violence among hospital staff nurses and the quality and safety of patient care. *Ph.D. dissertation*, University of California, San Francisco, United States—California. Retrieved November 27, 2010, from Dissertations & Theses @ University of California. (Publication No. AAT 3426213), 2010.

12. Buback D. Home study program: Assertiveness training to prevent verbal abuse in the OR. *AORN J*. 2004; 79:148–170.

13. McKenna BG, Smith NA, Poole SJ, Coverdale JH. Horizontal violence: Experiences of registered nurses in their first year of practice. *J Adv Nurs*. 2003; 42:90–96.

14. Hutchinson M, Vickers MH, Jackson D, Wilkes L. "They stand you in a corner; you are not to speak": Nurses tell of abusive indoctrination in work teams dominated by bullies. *Contemp Nurse*. 2006; 21:228–238.

15. Roche M, Diers D, Duffield C, Catling-Paull C. Violence toward nurses, the work environment, and patient outcomes. *J Nurs Scholarsh*. 2010; 42(1):13–22.

16. Moayed FA, Daraiseh N, Shell R, Salem, S. Workplace bullying: A systematic review of risk factors and outcomes. *Theor Issues Ergon Sci*. 2006; 7(3):311–327.

17. Friere P. *Pedagogy of the Oppressed*, 3rd Edition. New York: Continuum Publishing, 1971.

18. Clark, CM, Ahten, SM, Macy, R. Using problem based learning (PBL) scenarios to prepare nursing students to address incivility. *Clin Simul Nurs*. 2012; 9(3):e75–e83.

19. Griffin M. Teaching cognitive rehearsal as a shield for lateral violence: An intervention for newly licensed nurses. *J Contin Educ Nurs.* 2004; 35(6):257–263.

20. ANA. Healthy Nurse, Healthy Nation™ Grand Challenge. www.healthynursehealthynation.org/, 2017.

21. Brewer-Smyth K, Koenig HG. Could spirituality and religion promote stress resilience in survivors of childhood trauma? *Issues Ment Health Nurs.* 2014; 35(4):251–256.

22. Sanner-Stiehr E, Ward-Smith P. Lateral violence in nursing: Implications and strategies for nurse educators. *J Prof Nurs.* 2017; 33(2):113–118. doi:10.1016/j.profnurs.2016.08.007. Epub 2016 Aug 21. PubMed PMID: 28363385.

Section 3: Culture of Patient Safety

Clinical Vignette 1: A Husband's Worst Nightmare

Emily Bailey
Truman State University

Clinical vignette discusses the death of a patient due to failure at multiple levels and lays a foundation for the culture of patient safety.

THE CASE

Helen is a 50-year-old woman who came to the emergency room (ER) with chest pain for the past 1 h. Her husband Bob accompanied her and told the ER resident that they were driving to Las Vegas for their anniversary when her chest pain started suddenly. She has a chronic history of smoking. She has been smoking a pack of cigarettes for the past 20 years. She also has a past history of type 2 diabetes mellitus and hypertension for which she's taking medications inconsistently. She doesn't remember when she last saw her primary care physician. Physical examination was unremarkable. There was no chest tenderness, no murmurs, and gallops. S1 and S2 (heart sounds) can be heard on auscultation with no extra added sounds. An electrocardiogram (EKG) and telemetry along with serum troponins were ordered and were unremarkable at baseline. She was admitted to the telemetry floor, and a stress test along with every 4-h serum troponin level was ordered for the morning.

Overnight, the serum troponins began to creep up. The resident who was working two 36-h shifts did not follow up with laboratory results. The nurse who had recently joined and was intimidated by the attending did not communicate the abnormal lab results to either the resident or the attending. The morning nurse who assumed care of ten patients thought the resident was aware of the lab results and did not clarify further. Helen was taken to the cardiac lab for the scheduled stress test the next morning. The lab personnel failed to note the abnormal troponin levels because the resident did not mention it in his notes. During the stress test, the patient went into a cardiac arrest. Immediate Cardio Pulmonary

Resuscitation (CPR) was started, and resuscitation was done for an hour. Unfortunately, the patient passed away.

COMMENTS

This vignette provides an insight on how miscommunication, overworked staff, poorly designed electronic health records, inadequate documentation, patriarchal culture, and lack of culture of patient safety lead to patient harm. Here, we will discuss the use of safety culture assessment as a tool for improving the patient safety.

DISCUSSION

According to a recent study by Johns Hopkins, more than 250,000 deaths per year are due to medical errors in the United States alone.[1] If we were to place preventable adverse events on the U.S. Centers for Disease Control and Prevention's ranking of the leading causes of death, it would fall as the third leading cause of death in America after heart disease and cancer.[2]

Establishing an enhanced culture of patient safety within hospitals is the foundation by which change can occur. The road to increased patient safety is outlined by the four components of the patient safety culture model, as shown in Figure 1. All these components coincide with one another, with patient safety at the core.

The components of patient safety culture model include the following:

1. **Organizational culture:** The collection of core beliefs, attitudes, values, norms, and behavioral characteristics shared by individuals within an organization.
2. **Patient safety culture:** The result of a combination of individual and group norms, values, attitudes, beliefs, and perceptions that determine the level of commitment an organization has for health and safety.
3. **Patient safety climate:** The shared beliefs, attitudes, and perceptions of an organization toward the practices and processes by which patient safety is managed.
4. **Individual belief:** The attitude and perception of an individual within an organization toward patient safety.

Patient safety culture is a factor of "organizational culture," which is used to determine how committed an organization is regarding the management of health and safety.[3] The concepts used in the

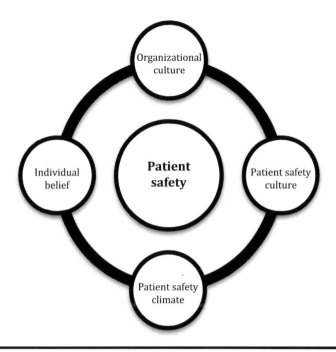

Figure 1   Patient safety culture model.[4]

definition of organizational culture are difficult to measure, which is why researchers rely on patient safety climate questionnaires to record employee perceptions about patient safety culture.[4] A positive patient safety climate has shown to be associated with positive patient safety, due to its reflection of the attitudes and beliefs held by each employee.

It is important to have a strong culture of patient safety within hospitals; patients should not have to worry about the quality of care they are receiving and should always feel confident they are in good hands. If employees are dedicated and have a strong sense of patient safety culture, patients can know with certainty that they are safe. Three underlying principles envelop a reliable culture:

1. Trust
2. Reporting
3. Improvement.

Coworkers exhibit mutual trust by reporting errors and incidents of potential danger, which leads to opportunities to learn and grow as an organization. This ultimately results in continuous improvement in patient safety.[5] Healthcare team members require a strong sense of trust, and patients should have that same level of confidence toward their healthcare providers. As a healthcare professional, one has a duty to do everything within his/her power to treat and improve the quality of life, ensuring the safety of the patient throughout the process. An incident of conceivable harm, medical error, or miscommunication has the potential to affect not only the patients but also those who love and care for them, such as loved ones and their healthcare providers.

Additionally, with preventable medical errors comes a phenomenon deemed, "second victim syndrome." When a medical professional is involved in a situation in which a preventable adverse event has occurred and become traumatized by it, they are referred to as the second victim. Research at the University of Missouri Health Care system found that almost one in seven medical professionals fit the description of second victims. It was found that 68% of second victims did not receive any institutional support. Because of these findings, a second victim support team was formed to ensure that when a clinician goes home after an unexpected occurrence, they do not go home to suffer alone. Healthcare systems with the strongest sense of safety culture support not only their patients but also their staff.[6]

A strong safety culture improves not only the healthcare outcomes of patients and clinicians but also the financial standing of institutions. Reports from the Department of Health and Human Services have found that advances in patient safety have led to an almost $20 billion decrease in costs.[7] This positive, significant monetary impact was measured over a course of four short years.

Two strategies that are promising in the realm of positively affecting the attitudes and beliefs the healthcare professionals have on patient safety are as follows:

- Walk-rounds
- Team training.

Out of eight studies done on walk-rounds, all reported an improvement in the staff perception of safety culture.[8] In a research study done by BMC Health Services, executive walk-rounds were found to have a positive effect on the safety climate attitudes of all nurses who participated in the sessions.[9] Team training also resulted in a statistically significant improvement in the safety of patient culture.[8] By simply training employees on how to communicate effectively and implementing walk-rounds as a mean of standard procedure, the safety of patients can improve significantly, emotional trauma can be avoided, and money can be saved.

REFERENCES

1. FastStats. 2018. Cdc.gov. Retrieved 7 November 2018, from www.cdc.gov/nchs/fastats/deaths.htm
2. News Release Archive. 2018. Hopkinsmedicine.org. Retrieved 7 November 2018, from www.hopkinsmedicine.org/news/media/releases/study_suggests_medical_errorsnow_third_leading_cause_of_death_in_the_us
3. Ulrich B, Kear T. Patient safety and patient safety culture: Foundations of excellent health care delivery. *Nephrol Nurs J.* 2014; 41(5):447–456, 505.
4. Morello RT, Lowthian JA, Barker AL, et al. Strategies for improving patient safety culture in hospitals: A systematic review. *BMJ Qual Saf.* 2013; 22:11–18.
5. Tsao K, Browne M. Culture of safety: A foundation for patient care. *Semin Pediatr Surg.* 2015; 24:283–287.
6. Scott SD. The Second Victim Phenomenon: A Harsh Reality of Health Care Professions. AHRQ Patient Safety Network. 2018. Psnet.ahrq.gov. Retrieved 7 November 2018, from https://psnet.ahrq.gov/perspectives/perspective/102/the-second-victimphenomenon-a-harsh- reality-of-health-care-professions
7. Agency for Healthcare Research & Quality. National Patient Safety Efforts Save 87,000 Lives and Nearly $20 Billion in Costs. 2018. Ahrq.gov. Retrieved 7 November 2018, from www.ahrq.gov/news/newsroom/press-releases/2015/saving-lives.html
8. Weaver SJ, Lubomksi LH, Wilson RF, Pfoh ER, Martinez KA, Dy SM. Promoting a culture of safety as a patient safety strategy: A systematic review. *Ann Intern Med.* 2013; 158:369–374.
9. Thomas EJ, Sexton JB, Neilands TB, Frankel A, Helmreich RL. The effect of executive walk rounds on nurse safety climate attitudes: A randomized trial of clinical units. *BMC Health Serv Res.* 2015; 5:28.

Clinical Vignette 2: A Big No-No

Emily Bailey
Truman State University

Clinical vignette discusses a case where the patient developed complications due to a surgical sponge left behind after a procedure. In addition, we will discuss patient safety issues in the operating room and use the example of aviation in improving patient safety.

THE CASE

Violet is a 25-year-old women who came to the emergency room (ER) with abdominal pain for the past 3 h. The pain is accompanied by fever and vomiting. Her temperature was 38°C, and her blood pressure was 100/60 mmHg. She was started on intravenous fluids and was given a stat dose of intravenous ondansetron. On examination, rebound tenderness was noted on her right lower quadrant. Complete blood count, serum pregnancy test, and C-reactive protein (CRP) along with computed tomography (CT) of the abdomen were ordered. Her urine pregnancy test was negative, white blood cells (WBC) count was 12,000 cells/mL, and CRP level was 11 mg/L. CT scan of the abdomen showed appendiceal wall enhancement and appendiceal wall thickening (>2 mm). The diagnosis of acute appendicitis was made, and the surgical team was consulted. She underwent appendectomy and was discharged subsequently.

Four months after the surgical procedure, she again came to the ER with right lower quadrant pain and fever. A CT scan was ordered, and it showed a tumor-like mass in the same area along with extensive abscess. Exploratory laparotomy was done, and a surgical sponge was removed from the abdominal cavity.

COMMENTS

This vignette provides an opportunity to discuss the safety issues in the operating room and the ways to mitigate these types of errors to avoid patient harm and lawsuits. Usually, before and after every surgery, instruments are counted by a nurse as a standard procedure to ensure all the instruments have been accounted for and nothing has been left behind in the patient. This could be solved by mandating a time pre- and post-procedure, creating a checklist in the operating room along with proper training of the team and incident reporting. We will also explore patient safety in the context of aviation practice.

DISCUSSION

A sentinel event can be defined as any unanticipated event in which death, physical injury, or psychological harm occurs or has the potential to occur.[1] Sentinel events can range anywhere from patient suicide, intravenous administration of the incorrect medication, wrong-site surgery, or operative/postoperative complications. Statistics calculated by the Joint Commission on Accreditation of Healthcare Organizations (JCAHO) found that the majority of sentinel events occur in general hospitals and psychiatric hospitals—68% and 11%, respectively. After reviewing a number of cases over a span of 11 years, the JCAHO discovered that 73% of sentinel events resulted in fatality, and 10% resulted in a loss of function.[2] Quality health information technology can reduce the prevalence of sentinel events because of the ability to send medical records and information electronically and communicate easily with patients and other physicians; however, if used inadequately or incorrectly, Health information technology (IT) can lead to further sentinel events.[3] Modified safety precautions taken in the field of aviation have shown a great promise in increasing patient safety.

The aviation field is comparable to healthcare in the sense that it requires great skill to keep individuals safe, and numerous precautions are necessary to ensure safety. It is important to note that although there are similarities between aviation and healthcare, healthcare differs substantially in terms of environment and complexity. Studies have shown that aviation protocols which have been adapted to fit the needs of the healthcare setting can have a great benefit in patient safety (Figure 1).

For instance, checklists play a major role in airline safety, and healthcare professions would benefit greatly from implementing them into routines. There are two principle types of checklists: normal and non-normal. Used for everyday flights in aviation, normal checklists can be used in healthcare either for nonemergent tasks where the list of tasks is too long to recall or for instances in which a process is likely to be interrupted. Normal checklists are used when the timing is not critical, and the environment allows

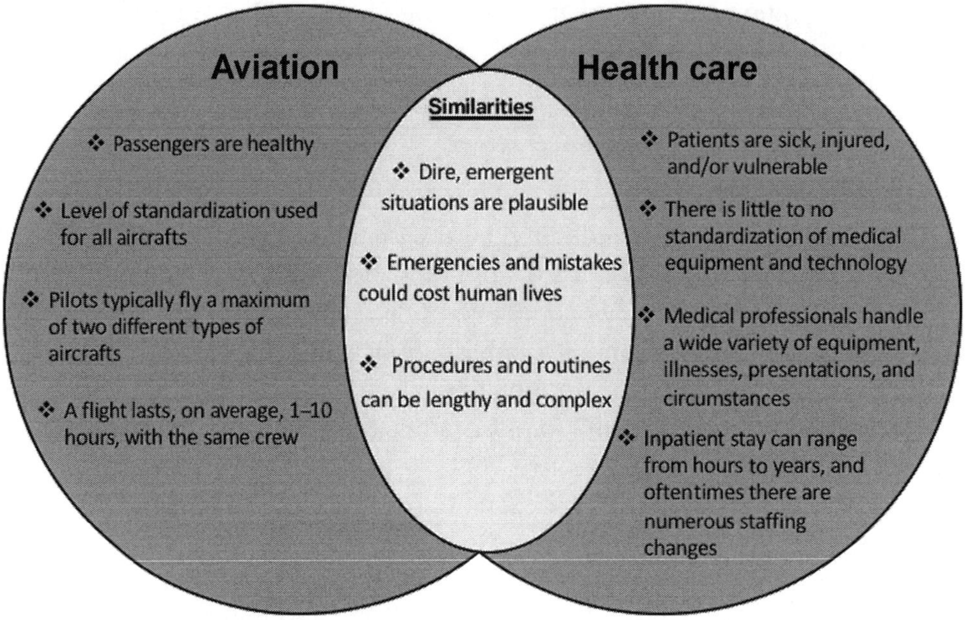

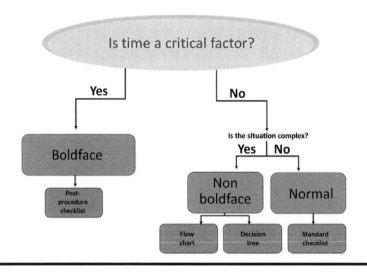

Figure 1   Compare and contrast: Aviation and healthcare.[4]

Figure 2   Determining which checklist to use.

for a physical list to be used.[5] Non-normal—or "emergency"—checklists can be broken down into two subcategories (Figure 2):

1. Boldface
2. Non-boldface

A **boldface** item calls for immediate action. If a procedure is not carried out quickly and correctly, the aircraft could be lost. In these situations, actions must be completed in such a timely manner that pilots *must* complete them by memory. Rigorous training and repetition engrave the process into the pilot's mind, until it becomes muscle memory. A checklist is used as soon as time allows in order to ensure all steps were completed correctly. In healthcare, we see boldface items utilized in patient resuscitation. Physical checklists are only used when the patient is not responding as expected, to ensure that all steps were executed in the correct order and fashion.[5] Here, we see intensive training as a key strategy in increasing patient safety.

A **non-boldface** checklist presents itself in the form of a flowchart or decision tree. Such checklists can be utilized for complex situations, when time isn't as constricted. In aviation, these are presented as color-coded decision trees and programmed into screens within the cockpit. Physicians have frequently used non-boldface charts for diagnoses, lists, and/or algorithms. These increase patient safety by potentially overcoming anchoring and confirmation biases by allowing a medical team to rule out potential diagnoses. A non-boldface item could also be used as a mnemonic.[5]

It is quite apparent that aviation and healthcare are widely different, and adopting a checklist or model from aviation without modifying it to meet healthcare standards would be ill-advised. However, it has been shown that if modifications to aviation protocols and procedures are deliberate, well-thought-out, systematic, and positive outcomes in healthcare will result. Economics is a key factor in healthcare, and studies have shown that such procedures save the healthcare industry a substantial amount of money— especially in legal fees.[4] There will always be factors of risk and danger for patients in healthcare, but we must seek ways to minimize these risks as much as we possibly can. It is a prime virtue to do no harm, and measures must be put into place to ensure this virtue is upheld.[6]

Aside from methods of aviation, utilization of the Universal Protocol in the operating room is crucial. The Universal Protocol consists of both a pre-procedure process and a surgical "time-out". The pre-procedure process confirms patient identity, surgical site, and description of procedure. A written form of consent is signed by the patient during this time, as well. A checklist is used here to ensure all necessary documents and information are accurate and available prior to patient transport to the operating room. The "time-out" is the final, standardized step of the Universal Protocol. During this time, the patient is awake and actively participating in the verification process, along with all the immediate members of the procedure team. All prior documentation, surgical information, and patient identification are reviewed once more, as a precaution. The use of the Universal Protocol increases patient safety significantly by reducing the prevalence of wrong-site or wrong-patient procedures.[7]

In addition to the Universal Protocol, checklists should be used in the operating room to ensure no surgical tools or items are left within the body where they can cause further damage in the future. The Association of perioperative Registered Nurses (AORN) has released a thorough checklist, which accounts for all items in an operating room. According to the AORN's standardized procedure, counts of all items, such as sponges, textiles, sharps, and instruments in the room, should be documented by a circulating registered nurse (RN). The circulating RN plays a crucial role in the surgical process by performing surgical counts before the procedure begins, when new items are added, before a cavity is closed, and so on. Additionally, he/she is responsible for informing the surgical team when the surgeon intentionally leaves items in the wound and sets up all instruments and supplies in a standard, organized way.[8] Use of such an in-depth checklist minimizes risk in the operating room exponentially, thereby increasing patient safety and resulting in a positive economic impact.

REFERENCES

1. www.jointcommission.org/assets/1/6/CAMH_2012_Update2_24_SE.pdf
2. www.the-hospitalist.org/hospitalist/article/123211/sentinel-events
3. www.jointcommission.org/ambulatory_buzz/what_you_can_do_to_prevent_health_it-related_sentinel_events/
4. Kapur, N., Parand, A., Soukup, T., Reader, T., Sevdalis, N. Aviation and healthcare: A comparative review with implications for patient safety. *Journal of the Royal Society of Medicine*. 2015; 0:1–10.
5. Clay-Williams, R., Colligan, L. Back to basics: Checklists in aviation and healthcare. *BMJ Quality and Safety*. 2015; 24:428–431.
6. Rutherford, W. Aviation safety: A model for health care? *Quality and Safety Health Care*. 2003; 12:162–163.

7. Stahel, P., Mehler, P., Clarke, T., Varnell, J. The 5th anniversary of the "Universal Protocol": Pitfalls and pearls revisited. *Patient Safety and Surgery*. 2009; 3:14.

8. www.aorn.org/guidelines/guideline-implementation-topics/patient-and-worker-safety/prevention-of-retained-surgical-items

Clinical Vignette 3: Alice in Wonderland

Nidhi Shankar Kikkeri
University of Missouri

Laura Qi
University of Missouri

Shivaraj Nagalli
Yuma Regional Medical Center

Clinical vignette discusses a medical error that happened due to a fatigued resident. In this chapter we will also discuss the impact of overworked health care providers and their effects on patient safety.

THE CASE

Mr. Clark is a 30-year-old male patient with a past medical history of chronic alcohol abuse and dependence, schizophrenia, seizure disorder, and depression. He is brought to the emergency department at 2 am by his wife after an accidental fall from the second floor of their house. An already busy emergency medicine resident who was in his 23rd hour of the shift was assigned to evaluate the patient. The resident physician, hoping this to be the last case before he calls for the day, finds the patient lethargic with Glasgow Coma Scale score of 9. His wife informs the resident doctor that his last alcohol drink was nearly 4 days prior.

A stat Computed Tomography (CT) head was ordered and reported as normal. Initial laboratory findings were remarkable for glucose level of 30 mg/dL and elevated creatinine kinase (CK) level. No trace of alcohol was found in his blood. Urine drug screen was normal. Intra venous (IV) thiamine and dextrose were administered with a partial improvement in his mentation. The resident admitted the patient to the general medicine ward.

The next morning, the patient is found moaning with pain and abdominal distention. The rounding physician finds him with acute urinary retention with paraplegia. A detailed neurological examination reveals additional findings of hyperreflexia over lower extremities. MRI thoraco-lumbar spine confirms spinal cord compression at T10 level.

COMMENTS

This patient initially had presented with fall from height and drowsiness. With the history of seizure disorder, chronic alcohol abuse, elevated CK, and normal CT brain, the initial diagnosis of alcohol withdrawal seizure was made. However, a simple physical examination of the back and neurological examination would have diagnosed the case in the Emergency Room (ER). The emergency medicine resident admitted to being tired toward the end of that shift. The patient underwent immediate surgical decompression. Although he is able to walk, he continues to depend on the walker.

DISCUSSION

The term "fatigue" in healthcare setting refers to a loss of interest, enthusiasm, and lack of efficiency at workplace, which has the potential to cause a negative impact on patient care.[1] The World Health Organization (WHO) defines burnout as a state of vital exhaustion and is coded as "Z73.0; Problems related to management difficulty" on International Classification of Diseases, 10th Edition (ICD-10).[2] Fatigue among healthcare workers is implicated as one of the major contributors to medical errors.

We like to bring the reader's attention to a tragic and very unfortunate case of LZ. It took the life of a young woman, which brought the much-needed focus on residents' burnout and their workload. In 1984, LZ was admitted to a famous teaching hospital in New York for flu-like symptoms but eventually succumbed to death due to serotonin syndrome.[1] She was under the care of two residents who were on their 36-h continuous shifts. Subsequent analysis into her death identified resident fatigue and lack of supervision as precipitating factors leading to her death. Further investigations led to the regulations passed by the Bell Commission in 1987, putting limitations to 80 h per week and 24 consecutive hours for residents in training at New York.[3,4]

More than a decade later, in 2003, the Accreditation Council for Graduate Medical Education (ACGME) implemented the above regulations and all residents to have at least one day off per week and not to be "on-call" more frequently than every third night.[3] Although fatigue is a common occurrence among all healthcare professions, here we discuss and focus on its causes among residents, their consequences, and strategies to deal with them effectively.

PREVALENCE

Evidence shows that physicians experience burnouts at higher incident rates than the general population.[5] The burnout rates among medical students and residents are approximately 28%–45% and 50%, respectively,[6–9] and can vary from 25% to 75% depending on subspecialties.[10] Recently, neurologists nationwide were surveyed by the American Academy of Neurology Burnout Taskforce, and approximately 60% of the respondents were found to experience at least one symptom of burnout.[11] There is an increased risk of substance abuse and suicide with increasing rates of stress among physicians.[12,13]

HOW TO MEASURE BURNOUT?

Maslach Burnout Inventory (MBI) continues to be most widely used and is considered to be the gold standard tool used in assessing the symptoms of burnout.[11,14] It involves taking a 15-min survey consisting of 22 survey questions, recognizing depersonalization, emotional exhaustion, and a decrease in personal accomplishments.[11,14,15]

FACTORS LEADING TO RESIDENT BURNOUT/FATIGUE

As indicated in Figure 1, resident fatigue can be precipitated by any one or combination of the following factors:

- Extended work shifts
- Excess workload

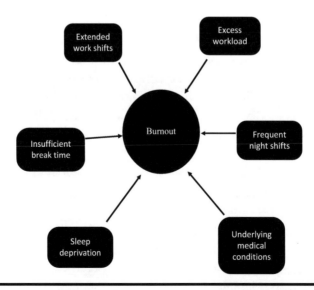

Figure 1 Picture illustrating the common causes leading to physicians' burnout.

- Underlying medical conditions
- Short staff/inadequate recruitment
- Unequal distribution of workload
- Insufficient break times
- Sleep deprivation
- Frequent changes to circadian rhythm

CONSEQUENCES OF RESIDENT BURNOUT

Resident fatigue can have adverse consequences on physical and mental well-being of residents themselves and patient care.

IMPACT OF BURNOUT ON RESIDENT WELL-BEING

- **Personality changes:** Excess work shifts leading to sleep deprivation bring changes in personalities such as irritability, disruptive behavior,[12,16] and a higher level of stress in resident life. It was noted to be worse in residents who have poor social and peer support, high patient load, and inadequate supervision from attending physicians.[17] It can lead to strain in personal relationships and cause mental health problems.[1,18]
- **Cognitive impairment:** Resident burnout causing sleeplessness leads to a short attention span, inability to focus, and impairment in cognitive abilities, psychomotor vigilance,[19] and fine motor skills.[20,21]
- **Daytime sleepiness:** Increased daytime sleepiness is associated with residents who work longer hours and have decreased sleep as reflected by higher scores on Epworth Sleepiness Scale,[22] Stanford Sleepiness Scale,[23,24] and visual analog scale.[24]
- **Attention deficit:** Extended work hours pose a threat to the safety of residents while driving; thereby increase the risk of motor vehicle accidents, phlebotomies increase the risk of needle stick injuries, and hence exposure to bloodborne pathogens.[20] A study found that daytime exposure to bloodborne pathogens was at the rate of 40 accidents per hour per 1,000 doctors in training,[25] and the risk was higher at night shifts[25,26] and during extended shifts (>24 h).

IMPACT OF BURNOUT ON PATIENT CARE

Physician burnout can adversely affect patient care. Physicians who experience burnout are more likely to prescribe wrong

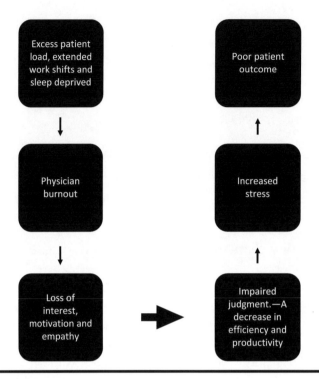

Figure 2 Flowchart describing the mechanism of physicians' burnout and its adverse effects.

medications, prescribe medications to unintended patients, not get the appropriate investigations, misinterpret laboratory reports, and encounter problems during handoffs. Surveys of interns indicate that more medical errors and attentional failures occur during extended shift rotations.[27]

Depersonalization is the term used for treating patients as objects, without empathy.[28] This can in turn strain the physician–patient relationship, gradually affecting the quality of patient care. Lack of interest in work and apathy can lead to the lack of motivation to follow up the patient with his laboratory reports or failure to communicate with other physicians involved in the patient's care, thereby increasing the probability of medical errors and adverse patient outcomes (Figure 2).[15]

In 2000, Williamson and Feyer studied the impact of sleep decprivation on performance and found that a person who has stayed awake for 24 h has the same level of diminished cognitive skill as that of someone who is intoxicated with alcohol and has a blood alcohol level of 0.10.[29]

In a randomized controlled trial by Landrigan et al., it was seen that serious medical errors made by interns were significantly more when they worked frequent extended shifts than when they worked shorter shifts (30 vs 16 h).[30]

There are studies that also evaluated the effect of "protected" sleep time on residents. One of which is a randomized controlled study, allowing residents to have a 5-h nap from 12:30 am to 5:30 am during an extended work shift resulted in decreased sleepiness and improved attention span on psychomotor testing.[31]

Studies to review the effects of 2003 ACGME work hour restrictions have shown an improvement in the resident quality of life,[31,32] burnout, motivation, time spent with family, and relationship with staff.[34]

DOES DUTY HOUR RESTRICTION REALLY IMPROVE PATIENT SAFETY?

In 2003, ACGME implemented regulations limiting residents to work not more than 80 h per week or 24-h limitation, no "on-call" more frequently than every third night, and have at least 1 day off per week. Following initial regulations, a systemic review conducted by Fletcher et al. found that there was an improvement in resident well-being, but changes in educational experience were less clear. Although mortality rates have improved since the time these regulations were imposed, it was attributed to overall improvement in delivery of quality of care than as a direct result of duty hour restrictions.[35]

Another systemic review by Ahmed et al., following ACGME's 2011 amendment of eliminating extended hour shifts for first-year residents, found no improvement in patient outcomes and also poor performance in board certification examinations by surgical residents following 2011 reform.[36]

Efforts to mitigate fatigue and sleep deprivation among residents often lead to more hand-offs and result in increased discontinuity of patient care, and the link between discontinuity and patient safety may also be harmful.[5,15]

However, another recent systemic review by Lin et al. in 2016 found that there was an improvement in resident well-being and patient safety as well but had perceived negative impact on resident education.[37]

Based on the results from randomized trials, Flexibility in Duty Hour Requirements for Surgical Trainees (FIRST) trial[38], and iCompare trial, which compared the effect of 2011 ACGME regulations versus less restricted hours in surgical and internal medicine residency programs, ACGME once again tweaked by allowing interns to work a full 24-h shift with an additional 4 h of transitioning care.[39]

STRATEGIES TO MITIGATE FATIGUE

It's important for residents or trainees to recognize the very much existence of resident fatigue and its adverse outcomes. Fatigue should not be considered as a sign of weakness in the abilities of a resident but should call for an evaluation of its precipitating factors.

Here, we list and recommend the following strategies that need to be adopted in all healthcare settings for its adequate recognition and management.

a. We recommend residency programs to provide a mandatory formal education on fatigue management.
b. Residents should be asked to take a break when they know they are tired. They can also take short naps between the end of daytime duties and initial on call handover.[1]
c. Use of burnout measuring scales such as MBI among residents.
d. Residents need to keep themselves well hydrated and have an adequate caloric intake to effectively work long hours. Trainees should be given opportunities to take a break and go out in natural light and get fresh air.[1]
e. Standardized handoff procedures can prevent medical errors significantly.
f. The hospital staff should be made aware that physicians need two full nights of sleep to recover from one night of sleep impairment. This should be kept in mind when the schedules of physicians are made.[1] This way they are not burdened with recurrent extended shifts or night shifts.
g. Residents can also use alternate transportation to go home after a long shift, rather than driving under fatigue, which can, in turn, increase the number of motor vehicle accidents.
h. An intriguing study found a higher quality of life and fewer reports of depersonalization and emotional exhaustion among residents and fellows at Mayo Clinic after a 12-week period of incentivized exercise program. This suggests that physical activity can be an effective approach for reducing burnout.[28,40]

i. Meditation can be a quick form of relaxation techniques for residents and physicians. Promoting the implementation of stress reduction programs can significantly reduce both medical errors and malpractice claims.[41,42]

j. Mindfulness, being able to focus on work amid distractions, promotes physician's ability to strengthen the patient–physician relationship.[28] Education and training in mindfulness-based stress reduction, relaxation techniques, and cognitive behavioral approaches in reducing stress are effective approaches in improving physicians' burnout, mood, and empathy.[28]

k. Continuous monitoring of compliance of duty hours. Establishment of helpline, providing easy web access to available resources in recognizing and managing burnout, could be of immense help to the residents.

l. Adequate peer and social support. Promoting physician engagement in defining causes (listen), finding and implementing solutions (act), and developing physician leaders (develop) can be the effective approaches in physician–organization relationships and reduce burnout.[28,43]

Fatigue among healthcare workers is a frequent occurrence. It is implicated as one among the common causes of medical errors in healthcare. Over years, the negative impact of physicians' burnout on their well-being and patient care is well evident and calls for a careful dissection of its causes and management. We believe that the physicians of tomorrow need to be aware of this existence and know how to manage it effectively.

Does recent amendment by ACGME in 2017 on duty hour restrictions improve resident burnout? Although previous statistical reviews have yielded conflicting and mixed results with duty hour restrictions on patient care (probably because of higher handoffs) and resident education, the resident well-being and quality of life have improved. It is strongly argued that work hour restrictions have limited the learning experiences for trainees.

This leads to a challenging task of creating a healthy and balanced work environment, which is needed for overworked healthcare professionals.

Reasonable work hours, good social and peer support, adequate supervision, promotion of sleep hygiene, preserving the continuity of care, and developing strategies in optimizing work schedules are necessary for mitigating physicians' burnout.

REFERENCES

1. Puddester D. Managing and mitigating fatigue in the era of changing resident duty hours. *BMC Med Educ.* 2014; 14(Suppl 1):S3. doi:10.1186/1472-6920-14-S1-S3; PMID: 25558784.
2. Geneva: World Health Organization; [Cited 2016 Feb 20]. World Health Organization. International Statistical Classification of Diseases and Related Health Problems. 10th Revision (ICD-10). [homepage on the Internet] Available from: http://apps.who.int/classifications/icd10/browse/2016/en#/Z70-Z76.
3. Agency of Healthcare research and Quality. Duty Hours and Patient Safety. https://psnet.ahrq.gov/primers/primer/19/duty-hours-and-patient-safety
4. Asch D, Parke R. The Libby Zion case: One step forward or two steps backward. *NEJM.* 1988; 318:771–775.
5. Spickard A Jr, Gabbe SG, Christensen JF. Mid-career burnout in generalist and specialist physicians. *JAMA.* 2002; 288:1447–1450.
6. Dyrbye LN, Thomas MR, Huntington JL, Lawson KL, Novotny PJ, Sloan JA, et al. Personal life events and medical student burnout: A multicenter study. *Acad Med.* 2006; 81:374–384. [PubMed].
7. Willcock SM, Daly MG, Tennant CC, Allard BJ. Burnout and psychiatric morbidity in new medical graduates. *Med J Aust.* 2004; 181:357–360. [PubMed].
8. Rosen IM, Gimotty PA, Shea JA, Bellini LM. Evolution of sleep quantity, sleep deprivation, mood disturbances, empathy, and burnout among interns. *Acad Med.* 2006; 81:82–85. [PubMed].
9. Shanafelt TD, Bradley KA, Wipf JE, Back AL. Burnout and self-reported patient care in an internal medicine residency program. *Ann Intern Med.* 2002; 136:358–367. [PubMed].
10. Martini S, Arfken CL, Churchill A, Balon R. Burnout comparison among residents in different medical specialties. *Acad Psychiatry.* 2004; 28:240–242. [PubMed].
11. Busis NA, Shanafelt TD, Keran CM, et al. Burnout, career satisfaction, and well-being among US neurologists in 2016 [published online ahead of print January 25, 2017]. *Neurology.* doi:10.1212/WNL.0000000000003640.
12. Shanafelt TD, Sloan JA, Habermann TM. The well-being of physicians. *Am J Med.* 2003; 114(6):513–519. doi:10.1016/S0002–9343(03)00117–7.
13. Dyrbye LN, Thomas MR, Shanafelt TD. Systematic review of depression, anxiety and other indicators of psychological distress among U.S. and Canadian medical students. *Acad Med.* 2006; 81(4):354–373.

14. Maslach C, Jackson SE, Leiter MP. *Maslach Burnout Inventory Manual*. 3rd ed. Palo Alto, CA: Consulting Psychologists Press, 1996.

15. Sigsbee B, Bernat JL. Physician burnout: A neurologic crisis. *Neurology*. 2014; 83(24):2302–2306. doi:10.1212/WNL.0000000000001077.

16. Dyrbye LN, Massie FS Jr, Eacker A, Harper W, Power D, Durning SJ, Thomas MR, Moutier C, Satele D, Sloan J, Shanfelt TD. Relationship between burnout and professional conduct and attitudes among US medical students. *JAMA*. 2010, 304:1173–1180.

17. Ford CV, Wentz DK. Internship: What is stressful? *South Med J*. 1986; 79(5):595–599. [PubMed: 3704727].

18. Wallace JE, Lemaire JB, Ghali WA. Physician wellness: A missing quality indicator. *Lancet*. 2009, 374:1714–1721.

19. Sharp KH, Vaughn GM, Cosby PW, Sewell CE, Kennaway DJ. Alterations of temperature, sleepiness, mood, and performance in residents are not associated with changes in sulfatoxymelatonin excretion. *J Pineal Res*. 1988; 5(6):499–512. [PubMed: 3225734].

20. Weiss P, Kryger M, Knauert M. Impact of extended duty hours on medical trainees. *Sleep Health*. 2016; 2(4):309–315. doi:10.1016/j.sleh.2016.08.003.

21. Ayalon RD, Friedman F Jr. The effect of sleep deprivation on fine motor coordination in obstetrics and gynecology residents. *Am J Obstet Gynecol*. 2008; 199(5):576 e571–575. [PubMed: 18822404].

22. Pikovsky O, Oron M, Shiyovich A, Perry ZH, Nesher L. The impact of sleep deprivation on sleepiness, risk factors and professional performance in medical residents. *Isr Med Assoc J*. 2013; 15(12):739–744. [PubMed: 24449976].

23. Saxena AD, George CF. Sleep and motor performance in on-call internal medicine residents. *Sleep*. 2005; 28(11):1386–1391. [PubMed: 16335328].

24. Arnedt JT, Owens J, Crouch M, Stahl J, Carskadon MA. Neurobehavioral performance of residents after heavy night call vs after alcohol ingestion. *JAMA*. 2005; 294(9):1025–1033. [PubMed: 16145022].

25. Parks DK, Yetman RJ, McNeese MC, Burau K, Smolensky MH. Day-night pattern in accidental exposures to blood-borne pathogens among medical students and residents. *Chronobiol Int*. 2000; 17(1):61–70. [PubMed: 10672434].

26. Ayas NT, Barger LK, Cade BE, Hashimoto DM, Rosner B, Cronin JW, et al. Extended work duration and the risk of self-reported percutaneous injuries in interns. *JAMA*. 2006; 296(9):1055–1062. [PubMed: 16954484].

27. Barger LK, Ayas NT, Cade BE, Cronin JW, Rosner B, Speizer FE, et al. Impact of extended- duration shifts on medical errors, adverse events, and attentional failures. *PLoS Med.* 2006; 3(12):e487. [PubMed: 17194188].

28. Deb A. Practical considerations in addressing physician burnout. *Continuum.* doi:10.1212/CON.0000000000000461.

29. Williamson AM, Feyer AM. Moderate sleep deprivation produces impairments in cognitive and motor performance equivalent to legally prescribed levels of alcohol intoxication. *Occup Environ Med.* 2000; 57(10):649–655.

30. Landrigan CP, Rothschild JM, Cronin JW, Kaushal R, Burdick E, Katz JT, et al. Effect of reducing interns' work hours on serious medical errors in intensive care units. *N Engl J Med.* 2004; 351(18):1838–1848. [PubMed: 15509817].

31. Volpp KG, Shea JA, Small DS, Basner M, Zhu J, Norton L, et al. Effect of a protected sleep period on hours slept during extended overnight in-hospital duty hours among medical interns: A randomized trial. *JAMA.* 2012; 308(21):2208–2217. [PubMed: 23212498].

32. Levine AC, Adusumilli J, Landrigan CP. Effects of reducing or eliminating resident work shifts over 16 hours: A systematic review. *Sleep.* 2010; 33(8):1043–1053. [PubMed: 20815185].

33. Fletcher KE, Underwood W III, Davis SQ, Mangrulkar RS, McMahon LF Jr, Saint S. Effects of work hour reduction on residents' lives: A systematic review. *JAMA.* 2005; 294(9):1088–1100. [PubMed: 16145030].

34. Hutter MM, Kellogg KC, Ferguson CM, Abbott WM, Warshaw AL. The impact of the 80-hour resident workweek on surgical residents and attending surgeons. *Ann Surg.* 2006; 243(6):864–871. discussion 871–865. [PubMed: 16772790].

35. Fletcher KE, Reed DA, Arora VM. Patient safety, resident education and resident well-being following implementation of the 2003 ACGME duty hour rules. *J Gen Intern Med.* 2011; 26(8):907–919.

36. Ahmed N, Devitt KS, Keshet I, et al. A systematic review of the effects of resident duty hour restrictions in surgery: Impact on resident wellness, training, and patient outcomes. *Ann Surg.* 2014; 259(6):1041–1053. doi:10.1097/SLA.0000000000000595.

37. Lin H, Lin E, Auditore S, Fanning J. A narrative review of high-quality literature on the effects of resident duty hours reforms. *Acad Med.* 2016; 91(1):140–150. doi:10.1097/ACM.0000000000000937.

38. Doolittle B. ACGME Duty Hours Not the Only Big Change in Requirements. https://knowledgeplus.nejm.org/blog/acgme-duty-hours-not-the-only-big-change-in-requirements/.

39. Bilimoria KY, Chung JW, et al. National cluster-randomized trial of duty-hour flexibility in surgical training. *N Engl J Med*. 2016; 374(8):713–727. doi:10.1056/NEJMoa1515724. Epub 2016 Feb 2.

40. Weight CJ, Sellon JL, Lessard-Anderson CR, et al. Physical activity, quality of life, and burnout among physician trainees: The effect of a team-based, incentivized exercise program. *Mayo Clin Proc*. 2013; 88(12):1435–1442. doi:10.1016/j.mayocp.2013.09.010.

41. Shanafelt TD. Enhancing meaning in work: A prescription for preventing physician burnout and promoting patient-centered care. *JAMA*. 2009; 302(12):1338–1340. doi:10.1001/jama.2009.1385.

42. Jones JW, Barge BN, Steffy BD, et al. Stress and medical malpractice: Organizational risk assessment and intervention. *J Appl Psychol*. 1988; 73(4):727–735. doi:10.1037/0021-9010.73.4.727.

43. Swensen S, Kabcenell A, Shanafelt TD. Physician-organization collaboration reduces physician burnout and promotes engagement: The Mayo Clinic experience. *J Healthc Manag*. 2016; 61(2):105–127.

Clinical Vignette 4: A Doctor's Curse

Suganiya Srikanthan
Saint James School of Medicine

The importance of infectious disease control and prevention is emphasized in healthcare training. Every individual on a healthcare team completes a training that details appropriate measures to take before patient interactions, including hand hygiene, prior to gaining access to a hospital work environment. However, many often lapse in the practice of proper hand hygiene. This case illustrates the harmful clinical consequences that can follow on failure to practice proper hand hygiene, and we will discuss the appropriate hand hygiene.

THE CASE

Mrs. Sarah Huckabee was a 70-year-old Caucasian woman with a past medical history of hypertension and type 2 diabetes that was brought to the emergency department from a nursing home for diarrhea with lower abdominal pain and fever. The nursing home reported that she was febrile and had three bouts of watery, non-bloody, non-bilious diarrhea with mucus since yesterday. The patient was brought in on a stretcher; however, she was still able to weakly verbalize her complaints. She reported abdominal pain to be 8/10, limited to her lower abdomen, constant, non-radiating, with no alleviating or aggravating factors, and no previous experience of similar symptoms. Vital signs were blood pressure of 110/79, heart rate of 101, temperature of 38.8°C (101.8°F), and respiratory rate of 19. Focused physical examination findings included dry mucous membrane and lower abdominal tenderness. The patient's only at-home medication was captopril 25 mg oral twice a day.

The nursing home physician was an on-call attending for the hospital to which Mrs. Huckabee was brought, and he made his last visit 1 week ago. At that time, Mrs. Huckabee had no complaints or abnormal clinical findings. The physician in the emergency department had admitted two other patients from Mrs. Huckabee's nursing home: they both had multiple bouts of diarrhea and fever similar to Mrs. Huckabee. The patients all recalled that the physician examining them rushed from the hospital and quickly examined them without using gloves. The hospital floor on which the nursing home physician worked had precautions for *Clostridium difficile* after a patient was infected. Mrs. Huckabee and the two other patients were also diag-nosed with *C. difficile* infection confirmed with toxin stool analysis.

The nursing home physician's preceding exposure to *C. difficile* and the subsequent link to three patients who all had similar clini-cal presentation and reported that the physician did not use gloves during his examination indicate inappropriate contact precautions to prevent transmission of *C. difficile* for patients in healthcare facilities.

COMMENTS

As can be seen in the clinical scenario, the physicians' lack of adherence to hand hygiene protocols in place for prevention of *C. difficile* infection leads to severe consequences for his patients. A simple task that takes a few minutes can have a great impact on the cascade of negative events that follow and shape the future of healthcare. If this precaution had been taken, the patients would not have made the emergency room visit, necessitating the use of resources including medical personnel, facilities, and equipment that would have otherwise been used to aid more dire patients.

DISCUSSION

There are many different options available to prevent the transmission of infectious diseases, and hand hygiene is one of the most effica-cious in reducing the incidence of gastrointestinal and respiratory infections. Education on hand hygiene has been identified as the most effective intervention in reducing the incidence of infectious dis-ease[1] and is provided to all the members of a healthcare team.[1] The consistent practice of proper hand hygiene prioritizes patient safety, and enforcement of hand hygiene protocol is important to yield and sustain benefits of this intervention. The most commonly utilized methods to prevent disease transmission before directly providing patient care are the use of alcohol-based hand sanitizer, use of medi-cal examination gloves, and handwashing with soap (nonantibacterial and bacterial are effectively the same in preventing infections).

There are multiple factors that need to be assessed to deter-mine the quality of healthcare. The Donabedian model is a quality paradigm of three factors assessing quality of hand hygiene: struc-ture, process, and outcome. Structure refers to the availability of resources to carry out appropriate hand hygiene, whereas process refers to the actual practice of hand hygiene. The outcome in the paradigm refers to both clinical consequences and business/finan-cial outcomes. The interconnections between the three different components of the Donabedian model as well as examples of each are clearly outlined in Figure 1.[2]

The structural component of this system is in relation to adequate provision of supply and education, thereby successful execution of hand hygiene. This involves carefully considered and planned placement of sinks with soap dispensers, alcohol-based sanitizers, gloves of various sizes provided in every patient room, mandatory hand hygiene information sessions, and strategically placed posters near these hand hygiene stations as well as routinely checking all dispensers for sufficient product availability.

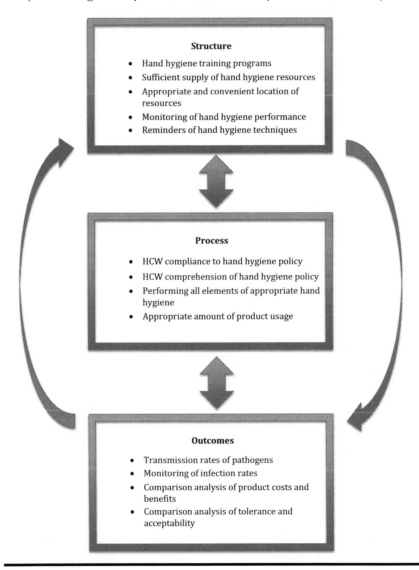

Figure 1   Donabedian model factors of hand hygiene.

The process in the Donabedian paradigm involves ensuring healthcare workers (HCWs) have an understanding of the hand hygiene education provided as well as compliance with the correct technique, use of appropriate volume of product, and ensuring implementation of alternative methods of hand hygiene when a certain form is not available.

Finally, interconnected with both structure and process, the outcome provides crucial data regarding the effects these factors had on infection rates, transmission rates, and costs and benefits of implemented products and services. All of these factors work in conjunction to help healthcare facilities develop the optimal system for hand hygiene promoting patient safety.[2]

Hand hygiene alternatives to handwashing with soap and water include the use of antiseptic wipes, rubbing alcohol, antibacterial liquid/foam sanitizer, and use of medical gloves. However, the protocol necessary for preventing the spread of *C. difficile* does not include the use of hand sanitizer or any alcohol-based rub, as alcohol is not effective in killing *C. difficile* spores. The current contact precautions for *C. difficile* are detailed in Table 1.[3]

The Centers for Disease Control and Prevention (CDC) recommends handwashing with soap and water, rubbing vigorously for at least 15 s, and covering all surfaces of the hands and fingers.[4] Clostridium difficile infection (CDI) may develop through a fecal–oral route of transmission or soon after antibiotic use, which can disrupt intestinal microbial flora.

A *New England Journal of Medicine* study estimated the incidence of CDI in the United States to be about 453,000 in 2011,

Table 1   Contact Precautions for Patients with Known or Suspected *Clostridium difficile*

- Patients infected with *C. difficile* should have a private room or share a room only with other patients infected with *C. difficile*.
- Healthcare providers (and possibly visitors) must use gloves and wear a gown over their clothing when entering the room and while taking care of patients with *C. difficile*.
- Shared medical equipment must be cleaned or dedicated.
- When leaving the room, hospital providers and visitors should remove their gown and gloves and clean their hands.
  - Proper hand hygiene is using soap and water (not alcohol-based hand rubs, as they are not sporicidal against *C. difficile*) in conjunction with gloves (as handwashing with soap and water may not completely remove *C. difficile* spores).

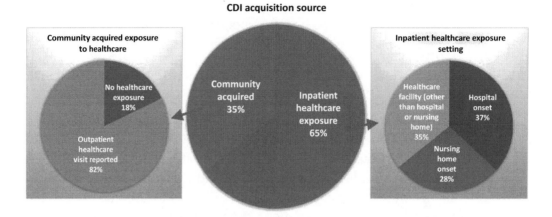

Figure 2 **Percentage of CDI acquisition source in community-acquired exposure to healthcare versus inpatient healthcare exposure setting.**

with a 6.4% mortality rate. In this study, there were an estimated 293,300 cases of healthcare-associated *C. difficile* and 159,700 community-associated cases of *C. difficile*, represented and further enumerated in Figure 2[5]:

As the above data illustrate, nosocomial infections account for the vast majority of CDI. *C. difficile* transmission in hospitals and long-term care facilities is rampant from contamination of hands, clothing, and stethoscopes in HCWs, to name just a few sources of infection. Research shows that handwashing with soap and water is superior to alcohol rub and antiseptic wipes, with respect to eliminating transmission risk of *C. difficile*.[6]

Despite the abundance of signs reminding both HCWs and visitors of medical facilities of hand hygiene, there is a lack of adherence in actual practice. A prominent example is in physicians, who are often limited in the time they spend with each patient. The increased time that is required to wash their hands and ensure they are fully dry before approaching the patient can significantly impact the amount of time devoted to patient care, though it is necessary for patient safety and accordingly patient care.[7] Practicing appropriate prevention strategies for infectious disease reduces potentially unnecessary usage of resources to diagnose and care for patients. These resources can be allocated to less preventable medical conditions. Hence, physicians washing their hands when necessary, despite the increased time required to do so, is the most efficient strategy for providing patient care.

To improve protocol compliance and prevent transmission of infection in any medical care facility, the statistics of hand hygiene program implementation, HCW compliance, and rates of infection need to be monitored. The Donabedian paradigm of quality care has been continuously adopted to uphold the standards of quality healthcare for all members of the healthcare team worldwide. Although Donabedian emphasized the importance of the three factors within his paradigm, the most important encompassing factor that links these elements and assures lasting changes is genuine care for one's patients.[8] This will help modify current practices to create sustainable and beneficial outcomes.

REFERENCES

1. Aiello AE, Coulborn RM, Perez V, Larson EL. Effect of hand hygiene on infectious disease risk in the community setting: A meta-analysis. *Am J Public Health.* 2008;98(8):1372–1381.
2. *WHO Guidelines on Hand Hygiene in Health Care: First Global Patient Safety Challenge Clean Care Is Safer Care.* Geneva: WHO; 2009. 2, Hand hygiene as a quality indicator for patient safety. Available from: www.ncbi.nlm.nih.gov/books/NBK144019/
3. www.cdc.gov/hai/organisms/cdiff/cdiff_faqs_hcp.html
4. www.cdc.gov/handhygiene/providers/index.html
5. Lessa FC, Mu Y, Bamberg WM, Beldavs ZG, Dumyati GK, Dunn JR, et al. Burden of Clostridium difficile infection in the United States. *N Engl J Med.* 2015;372(9):825–834.
6. Oughton MT, Loo VG, Dendukuri N, Fenn S, Libman MD. Hand hygiene with soap and water is superior to alcohol rub and antiseptic wipes for removal of Clostridium difficile. *Infect Control Hosp Epidemiol.* 2009;30(10):939–944.
7. Mcdonald LC, Gerding DN, Johnson S, Bakken JS, Carroll KC, Coffin SE, et al. Clinical practice guidelines for Clostridium difficile infection in adults and children: 2017 update by the Infectious Diseases Society of America (IDSA) and Society for Healthcare Epidemiology of America (SHEA). *Clin Infect Dis.* 2018;66(7):e1–e48.
8. Ayanian JZ, Markel H. Donabedian's lasting framework for health care quality. *N Engl J Med.* 2016;375(3):205–207.

Clinical Vignette 5: The Real Price of Smoking?

Ahmer Asif
University of Missouri

We will discuss a case of a patient fall and its consequences. We will also discuss the ways to improve fall protocol in the hospital.

THE CASE

Mr. Clarkson, who is an 85-year-old male with a known history of A-Fib (atrial fibrillation), MI (myocardial infarction), CABG (coronary artery bypass grafting), DM (diabetes mellitus), and smoking, admitted from emergency department (ED) to telemetry unit for cardiac monitoring after an episode of syncope at home. This episode was sudden in onset and lasted a few seconds, and the patient regained consciousness within no time. He had syncopal episodes in the past. Mr. Clarkson denies hitting his head during the fall or having any injuries. No aggravating or relieving factors that the patient or his wife mentioned except sudden standing from a lying position makes him feel dizzy. His wife reported that this is her husband's third admission in 6 months and he is getting weaker over time. Yesterday he had fallen at home prior to admission and complains of neck and back pain after the fall. She also complained that her husband is having some memory problems and he is not taking his prescribed medication the way he should and is becoming more fatigued. The wife reported that Mr. Clarkson takes more than ten medications for cardiac conditions, diabetes, including anticholinergics, antihypertensives, antiarrhythmics, and analgesics but he is now forgetting taking his medications. The patient also has problems with leg cramping upon walking. He has sleeping issues at night too and mostly sleeps in his chair.

He is a chronic smoker and smokes 1.5 PPD (pack per day) but does not drink alcohol. He is trying to cut off his smoking habit but it is not helping him much. Even in the hospital, the patient just could not help himself, insisted on going out for smoking every hour, and refused nicotine patch. The hospital staff except counseling him regarding smoking could not do much, in order to maintain their patient-generated post-discharge hospital ratings. The patient was well informed that he is at high fall risk and with the risk of injury. He was being monitored very carefully and all risk assessment tools and scores were being used. On the third day of admission when he went out for smoking, he was unaccompanied and tripped over a step and received multiple bruises and fracture of the hip joint. All this contributed towards making his hospital course very complicated.

COMMENTS

This clinical vignette enlightens the critical nature of *patient falls* in a healthcare facility, resulting in the patient having multiple injuries, that is, bruises, fractures, prolonging the patient hospital course, and increasing the cost of the hospital stay as well. It also highlights multiple factors contributing towards the patient falls such as smoking, cardiac history, noncompliance with medications, and old age. If a staff member while going for smoking accompanied the patient, he would have avoided the fall. Furthermore, this case emphasizes on the fact that hospitals allow their patients to go for smoking during their hospital stay just to maintain their patient-generated post-discharge ratings, which is one of the factors resulting in patient falls. However, multiple steps have been taken by the healthcare organizations to prevent the patient falls, but still a pressing need exists for more development on this issue.

DISCUSSION

A fall can be defined as an abrupt, unintended descent, with the patient having or not having the injury, resulting in the patient lying on the floor, on or against some other object, another person, or some other surface.[1] According to an estimation, in the U.S. hospitals, between 700,000 and 1,000,000 people fall each year.[2] Out of all those patients, from 30% to 35% bear an injury (e.g., fracture, head trauma) because of the fall, and roughly 11,000 falls are deadly.[3–7] Injuries resulting due to these falls can increase the hospital stay of almost 6.3 days,[8] as well as the cost for a somber fall with injury, approximately $14,056 per patient.[9] Falls can also lead to patient apprehension, loss of confidence in mobility and activities, social isolation, and eventually an elevated risk of falls (Figure 1). Centers for Medicare & Medicaid Services have identified the falls to be an avertable incident that should never happen.

Despite multiple efforts being done in the healthcare facilities, it is undeniable to state that patient falls is still a major problem. Avoiding the patient falls is a multifaceted and complicated issue

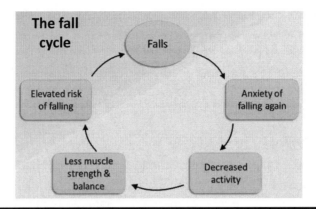

Figure 1   The fall cycle.

that demands the use of a robust approach to measure all the variables contributing potentially to the patient falls. Once the estimation of the variables has been done, the next step is the analysis of the data to conclude the primary causative factors. By following this process, multifaceted, focused, and stable improvements can be implemented in the healthcare facilities. Former studies have shown that focused interventions on discrete components or risks of falls have been ineffective[1] and that the fall reduction programs that have implemented simultaneous strategies to counter the multitude of aspects responsible for falls have been most effective. These strategies include improving the tools needed for the assessment of the fall risk, warranting the patient safety while toileting, making better the communiqué among staff members regarding fall risks, using mats and low beds, involving the patient's family within the context of care, and improving the level of education between staff and patient, to lessen the patient falls.[1]

BACKGROUND OF PATIENT FALLS

Over a span of the last six decades, hundreds of published research studies have focused broadly on patient falls. All of them aiming to make critical and other healthcare facilities a much better and safer environment for the patients. Specifically, these 50 years are considered historically to be a remarkable era where Western technologically advanced states have made substantial enhancements in the fields of medicine and patient safety. The upshot of these advancements was that major changes were needed and then applied to how healthcare workers are to be recompensed by third-party payers. So the query develops that why even after an enormous number of epidemiological studies on patient falls, the number of patient falls have not yet reduced leading to significantly fewer discharges with such incident?

Early on, for example, in the mid-1950s, the literature had just a few reports of patient falls. Since that time, multiple studies have been published all over the world. The states with subsequently significant developments in this regard are Canada,[10] Italy,[11] Australia,[12] Spain,[13] Taiwan,[14] United Kingdom,[15] and Switzerland.[16] Review of references of just one American[17] and one Australian[12] study makes it easier for us to determine that since the mid-1950s, essentially many hundreds of these papers have been added to the published writings. Undoubtedly, this advocates that patient falls is an issue of prime importance that generated a substantial interest predominantly among doctors and nurses to whom the assurance of healthcare facilities offering a safe and healthy environment for the public where they can have eminent patient care is of great concern.

CHALLENGES OF FALL PREVENTION?

Fall prevention among patients in hospitals and outside necessitates an interdisciplinary and multidimensional approach to care. More or less some measures of fall prevention care are greatly routinized but other features still need to be modified to the specific risk profile of each patient individually. No matter how talented and hardworking a physician is, he cannot prevent the patient falls by working alone. Relatively, this issue needs an active participation of numerous individuals, together with many disciplines and teams playing their part collectively in making the patient care better. In order to achieve this harmonization and coordination, first-class fall prevention requires structural principles and operational practices that should not only endorse the individual expertise but also the teamwork and communiqué. Mcclure et al., in 2009, proposed a model that can potentially set off changes on an enormous scale, create an effect that is normative, and attain a more stable distributive process. This model is particularly for healthcare facilities (hospitals, nursing homes) and involves prevention of fall and subsequent injury interventions at patient, unit, and organizational level[18,19] (Figure 2).

In addition to that, there needs to be a balance between fall prevention undertakings and other contemplations. This includes curtailing the restraints and sustaining the patient's mobility to

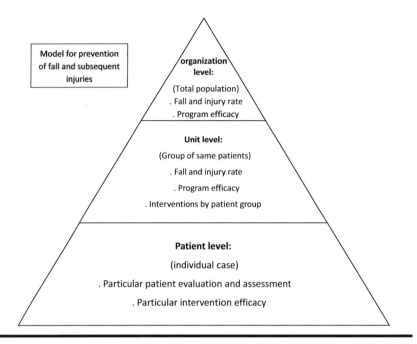

Figure 2   Model for prevention of fall and subsequent injuries.

improve the patient care. For that reason, all that we need is a system focus to make the required changes to improve the fall prevention. In summary, the five main challenging factors that need to be taken care of to prevent falls are that fall prevention

1. Needs to be more tailored and personalized
2. Needs to be balanced with other concerns and primaries for the patients
3. Needs to be balanced with the requirement to make the patient mobile
4. Needs an organizational, unit, and patient level approach altogether
5. Is one of the multiple actions required to save the patients from harm during their hospital stay.

CLASSIFICATION OF PATIENT FALLS

It is imperative to understand the causes of patient falls in order to devise a prevention program. Morse et al.,[20] in 1987, developed a classification system which is quite useful. According to it, patient falls can be categorized into three types:

1. **Physiological (anticipated):** Most of the inpatient falls fall into this category. These falls majorly happen in patients who have anticipated risk factors for falls, which can be recognized beforehand. It includes patients with altered mental status, frequent toileting needs, abnormal gait, or high-risk medications. Significant steps to take for the avoidance of falls in these patients are close supervision together with efforts to entertain the patient's risk factors.
2. **Physiological (unanticipated):** These falls mostly occur in patients who are at low risk of fall, due to an episode whose timing cannot be projected or estimated. This includes stroke, seizure, or a syncopal episode. Post-fall risk assessment along with measures to prevent injury and its recurrence is of high importance in these patients.
3. **Accidental:** These falls are majorly common in low-risk patients who suffer an environmental hazard. Their risk can be reduced by improving the environmental safety.

TOP CONTRIBUTING FACTORS OF PATIENT FALLS

Analysis of the literature revealed seven major factors—conditions recognized most repeatedly by healthcare facilities—contributing to falls and falls with injury. They are as follows:

1. Inadequate assessment of fall risk
2. Failure of the handoff communications
3. Issues with the call light
4. Issues with the toileting
5. Insufficient staff training, supervision, ranking, or skill mix
6. Deviation from adherence to conventional protocols and safety principles
7. Problems with the medications (sedatives, narcotics, stimulants, etc.)

WHAT ARE THE UNIVERSAL FALL PRECAUTIONS (FIVE P'S) AND HOW THEY CAN BE PERFORMED?

These precautions are the keystone of any healthcare facility having a fall prevention program, as they relate to all patients round the clock regardless of the fall risk. Implementation of these precautions necessitates training all hospital staff who deal with patients, irrespective of whether they are physicians. These

precautions swirl around keeping the patient's environment protected and relaxed. Sustaining a benign and calm environment is
the obligation of the hospital independent of a patient's specific
risks for falls because the inability to do so can put any patient at
risk. Hence, we can say that universal fall precautions comprise
the fundamentals of patient safety.

Universal fall precautions need to be performed from the
perspective of both the patients as well as the physical environment. An excellent basic strategy for the precautions that need
checking on the patient, for instance ascertaining the patient's
personal belongings are within reach, is hourly rounding. Hourly
rounding can be defined classically as hourly visits between 6
am and 10 pm and visits every 2 h between 10 pm and 6 am.
A nurse and a nurse assistant alternating with each other can
carry it out. If the patients at any time are sleeping, they are not
disturbed. Clinicians and nurses can use the five P's strategy during hourly bedside rounds. For example, the five P's could be as
follows:

1. **Pain:** Healthcare workers need to assess the patient's pain
   level. Medicine is prescribed if the patient is in pain.
2. **Personal needs:** Ask the patient for help using the toilet, for
   nutrition, for water, and for empty commodes/urinals.
3. **Position:** Assist the patient to get into a relaxed position or
   if immobile, then help the patient to turn to retain the skin
   continuity.
4. **Placement:** Focus that the patient's critical needs (e.g., call
   light, TV remote, books, newspapers, toileting equipment) are
   within the easy approach.
5. **Prevent fall:** Ask the patient or family members to put on call
   light if the patient needs to wake up.

USPSTF RECOMMENDATIONS FOR FALL PREVENTION IN OLDER ADULTS

The United States Preventive Services Task Force (USPSTF) has the
following recommendations for fall prevention community-dwelling
older adults (Table 1)[21]:

Table 1   Interventions to Prevent Falls in Older Adults (Age 65 or Older) (USPSTF)

Recommendations	Suggestions for Practice	USPSTF Evidence
The USPSTF recommends exercise interventions to prevent falls in community-dwelling adults 65 years or older who are at increased risk for falls.	Offer or provide this service.	There is moderate certainty that exercise confers a moderate net benefit in the reduction of falls.
The USPSTF recommends that clinicians selectively offer multifactorial interventions to prevent falls in community-dwelling adults 65 years or older who are at increased risk for falls.	Offer or provide this service for selected patients depending on individual circumstances. Patients and clinicians should consider the balance of benefits and harms based on the circumstances of prior falls, the presence of comorbid medical conditions, and the patient's values and preferences.	Existing evidence indicates that the overall net benefit of routinely offering multifactorial interventions to prevent falls is small.
The USPSTF recommends against vitamin D supplementation to prevent falls in community-dwelling adults 65 years or older.	Discourage the use of this service.	There is adequate evidence that the overall harms of vitamin D supplementation are small to moderate.

PRACTICES NEEDED TO BUILD A SUCCESSFUL FALL PREVENTION PROGRAM IN A HEALTHCARE FACILITY

For many years, fall prevention has been the focus of rigorous research and quality improvement practices that helped devise successful fall prevention programs. These efforts instigate by estimating the patient's risk of falls at an individual level. Several clinical estimation rules for identification of high-risk patients exist, but none of them were proven significantly precise. The Joint Commission suggests the underlying actions to facilitate healthcare organizations to make a fall prevention program and in turn prevent falls and fall-related injury. A successful program needs leadership assurance and a systematic, consolidated approach acquiring unremitting improvement and risk reduction. All healthcare facilities should consider the items listed as follows.

1. **Promote mindfulness of the need to prevent falls leading to injury:** Clinical and nonclinical staff need to be educated and communicated regarding the safety information at every level. Integrate safety precautions and insurances with the field of patient care and education.[22,23] It can be done by applying change management tools and ethics, including how to pull things together for success, make the change process easy, give the go-ahead to the staff, guarantee accountability, sustain progress, and get backing and commitment. In order to upkeep a vigorous change management effort, an administrative sponsor needs to be empowered to make sure the adequate resources and equipments, together with staffing and precautionary devices (e.g., alarms), as well as a clinical champion who can inspire investors and expedite staff receptiveness to patients asking for help.

2. **Establish and evaluate a multidisciplinary fall injury prevention team:** Establishment of an interdisciplinary fall prevention team is of significant value too. If there is already a one, then evaluate the members of this team to reassure the structural framework and capability to reduce injury risk from falls.[23,24] It is everyone's responsibility to reduce falls ending up in injury. Physicians, nurses, information technology, environmental services, pharmacy, patient advocates, quality and risk management, physical and occupational therapists, and other relevant shareholders should be involved in this.

3. **Practice a standardized, authenticated tool to recognize patient fall risk factors:** Usage of a standardized tool to figure out patient fall risk factors (e.g., Morse Fall Scale[25-27]

or Hendrich II Fall Risk Model,[28–30] preferably incorporated into the electronic medical record (EMR) is of highest clinical importance. The use of this tool should be followed by an inclusive and individualized evaluation of falls and injury risks. Make sure to include the patient's age, gender, level of function, and cognitive status in the evaluation. To ensure the interobserver reliability (the degree of evenness among observers), staff should be provided training on how to use the tool efficiently and accurately. Table 2 is a model of the Morse fall risk assessment tool.

Table 2   Morse Fall Risk Assessment Scale[31]

Item	*Item Score*		*Patient Score*
1) History of fall (immediate or previous)	No	0	
	Yes	25	_____
2) Secondary diagnosis (two or more medical diagnoses in chart)	No	0	
	Yes	25	_____
3) Ambulatory aid			
None/bed rest/nurse assist		0	
Crutches/cane/walker		15	
Furniture		30	_____
4) Intravenous therapy/heparin lock	No	0	
	Yes	20	_____
5) Gait			
Normal/bed rest/wheelchair		0	
Weak		10	
Impaired		20	_____
6) Mental status			
Oriented to own ability		0	
Overestimates/forgets limitations		15	_____

Total score: Tally the patient score and record
   0: No risk for falls
   <25: Low risk
   25–45: Moderate risk
   >45: High risk
			_____

4. **Development and implementation of individualized care plan after fall risk assessment:** After identifying the patient falls and injury risks using standardized tools, the next step is to develop a personalized plan of care and then implement treatment and interventions particular to a patient, population, or setting. Due to a risk of fall to some extent in all the hospitalized patients, the care plan must find out certain kinds of risks definite to a patient and treatments to decrease that risk. A fair risk evaluation drives deeper than screening and guides physicians to develop prevention strategies particular to acknowledged risk factors. For instance, the Veterans Health Administration's methodology ever since 2008 has been to evaluate patients for risks of fall, injury, and both fracture and nonfracture injury history.[32]

5. **Effective interventions and practices to be standardized and applied, comprising the following:**
   - *Standardized handoff communication process:* Role of standardized handoff communication process for sharing the patient risk for falls with an injury between healthcare workers is undeniable. This includes ascertaining specific areas of risk and patient-specific interventions to alleviate the risk.[33,34] For instance, subject to different settings, the course may comprise using whiteboards to communicate patient fall risks to nurses on all shifts; integrating tasks, warnings, records, and reminders into the EMR; or introducing a patient bedside shift report that contains patient falls risk fears.[35]
   - *Educating each patient individually:* One-on-one education of every patient at the bedside by qualified health experts using educational tools and materials covering fall risks and causes, protective approaches, and target setting and evaluation.[36]

6. **Conduct post-fall management:** Post-fall management includes a post-fall assessment; a system of reliable, translucent reporting; root cause analysis of falls,[22,23,25] which can notify improvement steps; and reassessment of the patient.
   - *Post-fall assessment:* Post-fall assessment is an organized way to gather information after a fall. It targets to determine whether there are injuries or other complications. A post-fall assessment should be conducted as early as possible

after the fall. Staff involvement is mandatory at all levels and, probably do involve the patient as well, to discuss the fall—what, how, and why (e.g. due to a medical condition or medication) it happened. In addition to this, the assessment should include the following:

- If suitable treatment was in place?
- Particular attention as to why the fall might have happened, including whether the call light was on and for how much time, nursing at the stage of patient fall, and which setting of care aspects were involved (e.g., toilet dimensions and slip and trip vulnerabilities).
- How is the care plan going to change?
- How parallel consequences can be evaded?

The clinical review should include a standard post-fall assessment tool that covers all the elements.[32]

- *Root cause analysis (report, combine, and analyze the causative factors continually to apprise improvement steps):* It is used in healthcare facilities to assess and comprehend what problems subsidized to error or undesired results. After a fall, you will gather data to reform the incident and conclude the causes of and causative factors to the fall. Transparent reporting, data aggregation, and analysis of the causative factors on a regular basis can help accelerate the improvement efforts. Analysis needs to be done in a systematic, data-driven way to determine issues that are important in your facility, and it will end up giving solutions for these factors. It helps the fall prevention team of the concerned setting to continuously reassess and update the methodology to patient fall prevention and injury mitigation.[24] For instance, veteran affairs department implemented a multidimensional approach for specific injuries related to the fall (bleed, hip fracture, head injury).[32]
- *Continual reassessment of the patient:* Continual reassessment of the patient, which includes prescription changes and evaluation of the cognitive and functional state over time, is also a part of the post-fall management. The Joint Commission's patient safety experts demonstrate that the mainstay of fall reduction is a continuous re-evaluation

of patients who have fallen so that one can figure out a change in the patient's medical illness that can precipitate an unfortunate patient outcome (such as an undiagnosed fracture or subdural hematoma).[23]

ROLE OF EXERCISE IN PREVENTING FALLS

With age, individuals lose the muscle strength that makes them prone to falls. It also dampens their reflexes, making it more tough for them to recoup their balance if they are about to fall. In order to regain the muscle strength and balance in such patients, the role of exercise is imperative. It not only can help you to stay active and sharp throughout the day but independent as well as. Following are some of the exercises that are noteworthy in this regard:

- **First steps:** Start by standing (against the wall), followed by warm-up (deep breathing), and then calf stretching and marching in place.
- **Strength improvement:** Regular exercise keeps you strong and healthy, and everyone can do it. Start slowly and then enhance your activity bit by bit. The exercises that improve strength are leg bending, knee bending, heel raise, sit-to-stand, and leg elevation.
- **Improve balance:** Following exercises help patients to improve balance. Start these exercises by holding on with both hands, then just one hand, then two fingers of one hand, and ultimately without using any hand. They include one-leg balance, toe-heel balance, hip circles, and heel-toe walking.
- **Tai chi:** It is an internal Chinese martial art practiced equally for its defense training and health benefits. In many societies, there are group exercise programs for older adults and classes such as tai chi. Role of tai chi in improving patient falls is increasing progressively.

Even though multiple administrations and healthcare organizations have taken positive steps towards mitigating the falls and subsequent injuries, still a pressing need exists to identify novel methods to reduce harm from falls in hospitals. The causative factors are both diverse and complicated. Apparently, the solutions seem to be quite rational and reasonable, and many of them are in practice as well, but organizations revealed a lack of definite implementation of the commonly used methods. The role of leadership provision and support is also crucial for the victory, specifically making sure that the ones included in the study had enough time for precise data collection and analysis. Its role is also essential in the implementation of advanced way outs. Complicated problems can be dealt using a robust approach because this warrants each individual organization to quantify and analyze the causative factors for patient falls and subsequent injuries, tending to recognize the unsurpassed, focused solutions for their healthcare organizations.

REFERENCES

1. Weinberg J, Proske D, Szerszen A, Lefkovic K, Cline C, El-Sayegh S, et al. An inpatient fall prevention initiative in a tertiary care hospital. *The Joint Commission Journal on Quality and Patient Safety* 2011;37(7):317–325.
2. Currie L. Advances in patient safety fall and injury prevention. In: Hughes RG, editor. *Patient Safety and Quality: An Evidence-Based Handbook for Nurses*. Rockville, MD: Agency for Healthcare Research and Quality (US); 2008.
3. Ash KL, MacLeod P, Clark L. A case control study of falls in the hospital setting. *Journal of Gerontological Nursing* 1998;24(12):7–9.
4. Fischer ID, Krauss MJ, Dunagan WC, Birge S, Hitcho E, Johnson S, et al. Patterns and predictors of inpatient falls and fall-related injuries in a large academic hospital. *Infection Control & Hospital Epidemiology* 2005;26(10):822–827.
5. Healey F, Scobie S, Oliver D, Pryce A, Thomson R, Glampson B. Falls in English and Welsh hospitals: A national observational study based on retrospective analysis of 12 months of patient safety incident reports. *BMJ Quality & Safety* 2008;17(6):424–430.
6. Hitcho EB, Krauss MJ, Birge S, Claiborne Dunagan W, Fischer I, Johnson S, et al. Characteristics and circumstances of falls in a hospital setting: A prospective analysis. *Journal of General Internal Medicine* 2004;19(7):732–739.
7. Schwendimann R, Bühler H, De Geest S, Milisen K. Falls and consequent injuries in hospitalized patients: Effects of an interdisciplinary falls prevention program. *BMC Health Services Research* 2006;6(1):69.
8. Wong CA, Recktenwald AJ, Jones ML, Waterman BM, Bollini ML, Dunagan WC. The cost of serious fall-related injuries at three Midwestern hospitals. *The Joint Commission Journal on Quality and Patient Safety* 2011;37(2):81–87.

9. Galbraith JG, Butler JS, Memon AR, Dolan MA, Harty JA. Cost analysis of a falls-prevention program in an orthopaedic setting. *Clinical Orthopaedics and Related Research* 2011;469(12):3462–3468.

10. Baker GR, Norton PG, Flintoft V, Blais R, Brown A, Cox J, et al. The Canadian Adverse Events Study: The incidence of adverse events among hospital patients in Canada. *Canadian Medical Association Journal* 2004;170(11):1678–1686.

11. Passaro A, Volpato S, Romagnoni F, Manzoli N, Zuliani G, Fellin R. Benzodiazepines with different half-life and falling in a hospitalized population: The GIFA study. *Journal of Clinical Epidemiology* 2000;53(12):1222–1229.

12. Hill KD, Vu M, Walsh W. Falls in the acute hospital setting—Impact on resource utilisation. *Australian Health Review* 2007;31(3):471–477.

13. Marta A-G, Miguel M-AJ, Carlos C-SJ, Carlos T-MJ. Circumstances and causes of falls by patients at a Spanish acute care hospital. *Journal of Evaluation in Clinical Practice* 2014;20(5):631–637.

14. Chen Y-C, Chien S-F, Chen L-K. Risk factors associated with falls among Chinese hospital inpatients in Taiwan. *Archives of Gerontology and Geriatrics* 2009;48(2):132–136.

15. Healey F, Scobie S, Oliver D, Pryce A, Thomson R, Glampson B. Falls in English and Welsh hospitals: A national observational study based on retrospective analysis of 12 months of patient safety incident reports. *Quality and Safety in Health Care* 2008;17(6):424–430.

16. Schwendimann R, Bühler H, De Geest S, Milisen K. Characteristics of hospital inpatient falls across clinical departments. *Gerontology* 2008;54(6):342–348.

17. Tideiksaar R. Falls in the elderly. *Bulletin of the New York Academy of Medicine: Journal of Urban Health* 1988;64(2):145–163.

18. Mcclure R, Turner C, Peel N, Spinks A, Eakin E, Hughes K. Population-based interventions for the prevention of fall-related injuries in older people. *The Cochrane Database of Systematic Reviews* 2005;(1):Cd004441.

19. Quigley P, White S. Hospital-based fall program measurement and improvement in high reliability organizations. *OJIN* 2013;18(2):5.

20. Morse JM, Tylko SJ, Dixon HA. Characteristics of the fall-prone patient. *The Gerontologist* 1987;27(4):516–522.

21. Force USPST, Grossman DC, Curry SJ, Owens DK, Barry MJ, Caughey AB, et al. Interventions to prevent falls in community-dwelling older adults: US preventive services task force recommendation statement. *JAMA* 2018;319(16):1696–1704.

22. Dupree E, Fritz-Campiz A, Musheno D. A new approach to preventing falls with injuries. *Journal of Nursing Care Quality* 2014;29(2):99–102.

23. Ganz D, Huang C, Saliba D, Miake-Lye I, Hempel S, Ganz D, et al. Preventing falls in hospitals: A toolkit for improving quality of care. *Annals of Internal Medicine* 2013;158(5 Pt 2):390–396.

24. Boushon B, Nielsen G, Quigley P, Rutherford P, Taylor J, Shannon D, et al. *How-to Guide: Reducing Patient Injuries from Falls.* Cambridge, MA: Institute for Healthcare Improvement; 2012.

25. Joint Commission. Preventing falls and fall-related injuries in health care facilities. *Sentinel Event Alert* 2015;(55):1–5.

26. Morse JM, Morse RM, Tylko SJ. Development of a scale to identify the fall-prone patient. *Canadian Journal on Aging/La Revue canadienne du vieillissement* 1989;8(4):366–377.

27. Morse JM. *Preventing Patient Falls.* New York: Springer; 2008.

28. Hendrich AL, Bender PS, Nyhuis A. Validation of the Hendrich II fall risk model: A large concurrent case/control study of hospitalized patients. *Applied Nursing Research* 2003;16(1):9–21.

29. Hendrich A, Nyhuis A, Kippenbrock T, Soja ME. Hospital falls: Development of a predictive model for clinical practice. *Applied Nursing Research* 1995;8(3):129–139.

30. Kim EAN, Mordiffi SZ, Bee WH, Devi K, Evans D. Evaluation of three fall-risk assessment tools in an acute care setting. *Journal of Advanced Nursing* 2007;60(4):427–435.

31. Morse JM, Black C, Oberle K, Donahue P. A prospective study to identify the fall-prone patient. *Social Science & Medicine* 1989;28(1):81–86.

32. Joint Commission. *Falls Toolkit.* US Department of Veterans Affairs: Joint Commission; 2015.

33. Dykes PC, Carroll DL, Hurley A, Lipsitz S, Benoit A, Chang F, et al. Fall prevention in acute care hospitals: A randomized trial. *JAMA* 2010;304(17):1912–1918.

34. Dykes PC, Carroll DL, Hurley AC, Benoit A, Middleton B. Why do patients in acute care hospitals fall? Can falls be prevented? *The Journal of Nursing Administration* 2009;39(6):299.

35. The Joint Commission Center for Transforming Healthcare: Targeted Solutions Tool® for Preventing Falls (accessed August 19, 2018).

36. Degelau J, Belz M, Bungum L, Flavin P, Harper C, Leys K, et al. Prevention of falls (acute care). Institute for Clinical Systems Improvement Health Care Protocol Updated April. 2012.

Clinical Vignette 6: A Rainy Night

Nidhi Shankar Kikkeri and Laura Qi
University of Missouri

Clinical vignette discusses a case where a stroke was missed on a scan as the attending did not read the report officially. We will also discuss radiological missed diagnosis and ways to improve hospital protocols for avoiding errors like this.

THE CASE

Ms. Katherine was a 34-year-old female with a past medical history of polysubstance abuse and hypertension. She was brought to the emergency room on a rainy night at 1 am by her friends with complaints of altered mental status of 2-h duration. Her friends reported that Katherine was with them the prior night and had been acting weird and confused after partying. She had also complained of a headache just few minutes before taking off for the night. Upon evaluation by emergency room physician, she was noted to be hypertensive, dehydrated, lethargic, and responding fairly to verbal commands. Her labs were consistent with hyponatremia, hypokalemia, and acute kidney injury. Drug screen was positive for methamphetamines and heroin. Blood alcohol level was significantly elevated. A noncontrast computed tomography (CT) brain was read by radiology resident as no acute changes were seen except for possible artifacts. The patient was diagnosed with acute toxic–metabolic encephalopathy. The patient was subsequently admitted to the medicine ward and was started on supportive care. Over the next 12 h, the patient continued to decline and is now unable to move any of her extremities and is mute. Neurology was consulted. A stat MRI (magnetic resonance imaging) brain revealed pontine hemorrhage involving ventral aspect of pons. The patient was finally diagnosed with locked-in syndrome secondary to pontine hemorrhagic infarct. A retrospective careful analysis of events revealed that initial CT brain had evidence of hemorrhage in the pons, which was reported as "possible" artifact, but the report was yet to be read by the radiology attending at the time of hospital admission.

COMMENTS

This patient was initially presented to the emergency department with headache and altered mental status. With the history of drug abuse, elevated ethanol levels, positive drug screen, and noncontributory CT brain report, her change in mentation was presumed to be due to metabolic derangements and illicit drug abuse. Serious neurological diseases are conveniently or easily missed by the reports of "artifacts" on imaging. Careful neurological examination of patients and their co-relation with imaging are necessary. CT often provides poor visualization of posterior aspects of the brain. Timely consultation of initial CT scan results with the radiology attending or an urgent MRI brain would have revealed diagnosis at initial presentation. The above patient continued to decline and died on day 16 of hospitalization due to aspiration pneumonia and hypoxic respiratory failure.

DISCUSSION

There has been an increasing use of imaging studies in making clinical decisions. An estimate of more than 80 million CT scans was performed in 2015, and approximately 1 in 14 patients arriving at the emergency room gets CT head.[1,2] This has created a huge challenge for the radiologists in effectively reading the scans and potentially missing subtle yet life-threatening findings and thereby precipitating a medical error.

An error is defined as a deviation from an expected norm. The term "patient safety" denotes the nonoccurrence of adverse events and the presence of measures to prevent them.[3] Institute of Medicine regards patient safety as indistinguishable from the delivery of quality healthcare.[4] Extreme diligence, expertise, and adequate training are necessary for delivering the highest quality of care by preventing radiological misinterpretations.

Malpractice refers to unprofessional misconduct and lack of skill in performing duties.[5] Majority of malpractice claims in the field of radiology are attributed to "missing" or "failure to diagnose." Overlooking and misinterpretation of radiologic images account for 40%–54% of radiology-related medical malpractice cases.[6,7]

In this article, we evaluate and identify leading factors in causing diagnostic errors in radiology and focus on the multidisciplinary collaborative approach to prevent them.

PREVALENCE

Radiological errors, unfortunately, are not uncommon. According to a report, nearly 4% of radiology reports contain errors.[5] As per Giacomo Sica et al., human and system errors account for 10% of fatalities in polytrauma patients with survivable injuries in a level I trauma center.[8] According to a study, discrepancy rates in the major and minor interpretation of CT scans between residents and staff radiologists amount to 1.7% and 2.6%, respectively, and overall resident miss rates range from 0.9% to 41%.[9–11]

CAUSES AND CONSEQUENCES

Reasons for missing crucial diagnosis and misinterpretation of radiological studies are multifaceted. Their identification, analysis, understanding the reasons, and formulating an action plan are necessary for avoiding these and thus can effectively help in timely diagnoses of crucial conditions.

Major factors can be categorized into the following:

A. Reader/observer-specific causes
   – Perceptual errors or underreading: Inability to recognize an abnormal finding
   – Errors due to lack of reasoning: Abnormal finding identified but failed to attribute to a specific cause
   – Errors due to faulty reasoning: Abnormal finding identified but attributed to wrong causes[12]
   – Errors due to poor communication: Abnormal finding identified but failed to report or communicate with ordering providers
   – Errors due to inadequate training and poor baseline knowledge
   – Errors resulting from long duty hours, fatigue, and observer burnout. Stress perceived due to errors would lead to more errors forming a vicious cycle.[13]
B. System-specific causes
   These are the errors which are not within the control of radiologists but arise and are secondary to the inadequate and improper health system and thereby affecting the judgment of the radiologists:
   – Inadequate clinical information of the patient[14]

- Poor quality images: This is often due to the inexperience of the radio technicians or failure of immobilization or poor technique.
- Inadequate staffing and excess workload: Studies have associated decrease in lung cancer detection with a decrease in viewing time, higher chances of error rates, and poor reporting.[12,15]
- Nonavailability of previous radiological studies: This often leads to challenges to teleradiologists whose interpretation and recommendations can significantly change based on the availability of prior imaging studies.[16]

According to Manning et al., majority of lung cancers missed on the chest radiography are due to complex nature of visual information available on chest imaging, making it difficult for the readers to distinguish between normal structures and pulmonary nodules.[16] Major causes of malpractice suits related to missing lung cancers involve chest radiographs in about 90% cases, whereas CT scans are attributed to remaining 10%. Observer performance, characteristics of the lesions, and difference in techniques are attributed to overlooking lung cancers according to a study by Fardanesh and White.[17]

As per the American College of Radiology Bulletin, about 30%–70% of the patients diagnosed to have breast cancer identified on the mammogram can be retrospectively traced back to initial mammograms which were reported as normal.[18] The most common lesions missed on mammograms are masses or densities (19%–64%), calcifications (18%–28%), mass with calcifications (2%), and architectural distortion (4%–12%).[19–22]

How to Investigate and Manage Diagnostic Errors Effectively?

We understand the importance of patient safety and the nature of consequences caused by medical errors attributed to overlooking of radiological images. These can have dire and negative outcomes as indicated in the abovementioned case. Establishment of error and safety management systems is crucial wherein errors are identified, reported, and carefully analyzed and measures are taken to prevent similar occurrences.[3]

Error reporting systems or Critical Incident Reporting Systems not only collect data but process the data and reflect the knowledge and

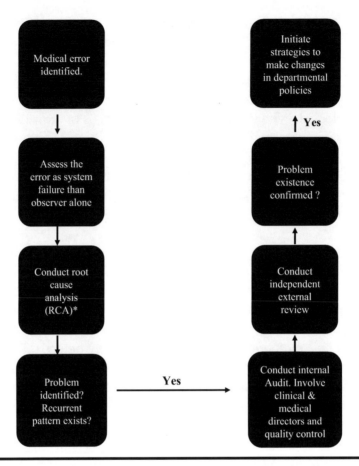

Figure 1 **Demonstration of an ideal hospital protocol in managing a diagnostic error.**[12,25]

insights thus gained back to the users, thereby improving the quality of care and patient safety.[23] The Joint Commission's Framework for Root Cause Analysis and Action Plan is one such reporting system which provides a comprehensive systematic analysis of an error.[24] The goal of error analysis is to identify learning opportunities in minimizing the degree of harm to the patients (Figure 1).

Here we discuss several strategies used to prevent future diagnostic errors:

1. Compiling a list of "don't-miss" diagnosis[23]: Diagnoses which are often critical but difficult to make yet can't afford to miss, either due to its potential negative consequences such as carotid artery dissection or a stroke where time is valuable and appropriate intervention is necessary to reduce the morbidity or mortality.

2. We call for use of automated screening checklists as a standard practice to reduce errors of omission, which would allow the observer to have a second look at frequently missed areas on the imaging studies. For instance, the inclusion of "blind spots" with a specific look at cerebral sulci, dural sinuses, orbits, cavernous sinuses, clivus, Meckel cave, brainstem, skull base, and parapharyngeal soft tissues as a part of every brain imaging would reduce the rate of false negative results.

3. Involvement of hospital administration in planning schedules of physicians to avoid overwork and burnout. Efforts need to be made to reduce the excess workload, adjusting duty hours and frequent distractions and interruptions.

4. Intense training of radiology residents, their proper supervision by attendings and their continuous involvement in medical education, and retraining of practicing radiologists in pattern recognition, repetition, and drills.[26]

5. Findings can be potentially missed due to "hindsight" or preformed bias and its potential to miss uncommon crucial findings. Cognitive debasing and metacognitive interventions have been advocated in avoiding this type of error.[26]

6. Establishing a standard protocol to communicate abnormal findings with the ordering provider in a timely manner and its appropriate documentation.

7. We call for better integration of electronic medical records and Picture Archiving and Communication Systems for better access to the clinical data of the patient to improve the accuracy and timeliness of reporting by teleradiologists.

8. Importance of discussions between the ordering provider and radiologists cannot be undermined when a discrepancy exists between clinical status and radiological reports.

9. Patient education and engagement with diagnostic possibilities and probabilities are necessities to minimize surprises. It also enhances patient's initiatives in question diagnosis when they are not responding as expected.[23]

10. Establishment of "safety nets" by creating a well-designed follow-up system in cases of diagnostic uncertainties to mitigate patient's harm.[23]

11. Providing upstream feedback to the radiologists/residents promotes the culture of safety, communication, and blame-free continuous learning environment.[23]

12. Utilization of second reading by neuroradiologist on CT and MRI studies when clinically indicated can significantly reduce errors. When in doubt, ask the experts!

Increasing use of diagnostic imaging has created an immense challenge to radiologists and poses a risk of misinterpretations and diagnostic errors. This has the potential to cause irreparable harm to the patient and has threatened the efficiency of healthcare system.

There is a need to identify the diagnostic errors and ways to minimize them. Minimizing diagnostic errors have shown to cut down the healthcare costs, improve hospital-wide mortality and morbidity rates, and are an indicator of an effective, successful healthcare system.[27]

Creating a patient safety culture in a healthcare setting is the foremost step. We recommend a multidisciplinary approach; an anonymous and more reliable reporting system; and identification of pitfalls, their analysis, and institution of departmental policies in minimizing the incidence of radiological errors.

James Reason describes errors as consequences of system failures rather than as consequences of individual attributes.[28] Being open minded in admitting errors, refraining from "blame-culture," the group practice of peer support in educational activities could help in improving the performance of radiologists.[27]

Intense and robust residency training continued educational programs, frequent mortality and morbidity meetings, and a comprehensive root cause analysis process are vital in decreasing the likelihood of future diagnostic errors thereby delivering quality healthcare.

REFERENCES

1. Allareddy V, Allareddy V, Nalliah RP. Epidemiology of facial fracture injuries. *J Oral Maxillofac Surg* 2011;69:2613–2618.
2. Berrington de González A, Mahesh M, Kim KP, Bhargavan M, Lewis R, Mettler F, Land C. Projected cancer risks from computed tomographic scans performed in the United States in 2007. *Arch Intern Med* 2009;169(22):2071–2077. doi:10.1001/archinternmed.2009.440. PMID 20008689.
3. Hoffmann B, Rohe J. Patient safety and error management: What causes adverse events and how can they be prevented? *Dtsch Arztebl Int* 2010;107(6):92–99. doi:10.3238/arztebl.2010.0092. Epub 2010 Feb 12.

4. Aspden P, Corrigan J, Wolcott J, et al, editors. *Patient Safety: Achieving a New Standard for Care.* Washington, DC: National Academies Press; 2004.

5. Pinto A. Letter from the guest editor: Errors and malpractice in radiology. *Semin Ultrasound CT MR* 2012;33(4):273–274. doi:10.1053/j.sult.2012.02.002.

6. Hamer MM, Morlock F, Foley HT, Ros PR. Medical malpractice in diagnostic radiology: Claims, compensation, and patient injury. *Radiology* 1987;164:263–266.

7. Berlin L. Malpractice and radiologists, update 1986: An 11.5-year perspective. *Am J Roentgenol* 1986;147:1291–1298.

8. Sica G1, Guida F, Bocchini G, Codella U, Mainenti PP, Tanga M, Scaglione M. Errors in imaging assessment of polytrauma patients. *Semin Ultrasound CT MR* 2012;33(4):337–346. doi:10.1053/j.sult.2012.01.012.

9. Yaniv G, Mozes O, Greenberg G, Bakon M, Hoffman C. Common sites and etiologies of residents' misinterpretation of head CT scans in the emergency department of a level I trauma center. *Isr Med Assoc J* 2013;15:221–225.

10. Borgstede JP, Lewis RS, Bhargavan M, Sunshine JH. RADPEER quality assurance program: A multifacility study of interpretive disagreement rates. *J Am Coll Radiol* 2004;1:59–65.

11. Wysoki MG, Nassar CJ, Koenigsberg RA, Novelline RA, Faro SH, Faerber EN. Head trauma: CT scan interpretation by radiology residents versus staff radiologists. *Radiology* 1998;208:125–128.

12. Brady A, Ó Laoide R, McCarthy P, McDermott R. Discrepancy and error in radiology: Concepts, causes and consequences. *Ulster Med J* 2012;81(1):3–9.

13. West CP, Huschka MM, Novotny PJ, et al. Association of perceived medical errors with resident distress and empathy: A prospective longitudinal study. *JAMA* 2006;296:1071–1078.

14. Berlin L, Berlin JW. Malpractice and radiologists in Cook County, IL: Trends in 20 years of litigation. *Am J Roentgenol* 1995;165(4):781–788.

15. Fitzgerald R. Error in radiology. *Clin Radiol* 2001;56(12):938–946.

16. Robinson PJ. Radiology's Achilles' heel: Error and variation in the interpretation of the Röntgen image. *Br J Radiol* 1997;70(839):1085–1098.

17. Fardanesh M, White C. Missed lung cancer on chest radiography and computed tomography. *Semin Ultrasound CT MR* 2012;33(4):280–287. doi:10.1053/j.sult 2012.01.006.

18. Berlin L. Dot size, lead time, fallibility, and impact on survival. Continuing controversies in mammography. *Am J Roentgenol* 2001;176:1123–1130.

19. Bird RE, Wallace TW, Yankaskas BC. Analysis of cancer missed at screening mammography. *Radiology* 1992;184:613–617.

20. Van Dijck JA, Verbeek AL, Hendriks JH, Holland R. The current detectability of breast cancer in a mammographic screening program. *Cancer* 1993;72:1933–1938.

21. Ikeda DM, Andersson I, Wattsgard C, Janzon L, Linell F. Interval carcinoma in the Malmo mammographic screening trial: Radiographic appearance and prognostic considerations. *Am J Roentgenol* 1992;159:287–294.

22. Harvey JA, Fajardo LL, Innis CA. Previous mammograms in patients with impalpable breast carcinoma: Retrospective vs blinded interpretation. *Am J Roentgenol* 1993;161:1167–1172.

23. Schiff GD, Kim S, et al. Diagnosing diagnosis errors: Lessons from a multi-institutional collaborative project. Advances in Patient Safety: From Research to Implementation (Volume 2: Concepts and Methodology). Rockville (MD): Agency for Healthcare Research and Quality (US); 2005 Feb.

24. www.jointcommission.org/framework_for_conducting_a_root_cause_analysis_and_action_plan/

25. Murphy JF. Root cause analysis of medical errors. *Ir Med J* 2008;101(2):36.

26. Bruno MA, Walker EA, Abujudeh HH. Understanding and confronting our mistakes: The epidemiology of error in radiology and strategies for error reduction. *Radiographics* 2015;35(6):1668–1676. doi:10.1148/rg.2015150023.

27. Pinto A, Acampora C, Pinto F, Kourdioukova E, Romano L, Verstraete K. Learning from diagnostic errors: A good way to improve education in radiology. *Eur J Radiol* 2011;78:372–376.

28. Reason J. Human error: Models and management. *BMJ* 2000;320(7237):768–770.

Clinical Vignette 7: Customer Service 101

Keerthana Kumar
University of Missouri

Hospitals necessitate profitability for continued and successful operation. Efforts to increase profitability in healthcare have been focused on increasing patient satisfaction, which is a practice that may result in poorer health outcomes. This case demonstrates the potential detriments that prioritizing patient satisfaction can have on patient safety, where an overmedicated patient sustained a fall after being allowed outside to smoke. We will discuss the protocols in place to avoid these situations.

THE CASE

Pamela was a 66-year-old woman with a past medical history of anxiety, osteoporosis, and fibromyalgia who was brought to the hospital by her husband after being in a motor vehicular accident. Pamela's husband was driving when they unavoidably hit a deer. Pamela's husband had no complaints or injuries, but Pamela had visible bruising and reported 10/10 pain in her right arm. X-ray revealed fracture of the right supracondylar humerus. Pamela was given hydrocodone for the pain and splinted after a closed reduction. Her vital signs were blood pressure of 145/86, heart rate of 86, respiratory rate of 16, and temperature of 36.6°C (97.8°F). Pamela was admitted for observation and her at-home medications were continued. Shortly after admission, Pamela told the nurse on the floor that she needed to smoke a cigarette, to which the nurse said okay and gave her instructions on acceptable smoking locations, and offered assistance which Pamela declined. In her walk to an acceptable smoking location, Pamela fell and hit her head. She was found to have a subdural hematoma from the fall.

Upon review of her medications, Pamela was found to be on hydrocodone (an opiate), amitriptyline (a tricyclic antidepressant for pain and anxiety), lorazepam (a benzodiazepine for anxiety), pregabalin (for pain), vitamin D, calcium, and diphenhydramine (for allergies). Pamela was a victim of polypharmacy, and the medications she was prescribed were largely given to increase her satisfaction as consumer, despite their negative consequences and with disregard to her overall health and well-being. Pamela was inappropriately medicated, as all of her formulary medications cause cognitive impairment, especially given her advanced age. Additionally, she was granted permission by the nurse for an unnecessary request with negative health consequences and given the autonomy for refusal of assistance despite her substandard mentation. The pervasive attempts to increase patient satisfaction with disregard to protocol and evidence-based recommendations culminated in Pamela's devastating fall.

COMMENTS

The combination of medications was inappropriate for Pamela's age. Benzodiazepines cause cognitive impairment, antihistamines such as diphenhydramine (and drugs with antihistamine affects including tricyclic antidepressants like amitriptyline) cause drowsiness, drugs with anticholinergic effects such as tricyclic antidepressants cause confusion and orthostatic hypotension, opiates such as hydrocodone cause dizziness and sedation, and all of these classes of medications should be used with caution in the elderly (age >65). This combination of medications was the likely cause of Pamela's fall.

DISCUSSION

Though hospitals can be havens for the ill and injured, contemporary healthcare facilities are businesses which accordingly necessitate profitability for continued and successful operation. Patient satisfaction in healthcare facilities has increasingly been prioritized in order to increase the profitability. This trend has been found to be associated with greater inpatient stays, increased healthcare expenditure, and increased mortality.[1]

Polypharmacy is especially a concern in older individuals who have a greater burden of comorbid illnesses and disabilities.[2] According to the 2015 U.S. Census Report, 14.9% of U.S. population is currently 65 years old or older, a rise from 13% in the 2010 U.S. Census Report, and from 2010 to 2015, the percentage change in the 62-year-old and above age group was close to 21% compared to 9.7% for the overall population.[3] In stark contrast, the number of clinicians with added qualifications in geriatrics has been at a plateau or even declining.[4] Aging is a non-modifiable risk factor for a slew of medical conditions, which can make healthcare management in older individuals especially challenging. This combination of understaffing and complex medication management are the areas of deficiency that have been shown to put patients at risk for adverse events.

Evaluating outcomes in order to optimize drug prescribing in elderly patients has become a challenging and complex public-health concern that requires a comprehensive approach to maximize benefit and minimize harm. Patient-centered care is critical, which discusses the goals of care with each patient and integrates therapies with patient preferences. A safety program study evidenced increased patient satisfaction and improved patient safety when pharmacists conducted follow-ups that included medical reconciliation, discussion of therapy goals, and patient education during follow-up, has shown to increase patient satisfaction and improve patient safety. Existing evidence supports an interdisciplinary approach, patient-centered care, and the implementation of patient safety programs in healthcare facilities. This multifactorial approach addresses shortages of healthcare providers for older adults and pharmacotherapy management with methods that will improve patient satisfaction, patient safety, and reduce unnecessary healthcare expenditures.[5,6]

Beyond medication management and understaffing, deficiencies in communication and the amount of time spent with patients are among the areas identified where deficiencies could put patients and risk for adverse events.[7] Processes for care and interpersonal dynamic are among the most important factors for caregivers and patients with regard to healthcare services. Table 1 illustrates the components of the patient experience that most affect the overall satisfaction.[8]

Table 1 indicates that the measure of patient satisfaction is an important component of healthcare beyond its effect on profitability, as these measures are indicators of healthcare quality, and by

Table 1   Patient Experiences Correlating to Satisfaction (in Order of Degree of Correlation)

1. Communication with nurses
2. Pain management
3. Timeliness of assistance
4. Explanation of medications administered
5. Communication with doctors
6. Cleanliness of room and bathroom
7. Discharge planning
8. Noise level at night

extension, patient safety. Improving patient experiences by focusing on care coordination and patient engagement will increase both satisfaction and outcomes.[9]

A major source of healthcare expenditure is falls in the elderly. Each year, approximately 30% of older adults fall, and this is projected to account for $54 billion in healthcare spending annually by 2020. Effective fall risk management should include early screening for risk factor assessment, prescribing customized interventions when necessary, and ensuring the implementation and compliance of these customized interventions. There are practice guidelines available to healthcare professionals and financial incentives to promote their adoption, though there remains a lack of adherence to these guidelines in clinical practice. Table 2 shows a breakdown of the current financial incentive models. There is concern that there is a lack of consistency in the different guidelines, which can increase the challenge to change clinical practice. The effectiveness of these models is yet to be assessed, as these models are relatively new and not fully adapted in the clinical practice.[10]

In addition to financial model incentives for providers, technology-based interventions are being developed and applied as more cost-effective methods of fall prevention.[11] In the inpatient setting, sitters have been found to be only marginally effective in reducing the cost-effectiveness of adverse outcomes, such as falls, and only marginal in improving patient satisfaction.[12] Video monitoring in particular has been identified as an inconspicuous method for preventing falls, particularly in inpatient settings, where it can reduce sitter costs and is

Table 2   Financial Incentive Models for Fall Prevention

Model	Origin and Incentive	Provider Duties	Recommended Procedures
Physician Quality Reporting System	• Established by the Centers for Medicare & Medicaid Services (CMS) in 2007 • A voluntary quality improvement program that encourages providers to report completion of clinical procedures	• Provider screens for fall risk (i.e., two or more falls within the past 12 months or any fall with injury in the past year) • If a patient is at fall risk, the provider conducts multi-factorial assessment. • Provider creates a plan of care for patients screening as a fall risk	• Identify falls history • Conduct Timed Up and Go test • Check vision • Measure orthostatic blood pressure • Review medication • Check home environment • Consider appropriate assistive device • Identify falls history • Discuss problems of falling or problems with balance or walking • Consider an assistive device • Assess orthostatic blood pressure • Suggest an exercise or physical therapy program • Suggest a vision or hearing test • Screen patient for fall risk • Provide balance, strength, and gait training • Identify falls history

(Continued)

Table 2 (*Continued*) Financial Incentive Models for Fall Prevention

Model	Origin and Incentive	Provider Duties	Recommended Procedures
Meaning-ful Use Incentive Program	• Launched in 2011 as part of the Affordable Care Act • CMS-run program that incentivizes providers to report specific core measures and select quality indicators • Incentive pay up to a total of $24,000–$44,000, depending on the year participation started • Providers who do not participate in Meaningful Use will be subject to a penalty fee	• Incentivize providers to: 1. Use electronic health records (EHRs) in a meaningful way 2. Enable exchanges of patient health information through EHRs 3. Submit indicators on quality of care • Provider screens for fall risk (i.e., two or more falls within the past 12 months or any fall with injury in the past year). • Provider discusses problems about falling or problems with balance or walking with patient. Provider develops a plan of care for falls for patients at risk	

(Continued)

Table 2 (Continued)   Financial Incentive Models for Fall Prevention

Model	Origin and Incentive	Provider Duties	Recommended Procedures
Medicare Annual Wellness Visit	• Launched in 2011 • Involves a series of prevention screenings including those for fall-related risk as well as for depression, cognition, and body mass index • Physicians who perform a wellness visit receive a higher reimbursement than a regular visit	• Provider screens for fall risk; provider provides health advice and referrals, as appropriate, to programs aimed at reducing risk factors for falls	
Accountable Care Organization Program	• Launched in 2011 • Created to help manage risk and incentivize prevention • Providers are incentivized to control costs by participating in a cost-saving plan	• Provider screens for fall risk (i.e., two or more falls within the past 12 months or any fall with injury in the past year)	

useful in the reduction of falls for patients who are cognitively impaired.[13]

REFERENCES

1. Fenton JJ, Jerant AF, Bertakis KD, Franks P. The cost of satisfaction: A national study of patient satisfaction, health care utilization, expenditures, and mortality. *Arch Intern Med.* 2012;172(5):405–411.
2. Marengoni A, Angleman S, Melis R, Mangialasche F, Karp A, Garmen A, et al. Aging with multimorbidity: A systematic review of the literature. *Ageing Res Rev.* 2011;10(4):430–439.
3. Ortman JM, Velkoff VA, Hogan H. *An Aging Nation: The Older Population in the United States.* United States Census Bureau, Economics and Statistics Administration, US Department of Commerce; 2014.
4. Warshaw GA, Bragg EJ, Shaull RW, Lindsell CJ. Academic geriatric programs in US allopathic and osteopathic medical schools. *JAMA.* 2002;288(18):2313–2319.
5. Ruiz-Millo O, Climente-Marti M, Navarro-Sanz JR. Patient and health professional satisfaction with an interdisciplinary patient safety program. *Int J Clin Pharm.* 2018;40(3):635–641.
6. Wenger NK, Doherty CL, Gurwitz JH, Hirsch GA, Holmes HM, Maurer MS, et al. Optimization of drug prescription and medication management in older adults with cardiovascular disease. *Drugs Aging.* 2017;34(11):803–810.
7. Rathert C, Brandt J, Williams ES. Putting the 'patient' in patient safety: A qualitative study of consumer experiences. *Health Expect.* 2012;15(3):327–336.
8. Boulding W, Glickman SW, Manary MP, Schulman KA, Staelin R. Relationship between patient satisfaction with inpatient care and hospital readmission within 30 days. *Am J Manag Care.* 2011;17(1):41–48.
9. Manary MP, Boulding W, Staelin R, Glickman SW. The patient experience and health outcomes. *N Engl J Med.* 2013;368(3):201–203.
10. Shubert TE, Smith ML, Prizer LP, Ory MG. Complexities of fall prevention in clinical settings: A commentary. *Gerontologist.* 2014;54(4):550–558.
11. Hamm J, Money AG, Atwal A, Paraskevopoulos I. Fall prevention intervention technologies: A conceptual framework and survey of the state of the art. *J Biomed Inform.* 2016;59:319–345.

12. Boswell DJ, Ramsey J, Smith MA, Wagers B. The cost-effectiveness of a patient-sitter program in an acute care hospital: A test of the impact of sitters on the incidence of falls and patient satisfaction. *Qual Manag Health Care*. 2001;10(1):10–16.
13. Cournan M, Fusco-Gessick B, Wright L. Improving patient safety through video monitoring. *Rehabil Nurs*. 2016. doi:10.1002/rnj.308.

Clinical Vignette 8: The Empty Crash Cart

Keerthana Kumar
University of Missouri

Emergency codes necessitate meticulous preparation for the best patient outcomes, as cardiac arrests are among the most quintessential examples of time-sensitive medical conditions where delays in treatment can result in fatality. This clinical vignette discusses a cardiac alert that went awry. We will further discuss methods to improve code teams and prevent errors using crew management techniques.

THE CASE

Ms.Kathleen is a 36-year-old diabetic women, undergoing hemodialysis three times a week for end stage renal disease. She is awaiting renal transplantation. Shortly before one of her scheduled sessions, Kathleen began experiencing extreme muscle weakness and chest tightness, which prompted her neighbor to drive her to the Emergency Department. Physical examination revealed diffuse weakness and crackles on lung auscultation. Heart rate was 54 beats/min. An electrocardiogram revealed widened QRS complexes with an irregular ventricular rhythm and tall T-waves. Hyperkalemia was suspected and calcium gluconate was administered, and during administration, Kathleen developed cardiac arrest with ventricular fibrillation. The nurse called a code blue, and crash cart was brought out by the newly hired cart nurse, and the physician called for the defibrillator. When the automatic external defibrillator (AED) was attempted, the electrodes were not attached. The cart nurse realized that she brought in a cart that was being restocked. She ran out and attempted to retrieve the fully equipped cart. By the time she returned with an adequately stocked cart, the AED did not detect a shockable rhythm and a time of death was called.

This error resulted in Kathleen's death, which could have potentially been prevented with a more rapid response time and simulation training of the newly hired staff.

COMMENTS

Code blues are called in emergency situations of cardiopulmonary arrest and require expeditious responses from the healthcare team. The factor which most contributes to improved outcomes is the time to resuscitation. There was an excessive period of lapse due to the crash cart nurse's error in bringing in the used crash, and Kathleen's death might have been prevented if resuscitation efforts were started earlier.

DISCUSSION

Cardiopulmonary arrests are situations where teamwork and adherence to established guidelines are vital to patient survival. Errors and oversights by any member of the team can have serious or fatal implications.[1]

The American Heart Association created the advanced cardiac life support (ACLS) training algorithm as practice guidelines for cardiac arrest, which are the standard of care in which support training is required at least every 2 years for healthcare providers. Effective training has been shown to include simulation of emergency situations for the use of the ACLS algorithm during rapid response situations. Simulation education enhances learning by increasing retention of knowledge and skills. Though the use of patient simulators is standard during ACLS training, mock codes would increase the effectiveness of training by recreating the stress factors in members of the healthcare team which may lead to underperformance during cardiac arrest. Mock codes are the most effective simulation education method for improving performance and outcomes in real-time situations, as well as for identifying potential errors in practice and proving solutions.[2,3]

Factors that have been identified as potentially contributing to inefficiency and chaotic or disorganized behavior during cardiac arrest codes include manifestations of stress or anxiety by healthcare team members, problems with equipment, and deficient training or practice of new skills. Manifestation of stress or anxiety includes disorganized behavior, regressive behavior, or overreaction to situations, including running elsewhere for supplies when they are located in the room.

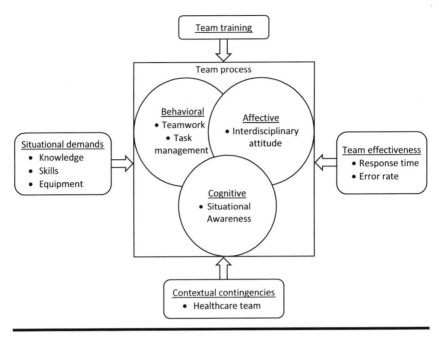

Figure 1   Conceptual framework of team effectiveness.[4]

Patient safety and quality of care have shown improvement when ACLS training is provided in conjunction with education on focused interdisciplinary management. Focused interdisciplinary education should include dedicated resources aimed at improving the dynamic interactions of a team, between the behavioral, cognitive, and affective components that constitute teamwork. Identification of these components along with contextual factors is critical for problem solving and conflict resolution, which are necessary for improving team effectiveness and ultimately patient safety (Figure 1).[4]

Proper preparation for situational demands of cardiopulmonary resuscitation (CPR) includes simulation training as described previously and having equipment ready and available. Medications and supplies must be immediately available for use in these situations, which are transported in a crash cart. A crash cart should contain all the essential supplies needed for CPR.[5] Table 1 includes the equipment included in a crash cart, and the specific topics of discussion in training that each piece of equipment should focus on, as well as the potential sources of error that the healthcare team should take vigilance against when preparing a crash cart (Table 1):[5,6]

Table 1   Crash Cart Equipment

Equipment Type	Specific Discussion Topic	Potential Sources of Error
Bag valve mask	• Mask fit • Oxygen administration • Assessing ventilation • Rescue breathing frequencies	• Deficient quantities of medication or other supplies • Absence of necessary supplies • Inconvenient organization of supplies
Oxygen	• Nasal cannula • Partial rebreathing versus non-rebreathing mask • Humidity • Using portable tank	
Crash cart	• Location of supplies • How to access supplies • How to exchange after use	
Defibrillator	• Turning it on • Charging it • Synchronizing • Running a strip • Changing the paper • Attaching the electrodes	
Suction	• Turning it on • Oral versus nasotracheal suctioning • Yankauer suction	

Accurate and rapid administration of CPR requires teamwork, organization, and effective training. As mentioned earlier, stress and anxiety contribute to errors that increase response time and negatively impact outcomes. Providing interdisciplinary training in nontechnical skills can improve behavioral, cognitive, and affective performance. Team preparedness through management training improves patient safety and quality of care. Examples of nontechnical skills to focus on when providing rapid response training are provided in Table 2.[4]

Table 2 Nontechnical Skills to Focus on When Providing Rapid Response Training

Task Management	Team Work	Situational Awareness

• Plan and prepare
  – Goal statements: "We need to oxygenate" or "We need to ventilate"
  – Verbalize a plan out loud or ask for advice
  – Get BVM (bag valve mask) ready before apnea occurs
• Prioritize
  – Start with airway, then breathing, then circulation
  – Call for help when patient is blue
  – Ensure chest rise with BVM
  – Check pulse with compressions
• Provided and maintain standards
  – Follow appropriate order of the steps of CPR: open airway, look/listen/feel, give two breaths for every 30 compressions, etc.
  – Use correct BVM size and mask size
• Identify and use resources
  – Ask for help
  – Lower stretcher and rail/move equipment
  – Silence the noise of baby or radio
  – Divide tasks of airway, circulation, IV management
	• Coordinate activities
	  – Tasks are verbalized
	  – Team members are respectful and cooperative
	  – All tasks divided equally
	• Exchange information
	  – Assessment findings are communicated
	  – Completion of tasks is verbalized
	  – Problems and difficulties are voiced
	• Use authority and assertiveness
	  – A leader is clearly designated
	  – Leader gives clear orders; delegates tasks
	  – Leader accepts advice
	• Assess capabilities
	  – Team members ask for help when struggling
	  – Leader recognizes ineffective performance and takes corrective action
		• Gather information
		  – Leader stands back and observes
		  – Leader asks for missing information or verifies information
		  – Leader is in a position to visualize the monitor
		• Recognize and understand
		  – Leader articulates a plan of action with goal statements
		  – Reassess oxygen saturation after administration
		  – Reassess A-B-Cs
		  – Reassess adequacy of ventilation/compressions
		• Anticipate
		  – Leader thinks aloud about possible causes
		  – Leader considers IV fluid
		  – Adequacy of IV site is assessed

These examples for improving team effectiveness and outcomes in rapid response situations have important implications for patient safety and care quality outcomes in the clinical setting. Patient safety will improve when contextual factors are taken in to account and interdisciplinary training reflects potential causes for inefficiency or errors.

REFERENCES

1. Huseman KF. Improving code blue response through the use of simulation. *J Nurses Staff Dev.* 2012;28(3):120–124.
2. Scaramuzzo LA, Wong Y, Voitle KL, Gordils-Perez J. Cardiopulmonary arrest in the outpatient setting: Enhancing patient safety through rapid response algorithms and simulation teaching. *Clin J Oncol Nurs.* 2014;18(1):61–64.
3. Dorney P. Code blue: Chaos or control, an educational initiative. *J Nurses Staff Dev.* 2011;27(5):242–244.
4. Jankouskas TS, Haidet KK, Hupcey JE, Kolanowski A, Murray WB. Targeted crisis resource management training improves performance among randomized nursing and medical students. *Simul Healthc.* 2011;6(6):316–326.
5. Nussbaum GB, Fisher JG. A crash cart that works. *Am J Nurs.* 1978;78(1):45–48.
6. Jankouskas TS. A continuous curriculum for building code blue competency. *J Nurses Staff Dev.* 2001;17(4):195–198.

Clinical Vignette 9: A Punch in the Face

Sireesha Murala
NTR University of Health Science

Clinical vignette discusses a case of a violent and difficult patient and the complications that came from it. We will also discuss protocols to prevent situations like this.

THE CASE

Mr. John is a 28-year-old male who was brought to the emergency room (ER) by his friends due to severe agitation, flushing, vomiting, drooling, and rapid breathing for the past few hours. His vital signs at presentation were as follows:

Vital Signs	Values
Blood pressure	146/88 mmHg
Pulse	122 beats/min
Respiratory rate	22 breaths/min

On examination, he was not oriented to time, place, and person. He appeared to be agitated and slightly depressed. Bilateral horizontal nystagmus was noted. Ten-panel drug test was ordered, and an intravenous line was established. He started vomiting again in the ER. Ondansetron was ordered, and as the nurse began to prepare and administer the medication, the patient suddenly became violent, disregarded the IV lines, and held the nurse in headlock while punching her repeatedly. The staff immediately alerted the security, the patient was put in a four-point restraints, and lorazepam was administered. His drug panel was positive for phencyclidine, and he was managed appropriately for it. On further questioning the patient's friends, they said they attended a party where Mr. John took an unknown substance to get high.

COMMENTS

In this case, the nurse was attacked, as there are no policies enforced on the patient safety in healthcare setting, especially in the emergency department (ED).[1]

The management of any intoxication should start with the initial resuscitation and stabilization of the neurological status of the patient.

The patient should then be restrained and sedated to avoid not only the violence against healthcare personnel but also self-inflicted injury. Security staff should be posted at every entrance of the ED, who intervenes to protect both the worker and the patient. Patient violence often results in physical injuries to the worker and the security staff, and raises the cost expenditure for the hospital.[2] These incidents can be decreased by placing the policies and educating the hospital staff about managing volatile and aggressive patients.

DISCUSSION

Workplace violence (WPV) is defined as "violent acts (physical assaults and threats of assaults) directed toward persons at work or on duty."[1] In hospitals, violence from the patients and patient visitors is also known as type II violence.[2] This phenomenon has become an epidemic in healthcare settings, especially in the ED.[1]

The signs and symptoms shown in Figure 1 are usually seen in an agitated and violent patient, and the staff attending to this patient's care have to be vigilant to avoid imminent danger to the fellow staff and other patients in the vicinity.[3]

Violent outcomes include screaming, cursing, yelling, spitting, biting, throwing objects, hitting or punching at self/others, and attacking/assault behavior.[3]

The management of a violent patient includes de-escalation of the situation by talking down, environmental manipulation, usage of physical restraints and/or seclusion, and usage of chemical restraints/pharmacological agents. Different types of restraints and their uses are shown in Table 1.[3]

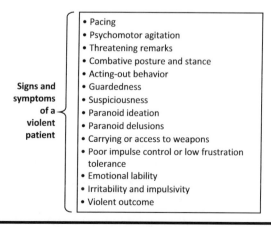

Figure 1   The signs and symptoms of a violent patient.

Table 1   Types of Restraints and Their Uses[3]

	Type of Restraints	*Use*
1	Physical restraints and seclusion	Use a four-point/five-point restraint as a last resort to avoid danger to themselves/to the staff
2	Chemical restraints	Used as primary therapy or in combination with other efforts of de-escalation Rapid tranquilization combines benzodiazepine and antipsychotic to achieve behavior control
3	Environmental manipulation	A quiet, individual room decreases the external stimuli and decreases the potential for a violent event

Every emergency care setting should have an in-service training program on the use of restraints, to whoever is involved in the care of the patients. The procedure must be performed safely and effectively while conveying calmness and confidence to the staff. However, restraints should never be used as a punishment, to calm a demanding/disruptive patient, for the convenience of the staff, and as a substitute for any treatment regimen.[3]

Health professionals often reported feeling unsupported by their institutions. WPV in the ED should start with the guiding principles (Table 2) and priority focus areas (Table 3), as shown below.[1]

Table 2   Guiding Principles on Mitigating Violence at Workplace

- Violence happens anywhere.
- Positive patient outcomes are promoted by healthy work environments
- All aspects of violence should be addressed (among patients, families, and colleagues).
- WPV should be addressed with a multidisciplinary team.
- All the members of the organization should uphold the behavior standards.
- If an issue which may lead to WPV is raised, the organization should address it promptly.
- Collaboration of nurses and other healthcare professionals should be maintained at all levels.
- Effectiveness of nursing and patient care increases by addressing the WPV.

Table 3   Five Priority Focus Areas[1]

	Five Priority Focus Areas	*Elements*
1	Behaviors to promote at workplace	• Respectful communication • Mutual respect • Honesty, trust, and beneficence
2	Promotion of zero-tolerance framework	• Top-down approach should be supported by the organization • Policies should define what actions are not tolerated and their consequences for violations of those specific enacted policies • All policies should be clearly understood and are applicable to each person in the organization • Lateral violence should be prohibited, regardless of the role and position of the individual in the organization
3	Ownership and account-ability elements	• Personal accountability is promoted, so that each person is responsible for reporting and responding to those incidents at workplace • Staff input should be included in developing a zero-tolerance policy • Each person in the organization has clearly defined universal standards of behavior and is equally accountable • Chain of command should be followed in reporting any incidents of violence, which would enforce the zero-tolerance policy
4	Training and education of essential elements on WPV	• Personal and organizational readiness to learn • Evidence-based, organizational supported, and readily available tools and interventions • Skilled and experienced facilitators who can understand the specific issues and audience • Training should be encouraged on early recognition and de-escalation of potential violence at workplace • Specific simulated case studies pertaining to healthcare should be demonstrated to understand the actions in violent situations

(Continued)

Table 3 (*Continued*)   Five Priority Focus Areas[1]

	Five Priority Focus Areas	*Elements*

5	Outcome metrics of the program's success	• Patient safety scores and top-ranked staff
		• Decrease in the incidence of harm from violent behavior
		• Reports of feeling safe survey among the staff in the entire organization
		• In healthcare setting, patients and families would report feeling safe
		• Staff would feel comfortable in reporting violent incidents and involving persons of authority
		• The following culture change indicators are reflected by the organization:
		  – Employers are engaged
		  – Employees are satisfied
		  – HCAHPS score increases

HCAHPS, hospital consumer assessment of healthcare providers and systems.

Simulation-based interprofessional team training would improve staff attitude toward patient care with behavioral emergencies in the ED.[4] Rapid training program promotes effective communication skills to control internal (patient), external (environmental), and interactional (situational) factors. Hybrid educational intervention on WPV tailored to the ED staff is a useful strategy to achieve better learning outcomes. Security guards should be included in the rapid response teams along with physicians, nurses, social workers, technicians, human resources personnel, members of administration, and risk management personnel. ED staff perceived the presence of security officers to be supportive, but the effectiveness of maintaining a safe work environment in the ED is not.[1]

Haddon matrix combines the epidemiologic concepts of the host (employee), vector and vehicle (patient/visitor) factors, and physical/social environmental factors to promote primary, secondary, and tertiary prevention of aggressive/violent incidents in the ED. Application of Haddon matrix in preventing ED violence is shown in Table 4.[1]

Table 4 Application of Haddon Matrix in Preventing ED Violence[1]

	Host (Employee) Factors	Vector and Vehicle (Patient/Visitor) Factors	Physical/Social Environmental Factors
Before assault	• Education and training • Policy and procedures • Preventing aggressive behavior • De-escalation and conflict resolution • Managing aggression	• Communication to patients and visitors that violence will not be tolerated and potential consequences of violent behavior • Minimize anxiety for waiting patients and visitors by communicating with them every 30 min	• Develop and communicate policy to all the employees that violence is never acceptable • Development and implementation of violence policies and procedures • Education of the manager • Security/police response/policies and education • Monitoring access to ED • Alert ED staff when previously violent patients visit the ED again • Quiet area/environment • Special areas for aggressive patients/safe room for criminals • Enforce visitor policies (number of visitors)
During assault	• Education and training • Nonviolent crisis intervention	• Isolate perpetrator from others	• Security/police plan • Implement procedures for dealing with violent events
After assault	• Critical incident debriefing • Mandatory reporting of all physical assaults and physical threats	• Reporting to security/police • Maintain patient's/visitor's name for alerting staff upon return visit	• Create procedure for investigating physical threats • Create procedure for reviewing violent event

Further research and studies are needed to identify training strategies, best clinical approaches, and security measures to design and promote a safe work environment in the ED.[1]

REFERENCES

1. Ramacciati N, Ceccagnoli A, Addey B, Lumini E, Rasero L. Interventions to reduce the risk of violence toward emergency department staff: Current approaches. *Open Access Emergency Medicine* 2016;8:17–27.
2. Arnetz JE, Hamblin L, Russell J, et al. Preventing patient-to-worker violence in hospitals: Outcome of a randomized controlled intervention. *Journal of Occupational and Environmental Medicine* 2017;59(1):18–27.
3. Petit JR. Management of the acutely violent patient. *Psychiatric Clinics of North America* 2005;28(3):701–711, 710. Review.
4. Wong AH, Wing L, Weiss B, Gang M. Coordinating a team response to behavioral emergencies in the emergency department: A simulation-enhanced interprofessional curriculum. *Western Journal of Emergency Medicine* 2015;16(6):859–865.

Clinical Vignette 10: As the Kings So Are the Subjects

Sireesha Murala
NTR University of Health Science

Clinical vignette discusses a case where a medical error happened due to incompetence from the clinic director. We will discuss the importance of leadership to develop a culture of patient safety.

THE CASE

Mrs. Julie is a 45-year-old female who came to the outpatient service for a yearly follow-up. She has a history of severe asthma and is getting worse despite using inhaled long-acting bronchodilator, salmeterol, and inhaled corticosteroids. She got her yearly flu shot, and her examination was unremarkable. She complained that her asthma attacks are more frequent than usual, and her current regimen seems to be not helping much. The physician ordered oral corticosteroids, and because the patient wanted to hand-carry the prescription, the physician asked his nurse to collect the prescription from the printer in a different room and hand it over to the patient.

The physician got a call from an emergency care unit about the patient that she had a severe unprovoked asthma attack and died because of it. He was informed that she took propranolol as her primary care provider prescribed it. The physician later found out that a different prescription was given out by the nurse without checking the patient's name and prescription.

COMMENTS

In the above clinical vignette, the patient died due to a medical error from the side of clinic director.

As the physician has ordered, the nurse gave out a prescription of a different patient. As the patient is an asthmatic, propranolol is contraindicated due to the risk of bronchospasm, which ultimately leads to death of the patient. The cause is the location of the printer in a different room, far from the nursing station and physician's room. The chief nurse had already reported the difficulties with checking in and out of patients as the nursing station is far from the patient waiting area. Even then, the clinic director had made no changes to prevent these hazards in patient safety. If the clinic director had taken the leadership and put a sequential flow of the patients and arranging the nursing station close to the physician's room and printer area, this error could have been avoided. Team training and executive management would prevent these errors in the future.

DISCUSSION

In primary care, the key for high-quality, safe, and effective healthcare is the relationship between the clinician and the patient.[1] The concept of patient safety depends on clinical staff safety attitudes, beliefs, and knowledge. It is important to consider safety more than a mere absence of accidents.[2] Development of safety culture is the core element among many other efforts to improve patient safety in acute healthcare settings like emergency departments.[3]

In Primary Care Settings, the Breakdown of Patient Safety Is shown as follows[1]:
• Among outpatients, 1 in 20 experienced a diagnostic error. • Diagnostic errors were reported in 55% of outpatient visits. • Adverse drug reactions 1 in 9 admissions in ED. • Medication errors are reported in an estimated 160 million of patients from primary care. • After a primary care visit, 80% of patients have immediately forgotten their diagnosis.

The four evidence-based strategies that promote the engagement of patients and families to improve the safety are shown as follows:[1]

■ Be prepared and engaged
■ Create a safe medicine list together
■ Teach-back
■ Warm handoff plus

Patient safety culture (PSC) is defined as the willingness and ability of the organization to understand safety and hazards. Layers of PSC include organizational dimensions, social processes, and psychological dimensions and are shown in Table 1. Patient safety requires steering and controlling the organization and mindful use of both social processes and psychological dimensions.[2]

Table 1   Layers of PSC and Their Dimensions[2]

	Layers	*Dimensions*
1	Organizational dimensions	• System of organizational management • Promotion of safety through the actions of the management • Immediate superior actions • Cooperation practices • Free flow of information and communication • Organizational learning practices • Training and competencies management • Resources management • Change management • Third parties/subcontractors management • Flow of information and collaboration between units and professional groups
2	Social processes	• Collective sensemaking • Maintenance of social identity • Local adaptation and optimization • Cues normalization • Embedding of conceptions
3	Psychological dimensions	• Perceived meaningfulness of one's own work • Sense of personal responsibility and control over one's own work and its results • Organizational knowledge and the expectations of their own work • Knowledge on the hazard mechanisms and hazards which can turn into actual harm • Safety knowledge and means to achieve it • Organizational core task knowledge and its requirements and constraints

PSC does not include situational performance of the individual workers but is more about the potential than actual performance. PSC affects the patient safety in each case by creating the work preconditions and influencing the situational possibility of safe actions.[2]

Table 2   Patient Safety Strategies and Their Benefits[3]

	Strategies	*Benefits*
1	Team training	• Optimizes teamwork processes such as cooperation, communication, collaboration, and leadership • Focuses on attaining skills, or attitude and knowledge • Studies reported a significant improvement in staff perceptions of safety culture
2	Executive walk-rounds	• Shows leadership commitment to safety; fosters trust and psychological safety; and provides support to the frontline care providers to effectively address any treats to patient safety • Studies reported an improvement in staff perceptions of safety culture
3	CUSP	• Pairs adaptive (team training) and technical interventions (clinical care algorithms), which would improve patient safety and quality • It includes executive engagement and team training, with specific strategies to translate evidence-based clinical care into practice

PSC includes interventions in leadership principles, teamwork, and behavior change. Multifaceted strategies with interventions such as team training, executive walk-rounds or interdisciplinary rounding, and comprehensive unit-based safety program (CUSP) would promote the culture of patient safety. Table 2 shows these patient safety strategies and their benefits.[3]

Organizations should incorporate the above elements to promote and improve the safety culture and should be evaluated across multiple outcomes. Future research is needed to investigate safety culture as a cross-cutting factor to moderate the effectiveness of patient safety practices.[3] PSC research benefits from a focus on concerning concepts of the organization and patient safety.[2]

REFERENCES

1. Guide to Improving Patient Safety in Primary Care Settings by Engaging Patients and Families. Content last reviewed July 2018. Agency for Healthcare Research and Quality, Rockville, MD. www.ahrq.gov/professionals/quality-patient-safety/patient-family-engagement/pfeprimarycare/index.html. Accessed on July 17, 2018.
2. Reiman T, Pietikäinen E, Oedewald P. Multilayered approach to patient safety culture. *Qual Saf Health Care* 2010;19(5):e20.
3. Weaver SJ, Lubomksi LH, Wilson RF, Pfoh ER, Martinez KA, Dy SM. Promoting a culture of safety as a patient safety strategy: A systematic review. *Ann Intern Med* 2013;158(5 pt 2):369–374.

Clinical Vignette 11: The Encrypted Message

Keerthana Kumar
University of Missouri

Abbreviations, acronyms, and other forms of shorthand are designed to make communication more efficient, especially to save time and energy for the person trying to communicate information. Unfortunately, there is often a loss of clarity that accompanies abbreviations. The lack of clarity that accompanies medical shorthand can result in miscommunication and medical errors that negatively impact patient safety and productivity. We will discuss examples of the failures in communication and the potential errors that can occur through the use of abbreviations, acronyms, and other shorthand symbols in medicine.

THE CASE

Gordon was a 74-year-old gentleman with a past medical history of hypertension and hyperlipidemia who was brought to the local emergency room by his wife after falling in the bathtub. Gordon reported a 9/10 aching, non-radiating pain in his right lower leg, and denied any other symptoms or prodromal symptoms surrounding the fall. Physical examination revealed bruising and swelling of the right knee and an inability to bear weight on the right side. X-ray of the right knee revealed tibial plateau fracture. Vital signs were blood pressure of 176/97, heart rate of 72, respiratory rate of 18, and temperature of 36.7°C (98.1°F). At home, medications were aspirin, atorvastatin, and prazosin. Gordon was given morphine sulfate for the pain and labetalol to lower his blood pressure. The knee swelling reduced, and urine analysis was within normal limits. A splint was created and placed over his right leg, and blood pressure had lowered. Gordon then reported a 4/10 pain, although it was stated he was ready to go home. Gordon was being prepared for discharge and was made an outpatient follow-up appointment to be seen in 10 days. He was given a prescription for morphine on discharge that read "MSO4 2mg PO q4hrs PRN, q #10, Refills 0."

When Gordon came for his follow-up appointment, he reported distress and extreme pain following discharge that the morphine did not eliminate. He reported using Tylenol in conjunction with the morphine, to which there was still constant 7/10 pain the first 2 days following discharge, and his systolic blood pressure on home measurement was consistently in the 160s due to pain. When the doctor examined his prescription bottle, Gordon was given 10 pills for "Magnesium Sulfate 2mg PO q4hrs PRN," which is a very low, subtherapeutic dose of magnesium sulfate.

COMMENTS

Gordon was unnecessarily in pain due to the abbreviation for morphine sulfate used while writing his prescription, which is an abbreviation prohibited for use by healthcare providers. Gordon's history of hypertension combined with pain from his fracture was the likely cause of his high blood pressure readings, and gave even more importance to pain control as a healthcare goal for Gordon.

DISCUSSION

Errors in writing prescriptions are prevalent and result in up to 7,000 deaths per year.[1] In response to the need for improvement in written/electronic communication, the Joint Commission on Accreditation of Healthcare Organizations developed the official "Do Not Use" list of abbreviations in 2004 (Table 1) and subsequently a list of additional abbreviations for possible future inclusion (Table 2):

Table 1 Official "Do Not Use" List.[1] Applies to All Orders and All Medication-Related Documentation That Is Handwritten (Including Free-Text Computer Entry) or on Preprinted Forms

Do Not Use	Potential Problem(s)	Use Instead
U (unit)	• Mistaken for "0" (zero), the number "4" (four), or "cc"	• Write "unit" IU (International Unit)
IU (International Unit)	• Mistaken for IV (intravenous) or the number 10 (ten)	• Write "International Unit"
Q.D., QD, q.d., qd (daily) Q.O.D., QOD, q.o.d, qod (every other day)	• Mistaken for each other • Period after the Q mistaken for "I" and the "O" mistaken for "I"	• Write "daily" • Write "every other day"

(Continued)

Table 1 (*Continued*)   Official "Do Not Use" List.[1] Applies to All Orders and All Medication-Related Documentation That Is Handwritten (Including Free-Text Computer Entry) or on Preprinted Forms

Do Not Use	Potential Problem(s)	Use Instead
Trailing zero (X.0 mg)[a] Lack of leading zero (.X mg)	• Decimal point is missed	• Write X mg • Write 0.X mg
MS, MSO$_4$, and MgSO$_4$	• Can mean morphine sulfate or magnesium sulfate • Confused for one another	• Write "morphine sulfate" • Write "magnesium sulfate"

[a] Exception: A "trailing zero" may be used only where required to demonstrate the level of precision of the value being reported, such as for laboratory results, imaging studies that report size of lesions, or catheter/tube sizes. It may not be used in medication orders or other medication-related documentation.

Table 2   Additional Abbreviations, Acronyms, and Symbols[2] (For Possible Future Inclusion in the Official "Do Not Use" List)

Do Not Use	Potential Problem(s)	Use Instead
> (greater than) < (less than)	• Misinterpreted as the number "7" (seven) or the letter "L" • Confused for one another	• Write "greater than" • Write "less than"
Abbreviations for drug names	• Misinterpreted due to similar abbreviations for multiple drugs	• Write drug names in full
Apothecary units	• Unfamiliar to many practitioners • Confused with metric units	• Use metric units
@	• Mistaken for the number "2" (two)	• Write "at"
cc	• Mistaken for U (units) when poorly written	• Write "mL" or "ml" or "milliliters" ("mL" is preferred)
μg	• Mistaken for mg (milligrams) resulting in one thousandfold overdose	• Write "mcg" or "micrograms"

Frequency of selected abbreviations associated with errors

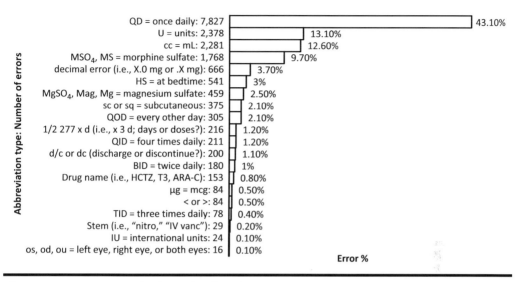

Figure 1 Frequency of selected abbreviations associated with errors.

Despite the availability of the "Do Not Use" list, noncompliance remains an issue (by 23%) during Joint Commission surveys. In a Joint Commission analysis on 18,153 classifiable errors, the frequency of the errors reported is shown in Figure 1.[1]

Even beyond medical management, the use of abbreviations and acronyms is often detrimental and almost always results in some misinterpretation.[3] Electronic health records (EHRs) are less prone to medical errors from abbreviation use compared to paper.[4] The risk of misinterpretation in EMRs, although less than written, still commands vigilance to reduce medical errors, particularly with regard to drug names, dosages, and scheduling. The Joint Commission additionally has the following recommendations for improving communications through minimization of abbreviation use[1]:

■ Initiate a campaign to eradicate the use of abbreviations in clinical practice; an interdisciplinary approach is essential.
  – Use "Dear Doctor" letters.
  – Post prohibited abbreviation lists on hospital identification badges, in patient charts, newsletters, an intranet site, computer screen savers, and announcement boards.
  – Use peer-initiated accountability.
  – Give rewards for nonusage.

- Educate staff on the harmful effects of abbreviations.
- Minimize the use of abbreviations; write out the drug name, schedule, and unit of measure.
  - Prohibit use in patient charts, preprinted order forms, and computer programs.
- Clarify intent to avoid misinterpretation if abbreviations are found.
- Introduce computerized physician order entry in a manner that minimizes the use of abbreviations.
- Review all computer-entry software for potential abbreviation issues.
- Prohibit the use of abbreviations in all facility publications (e.g., newsletters).
- Include industry, organizational, educational, and professional bodies in error-prone abbreviation awareness and avoidance, as the multifaceted nature of healthcare requires a global approach.

Education of these recommendations and rules is essential, but enforcement is required to ensure compliance.[5] The Joint Commission recommends minimization of abbreviation use and prohibits use of drug abbreviation in patient charts and computer programs, and reviewing all computer-entry software for potential abbreviation use. The utilization of computer programs with hard-stop alerts will promote patient safety by precluding inappropriate abbreviation use. Embedding alerts within an electronic progress note program has been shown to reduce the use of abbreviations to a much greater extent than alerts with an autocorrection feature.[6] Additionally, subjects aware of being monitored for noncompliance have been found to be significantly more likely to comply with rules with regard to abbreviation use.[6] We can conclude that EHR system alerts will assist in the reduction of medical errors through abbreviation use. However, patient safety will be best established by a global approach that promotes a multifaceted awareness and avoidance of abbreviation use from the healthcare team.

REFERENCES

1. Brunetti, L., Santell, J.P., and Hicks, R.W., The impact of abbreviations on patient safety. *Jt Comm J Qual Patient Saf*, 2007. 33(9): pp. 576–583.

2. www.jointcommission.org/assets/1/18/dnu_list.pdf
3. Shiffman, S., et al., Pharmacist and physician interpretation of abbreviations for acetaminophen intended for use in a consumer icon. *Pharmacy (Basel)*, 2015. 3(4): pp. 169–181.
4. Cheung, S., et al., Audit on the use of dangerous abbreviations, symbols, and dose designations in paper compared to electronic medication orders: A multicenter study. *Ann Pharmacother*, 2018. 52(4): pp. 332–337.
5. Traynor, K., Enforcement outdoes education at eliminating unsafe abbreviations. *Am J Health Syst Pharm*, 2004. 61(13): pp. 1314, 1317, 1322.
6. Myers, J.S., et al., A randomized-controlled trial of computerized alerts to reduce unapproved medication abbreviation use. *J Am Med Inform Assoc*, 2011. 18(1): pp. 17–23.

Section 4: Electronic Medical Records and Patient Safety

Clinical Vignette 1: Rubik's Cube

Anudeep Yelam
University of Missouri

Clinical vignette discusses the medical errors due to problems with electronic health record (EHR) notification resulting in delayed diagnosis. In addition, we will discuss different causes of EHR-related medical errors.

THE CASE

Peter, a 64-year-old male with a history of hypertension and chronic kidney disease, came to outpatient service with a history of generalized weakness and easy fatigability for 1 month. He is taking enalapril for his hypertension and atorvastatin for his high low density lipoprotein (LDL). Complete blood count, complete metabolic profile, and renal function tests were ordered. His renal function tests were abnormal with elevated serum creatinine, blood urea nitrogen (BUN), and increased proteinuria.

Serum creatinine	2.5 mg/dL (normal: 0.8–1.2 mg/dL)
BUN	32 mg/dL (normal: 7–22 mg/dL)
Urine protein	3+

On review of records, it was noted that the laboratory results were reported in the EHR but the physician failed to follow up on the results because the EHR did not alert to the abnormal results, and this delayed the staging of his chronic kidney disease and appropriate management.

COMMENTS

In the above case scenario, the patient's abnormal laboratory values have not been notified or followed up by the physician in time resulting in delayed diagnosis. This could have been prevented if the physician had direct access to the primary report or through automated notifications.[1]

DISCUSSION

Follow-up of laboratory test results is a major patient safety concern. Many EHRs may not be able to alert the physicians to the abnormal patients' laboratory results. The results are usually phoned or in some cases sent to the providers' EHR inbox. However, there is always a chance of human error, and checking the results manually may not always be feasible. EHRs can potentially address this through the implementation of robust quality assurance systems to monitor critical alert follow-up rates[2] and the use of dual notifications for alerts judiciously.[1]

EHRs are designed to provide better healthcare and decrease healthcare costs. Despite EHR implementation in improving patient safety, recent literature has revealed potential safety hazards associated with its use, referred to as e-iatrogenics.[3] The errors related to EHR should be proactively addressed. If not, millions of patients may be affected owing to the increased adoption of EHRs. Here, we focus on errors related to EHR use.

EHR-related medical errors can be divided into two types (Table 1):

1. System-related errors
2. User-related errors

System-related errors: These could be either due to EHR system design flaws or failure/lack of alerts and alarms (Table 1). Expanding capabilities of EHR requires complex software, which increases the chance of software failures that have the potential to harm patients. EHR system contains all the patients' records, and a glitch in it can result in an inaccurate entry of patients' allergies, medications, or mix-up of patients' data, which results in unintended consequences. Also, proper alert systems are mandatory to prevent patient harm. A system should be able to notify duplicate entries of medications, mix-up of patients' names, and so on, and the failure to do so can result in adverse outcomes.

Although EHR systems do not directly impact patient care without human intervention, the technology is often so complicated that users sometimes cannot analyze or understand its

Table 1   EHR-Related Medical Errors due to System Factors[5]

Error Related to	Comments	Examples
Technical and design issues	EHR system requires the development of complex software, and these are prone to numerous bugs and glitches.	The possibility of missing or corrupted data due to a software issue as in case of laboratory results being displayed incorrectly with an extra character.
Failure or lack of alerts and alarms	Proper alert systems are mandatory to prevent adverse outcomes.	A baby died from a massive drug overdose as a result of a transcription error that occurred when a handwritten order was transcribed incorrectly into the computer. This could have prevented if automated alerts had been activated.

computations and therefore cannot exercise competent human intervention.[4] For example, providers can rely on algorithm-generated diagnosis and treatment recommendations without fully acknowledging how the system was developed.

User-related errors: In addition to EHR technical flaws and design issues that can contribute to suboptimal healthcare delivery, errors can also result due to improper system use. These occur due to the complexity of the system, inadequate training, lack of user-friendly interface, and so on. A provider sometimes can select an item next to the intended one in the drop-down menu, such as selection of wrong patient or medication.[6] This type of error is called "adjacency error" and is not seen with paper-based records. EHR systems provide with functionalities to ease the workflow such as copy and paste, templates, and clinical decision support systems (Table 2). However, when this function is used inappropriately it can result in improper documentation, medical errors, or allegations of fraud. Copy/paste and usage of templates are the most common EHR-related user errors.

Copy and paste user-related error: This is also known as cloning or carrying forward. Incorrect use of copying/pasting text from

Table 2   EHR-Related Medical Errors due to User Factors[5]

Error Related to	*Comments*	*Examples*
Copy and paste errors (also known as cloning or carrying forward)	Inappropriate use of copy and paste functionality can result in inaccurate and false data entry, which results in poor decision-making.	Copying and pasting the same note for several days in a row nearly resulted in an unneeded change in the patient's antibiotic regimen because the note had not been updated to reflect the fact that patient's abscess had been already drained.
Templates	Templates are intended so that the physician can manage the workflow efficiently, thus saving time and focus on what is important (the patient care). But unintended consequences can occur if not used correctly.	• Patient had papilledema on examination, but the physician missed to enter it in the standard template. • Amputees EHR noted that his extremities were normal.
Clinical decision support system	Use of decision support systems may lead to errors of omission, whereby important data will be missed because the system does not prompt one to notice the information, or when the individual does what the system prompts them to do, even when it contradicts their medical knowledge, training, and other available information. This is called "automation bias."	The computer application interpreted the EKG as normal when the patient, in fact, had a conduction block. This influenced the decision- making of a resident leading to incorrect documentation.

(Continued)

Table 2 (*Continued*)   EHR-Related Medical Errors due to User Factors[5]

Error Related to	Comments	Examples
Alert fatigue	The alerts are designed to notify users to clinically significant errors or potential adverse events. However, the EHR can sometimes overwhelm the physician with alerts of little practical significance and cause alert fatigue.	A physician prescribed a penicillin antibiotic ignoring the alert notification of patient's allergy to the medication. This could be because many of the displayed alerts were of little practical significance and were also excessive and disruptive to the prescriber, thus missing the most important notification.

various locations in the EHR, either from the same or from the previous patient encounters, can result in the following[5]:

1. Inaccurate or outdated information
2. Propagation of false information
3. Internally inconsistent progress notes
4. Unnecessary lengthy progress notes

The inappropriate use of copy/paste function leads to disorganized, cluttered, and irrelevant information being displayed, making it difficult to locate relevant information[7] and understand the patients' illness. This ultimately results in poor decision-making as well as malpractice litigation. A study in the *Journal of the American Informatics Association* found that approximately 80% of sign-out notes and 55% of the notes contained copied text.[8]

Inappropriate template use-related error: This is built into the EHR so that the provider doesn't miss the elements essential in demonstrating appropriate care. Usage of these standard paragraphs and text, though, helps the provider to manage the workflow and time; inappropriate use can result in unintended consequences. It can also result in an inaccurate entry of events or sometimes miss the entry of actual events. In addition to the reduced quality of care or increased liability exposure, pre-populated templates in advance can also cause overdocumentation, which leads to higher level services than actually provided to be billed.

REFERENCES

1. Singh, H., et al., Timely follow-up of abnormal diagnostic imaging test results in an outpatient setting: Are electronic medical records achieving their potential? *Arch Intern Med.* 2009. **169**(17): pp. 1578–1586.
2. Singh, H., et al., Notification of abnormal lab test results in an electronic medical record: Do any safety concerns remain? *Am J Med.* 2010. **123**(3): pp. 238–244.
3. Weiner, J.P., et al., "e-Iatrogenesis": The most critical unintended consequence of CPOE and other HIT. *J Am Med Inform Assoc.* 2007. **14**(3): pp. 387–388; discussion 389.
4. Hoffman, S. and A. Podgurski, Finding a cure: The case for regulation and oversight of electronic health record systems. *Harvard J Law and Technol.* 2008. **22**: p. 65.
5. Bowman, S., Impact of electronic health record systems on information integrity: Quality and safety implications. *Perspect Health Inf Manag.* 2013. **10**(Fall): p. 1c.
6. Committee on Patient Safety and Health Information Technology, Institute of Medicine. *Health IT and Patient Safety: Building Safer Systems for Better Care*, Washington (DC): National Academies Press (US). 2011.
7. O'Malley, A.S., et al., Are electronic medical records helpful for care coordination? Experiences of physician practices. *J Gen Intern Med.* 2010. **25**(3): pp. 177–185.
8. Wrenn, J.O., et al., Quantifying clinical narrative redundancy in an electronic health record. *J Am Med Inform Assoc.* 2010. **17**(1): pp. 49–53.

Clinical Vignette 2: A Hurried Miss

Anudeep Yelam
University of Missouri

Clinical vignette discusses a case where an echocardiogram report was not fully read due to the way it was presented on the EHR, which resulted in a preventable stroke. In addition, we will discuss the ways to mitigate EHR-related errors.

THE CASE

Sid is a 34-year-old male from India and was brought to the emergency room (ER) by his wife with complaints of increased heart rate and shortness of breath for the past 1 week. He had a history of sore throat during childhood which was inadequately treated. Electrocardiogram was ordered along with serum troponins that were normal. The patient was admitted into inpatient service for further workup. An echocardiogram was ordered, and the results were sent through EHR. The provider read just the conclusion of the report missing the mention of mild mitral stenosis in the detailed body of report and was discharged with a diagnosis of panic attack.

The patient was seen again in the ER with stroke after few months during which EKG showed irregularly irregular P waves and severe mitral stenosis on echocardiogram. If there was a way by which EHR could highlight the presence of mild mitral stenosis in the detailed report and had it been also included in the conclusion of the report, the stroke could have been prevented.

COMMENTS

In this case, the mitral stenosis on echocardiogram was missed, which resulted in stroke because the physician did not read the complete report due to the way it was presented on the EHR.

The EHR has two components when displaying the imaging or diagnostic reports: the descriptive part which includes a detailed report and the conclusion part which only includes the most important findings. Not all the findings are reported in the conclusion hoping the provider who requested the test would read the report in its entirety. But this is not always possible because of the busy clinic/hospital schedules and the way the report is presented in the EHR, string of long detailed text. This can be solved by developing and implementing algorithms/artificial intelligence programs to identify and highlight the positive findings in the body of the report be included automatically in the final conclusion of the report that have to be signed/attested by the reporting physician before adding/saving it into the EHR.

DISCUSSION

Health information technology and EHRs are here to stay. While new approaches to EHR are likely to emerge, healthcare organizations should ensure both safety of their current technology and its usage today. Several resources are available to assist healthcare organizations like SAFER guides developed by the office of the National Coordinator for Health Information Technology.[1] It consists of nine guides organized into three groups: foundational guides, infrastructures guides, and clinical process guides. These provide assessment checklists and structure for teams to assess and improve their systems. The agency for healthcare research and quality also produced guidelines for reducing unintended consequences of EHR.[2]

Below are few of many ways to mitigate EHR-related errors:

Type of Error	Ways to Reduce EHR-Related Errors
EHR system design flaws	To reduce EHR system design flaws and unintended consequences: • An industry standard should be established.[3] • Federal regulations should be put in place to establish approval and monitor EHR system standards and implementation specifications. • EHR system vendors should employ design and usability standards that optimize system safety, efficacy, and information integrity.
User-related	• EHR usability should be included in the EHR certification process. • Healthcare organizations should ensure that all users receive thorough training on system use. • Internal reporting system to identify problems using EHR, EHR-related errors, and issues should be established.

(Continued)

Type of Error	Ways to Reduce EHR-Related Errors
Documentation recording process	• Highlight all "pasted" material, and source attribution for copied text should be recorded. • A "zero-tolerance" policy on unethical copying practices should be adopted by the organization.[4] • Policies should be designed to minimize the insertion of patient data available elsewhere in the records and discourage copying as a way of improving clinical productivity.[4]
Alerts	Only important alerts such as medication allergies, abnormal laboratory values, and significant drug interactions should be notified instead of overwhelming and excessive alerts that are of less practical significance.

EHRs provide opportunities to transform healthcare if the systems are properly designed and used and the data in the systems are accurate. Although there are guidelines and principles to improve patient safety, these are not put into widespread practice. Policy makers, EHR vendors, and healthcare providers must all work together to ensure better practices and better patient care.[4]

REFERENCES

1. SAFER Guides. Available at: www.healthit.gov/topic/safety/safer-guides. Accessed on July 25, 2018.
2. Agency for Healthcare Research and Quality Guidelines. Available at: www.healthit.gov/unintended-consequences/. Accessed on July 25, 2018.
3. Committee on Patient Safety and Health Information Technology, Institute of Medicine. *Health IT and Patient Safety: Building Safer Systems for Better Care*, Washington (DC): National Academies Press (US). 2011.
4. Bowman, S., Impact of electronic health record systems on information integrity: Quality and safety implications. *Perspect Health Inf Manag.* 2013. **10**(Fall): p. 1c.

Clinical Vignette 3: A Case of Mistaken Identity

Anudeep Yelam
University of Missouri

Clinical vignette discusses a case where report was sent to a different provider and resulted in worsening of her disease symptoms. We will discuss about the Centers for Medicare & Medicaid Services mandated meaningful use (MU) and its impact on patient safety. We will also talk briefly about Medicare Access and Children's Health Insurance Program Reauthorization Act (MACRA).

THE CASE

Mary, a 60-year-old female, came to the outpatient clinic with numbness and tingling of the lower extremities along with painless ulcer in the bottom of her feet for 6 months. She has a history of diabetes for 10 years for which she's using insulin regularly. On examination, muscle tone, bulk, strength, and deep tendon reflexes are all normal bilaterally throughout. On sensory examination, there is decreased sensation in the feet till below the knee bilaterally as well as decreased sensation in the hands bilaterally. She has steppage gait, negative Romberg's sign, and normal finger nose test. HBA1C and nerve conduction studies (NCS) with electromyography (EMG) were ordered.

NCS/EMG is done by outside specialist, and the results were sent to a different provider because of patients' first name mix-up. The patients' primary care physician never received the results. After a couple of months, the patient again saw the primary care physician with worsening of her symptoms.

COMMENTS

This case provides an opportunity to examine the identification mix-ups within EMR and their impact on patient safety. This doesn't mean the EMR failed here. Rather, the errors were because of lack of proper safeguards against misidentification and weak linkages of the EHRs. A system has to be in place so that the EHR can alert the provider/technician on misidentification.

In order to improve the patient safety, quality, and efficiency of healthcare organizations, health information technology, particularly EHR, was mandated by the federal incentive program, which defined MU in three stages for timely adoption of EHR use as described in the discussion below. However, despite the widespread adoption of EHR systems, only few hospitals have met all the criteria because the implementation and development of MU for EHR is still an ongoing process.[1] Data on overall improvements in patient outcomes associated with EHR implementation are yet to be determined and documented.[2]

DISCUSSION

Health Information Technology for Economic and Clinical Health (HITECH) Act prompted widespread adoption and use of EHR technology.[3] Since the passage of HITECH Act, hospital adoption of EHRs has grown rapidly.[1] Under this EHR incentive programs, eligible professionals and hospitals can receive financial incentives for adoption and MU of EHRs.

In primary care, MU consists of three stages:

1. Stage 1: Transferring data to EHRs and being able to share information
2. Stage 2: Including new standards such as online access for patients to their health information and electronic health information exchange between providers
3. Stage 3: Implementation

The following are the components of MU:

1. Use of certified EHR in a meaningful manner (e.g., e-prescribing)
2. Use of certified EHR for electronic exchange of health information to improve the quality of healthcare
3. Use of certified EHR to submit clinical quality measures

MU uses certified EHR technology to (Figure 1)

- Improve quality, safety, and efficiency, and reduce health disparities.
- Engage patients and families in their healthcare.
- Improve care coordination.
- Improve population and public health.
- Ensure adequate and privacy and security protection for personal health information.

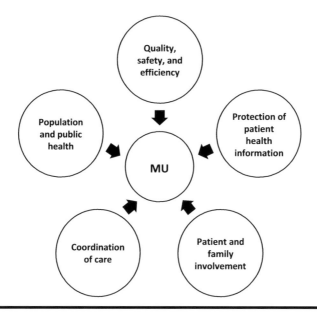

Figure 1   Meaningful use (MU) and its goals.

MACRA replaced Medicare reimbursement schedule with a new pay for performance program that is focused on quality, value, and accountability. There are two types of Medicare payments: Merit-Based Incentive Payment System (MIPS) and Alternative Payment System.

MIPS components include four performance categories (Figure 2):

Figure 2   Merit-Based Incentive Payment System (MIPS) performance categories.

1. Quality
2. Advancing care information
3. Clinical improvement activities
4. Cost

The advantage of MACRA is that it promotes connectivity between patients and providers through the use of health technology. It prioritizes positive outcomes of the patients and weighs the quality of care as it links providers' pay to their performance.

REFERENCES

1. Adler-Milstein, J., et al., More than half of US hospitals have at least a basic EHR, but stage 2 criteria remain challenging for most. *Health Aff (Millwood)*. 2014. **33**(9): pp. 1664–1671.
2. Yanamadala, S., et al., Electronic health records and quality of care: An observational study modeling impact on mortality, readmissions, and complications. *Medicine (Baltimore)*. 2016. **95**(19): p. e3332.
3. Buntin, M.B., S.H. Jain, and D. Blumenthal, Health information technology: Laying the infrastructure for national health reform. *Health Aff (Millwood)*. 2010. **29**(6): pp. 1214–1219.

Chapter 4

Understanding Diagnostic Errors

Diagnostic errors and cognitive bias account for a huge economic and healthcare burden in the United States. This chapter discusses different types of diagnostic error and cognitive bias with their impact on the healthcare system. Each clinical vignette in the following chapter highlights medical error due to cognitive bias mainly focusing on the anchoring bias, availability bias, heuristics, framing effect, overdiagnosis, and overconfidence. Further, this chapter details the ways to mitigate the diagnostic error and improve the quality care for patients. It also highlights the use of various tools such as software programs to improve the diagnostic accuracy.

Clinical Vignette 1: Is First Love the True Love?

Harleen Kaur
University of Missouri

Clinical vignette discusses anchoring bias and gives a background on diagnostic errors.

THE CASE

Ms. Emily, a 22-year-old female, presents to the clinic with symptoms of headache, myalgia, fatigue, and difficulty in sleeping, and says "I have pain everywhere in my body." She adds that she works as a waitress at a local restaurant and has difficulty in working because of the fatigue and body ache. Dr. Gordan, a 62-year-old physician, is her primary care provider. He usually has a busy clinic with less ancillary staff to support the clinic. After listening to the patient information, Dr. Gordon told her that she might be suffering from fibromyalgia and prescribed her Savella (milnacipran) 25 mg dose at bedtime and asked her to follow up in 2 weeks if symptoms don't improve. After 2 weeks, Ms. Emily again returned to the clinic without much improvement in symptoms. Dr. Gordon increased the dose of Savella to 50 mg and advised her to take over-the-counter B-complex vitamins as well. Ms. Emily returned to the clinics in 3 weeks with the symptoms of rash developing on her face and arms. Dr. Gordon got concerned and further asked her about any other complaints she had, to which she added, "I sometimes get ulcers in the mouth, but they come and go by themselves and I don't have take anything for them." Dr. Gordon further asked, if she had any family history of autoimmune disease, to which she said, "My mother passed away when I was young, she had some disease, I don't know the name, but my grandma told she was not able to conceive for a long time, had multiple miscarriages and I was her only child." Dr. Gordon replied, "sorry to hear about that, but do you have any idea what happened to her?". Ms. Emily further added, "I don't know much, I was only 12, but what I heard from others was that she had kidney failure." After the detailed history, Mr. Gordon ordered diagnostic workup which included complete blood count, autoimmune panel, liver function test, and kidney function test along with vitamin D level. The diagnostic report suggested moderate anemia with a hemoglobin level of 10.6 g/dL (moderate anemia range: 8–10.9 g/dL) and a low vitamin D level of 29 ng/mL (30–100 ng/mL), and the auto-immune panel showed positive ANA (antinuclear antibody) titers. Dr. Gordon further explained Emily about the significance of rise in ANA titers and need for possible blood workup to rule out autoimmune disease such as systemic lupus erythematosus (SLE).

COMMENTS

The clinical scenario presents *anchoring bias*-related diagnostic error which occurred because of the possible initial impression about the patient symptoms and confirmed it into final diagnosis without looking into the whole picture and going through a detailed diagnostic workup. In this clinical scenario, the given explanation about Emily's mother, one can raise a possibility of SLE with antiphospholipid antibodies resulting in multiple abortions with possible disease flare-up leading to kidney failure. Due to the busy clinic schedule, the physician did not pay much attention to enquire about the family history in this case. If the physician would have taken a detailed history along with complete diagnostic workup on the first appointment visit, the delay in diagnosis and misdiagnosis could be prevented.

DISCUSSION

Diagnostic error is a healthcare burden affecting the quality of patient care in not only the United States but also worldwide.[1] In the United States, 12 million diagnostic errors have been reported annually,[2] which results in a significant economic burden of $100–$500 billion to U.S. healthcare system annually.[3] The diagnostic error in healthcare is defined, by the U.S. Institute of Medicine Committee, as the inability to establish a definitive diagnosis/explanation of the patient's healthcare problem(s) or ineffective communication of the explanation to the patient.[4] The diagnostic errors can result from underdiagnosis, missed diagnosis, or delayed diagnosis, each one of which potentially affects the patient care. A retrospective review performed by Singh et al. on 209 patients concluded that 7% of the most common missed diagnosis was pneumonia in ambulatory patient settings.[6] They also highlighted that 6% of primary cancer was missed diagnosis in their study.

In this chapter, we try to highlight the causes of diagnostic errors we deal with in day-to-day practice and strategies to overcome them to improve patient quality care.

PREVALENCE

The prevalence of diagnostic error is estimated to be in the range of 5%–15%.[5] Seventeen percentage of preventable diagnostic errors were accounted in hospitalized patients by the Harvard Medical School Study.[6] Singh et al. performed a survey on 726 pediatricians and concluded that half of the pediatricians made a diagnostic error once or twice a month and half reported diagnostic error that caused potential harm to the patient nearly once or twice a year.[7] Diagnostic error in healthcare system not only causes potential harm to patient quality but also is the second leading cause of malpractice-related legal suits against the hospital.[8]

CAUSE OF DIAGNOSTIC ERRORS

The cause of diagnostic error can be divided into three main factors: **cognitive errors, no fault errors, and system errors** (Figure 1).[5] The cognitive and system factors may coexist and

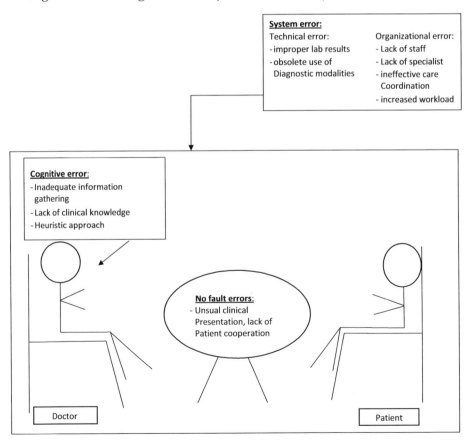

Figure 1   Causes contributing to the diagnostic error in the healthcare system.

interact with each other, resulting in many cases of diagnostic errors. Also, it is highly likely for the diagnostic errors to occur if there is unfamiliarity with the patient, if coexisting morbid disorders confuse the clinical picture of the illness, or if there is any atypical manifestation of the disease.[9] Each one of them is explained in detail as follows:

Cognitive errors: Inability of the clinician to reach a diagnosis because of lack of knowledge, improper clinical encounters, or inaccurate clinical acumen.[10] Heuristic approach used by the physicians to use shortcuts to quickly reach to the diagnosis may result in underdiagnosis or misdiagnosis. Heuristic approach may result in various types of bias such as anchoring bias or availability bias.

System errors: The diagnostic errors can be attributed to the negligence on the part of the hospital settings which may be in the form of technical incompetency such as incorrect lab results, delayed imaging result, or organizational failures such as lack of specialists, failure to coordinate care, lack of ancillary staff, increased workload on the physicians, and obsolete testing modalities.[10]

No fault errors: Such type of errors are attributed to the unusual/atypical clinical presentation of the patient and lack of patient cooperation in which case it may be very unlikely to reach to an affirmative diagnosis.

APPROACH TO IMPROVE THE DIAGNOSTIC ERRORS

The initial protocol of the diagnostic process includes detail history taking, abnormal physical findings, and abnormal prior radiological and laboratory findings (*perception*) followed by the analysis of the clinical picture and generating the most likely diagnosis or the differential diagnosis (*hypothesis generation*) and then evaluating the list of initial diagnosis with series of blood workup and radiological investigation (*data interpretation*) to finally confirm the clinical diagnosis(*verification*).[11]

Rush et al. have introduced the approach of *CARE model* (Communicate, Assess for biased reasoning, Reconsider differential diagnosis, and Enact a plan) to reduce the diagnostic error in hospital settings and improve the quality of care for the patients.[12] The model includes:

1. Communication

A detailed history is the most important step towards accurate diagnosis. Sir William Osler quoted, "Listen to the patient, he is telling you the diagnosis."[13] In clinical setting, most of the misdiagnosis occurs due to the lack of communication between the physician and the patient, and miscommunication in handling patient information among the caregivers. In 2012, the Joint Commission attributed 80% of the diagnostic errors occur because of the ineffective handling of the patient information during handoffs and patient transfer.[14] For example, the first case of *Ebola virus* in the United States resulted in the death of Thomas Eric Duncan due to rapid progression of the disease, but in this case, travel history was the key clue to approach the diagnosis of the disease which was documented by the nurses, but was not effectively communicated to other healthcare provider and nursing staff.[15] Hence, effective communication is the key strategy in preventing diagnostic error and providing effective quality care to the patients.

2. Asses for Biased Reasoning

In clinical settings, the use of heuristic approach or shortcuts to reach the diagnosis can result in missed diagnosis or underdiagnosis, resulting in diagnostic error due to cognitive bias. The most common bias encountered in clinical setting is anchoring bias (88%) followed by the availability bias (76%).[16] *Anchoring bias* is the tendency to strongly recommend the initial diagnosis as the final diagnosis, without making effort to consider other potential differential diagnosis and ultimately resulting in *premature closure* of the case. Anchoring bias can result in irrelevant test and treatment modality and underdiagnosis or missed diagnosis of the case. *Attribution bias* can arise from the failure to consider all possible sources for the patient problem. The physician is so well versed with the patient history since a long time that he does not want to potentially consider all differential diagnosis for the patient problem. *Availability bias* arises from focusing on the most common diagnosis as the final diagnosis of the patient problem.

3. Reconsidering Differential Diagnosis

Reevaluation of all the patient complaints and diagnostic testing can be helpful in preventing premature closure of the case and diagnostic error. The *dual process theory* of the clinical reasoning states that there are two types of clinical reasoning that can help to prevent the diagnostic error. *System I* (intuitive or nonanalytical) is a time-effective approach to conclude the diagnosis of most common clinical presentation of the complaints. However, there are still chances of premature closure of the case with this approach. *System II* (analytical) uses more analytical clinical reasoning to effectively reach to the diagnosis of the clinical presentation.[17]

4. Enact a Plan

After the complete evaluation of the patient complaints, initiation of a treatment plan with effective communication of the patient information among the healthcare team is the key strategy. Rush et al. also focus on the importance of *health literacy* in effectively executing the treatment plan.

REFERENCES

1. Singh H, Schiff GD, Graber ML, et al. The global burden of diagnostic errors in primary care. *BMJ Qual Saf* 2017;26:484–494. doi:10.1136/bmjqs–2016–005401.

2. Singh H, Meyer AN, Thomas EJ. The frequency of diagnostic errors in outpatient care: Estimations from three large observational studies involving US adult populations. *BMJ Qual Saf* 2014;23:727–731.

3. Newman-Toker DE. Diagnostic value: The economics of high-quality diagnosis and a value-based perspective on diagnostic innovation [lecture]. *Modern Healthcare 3rd Annual Patient Safety & Quality Virtual Conference*; June 17, 2015; online e-conference.

4. Committee on Diagnostic Error in Health Care, Institute of Medicine. Improving diagnosis in health care. September, 2015. Available from: https://iom.nationalacademies.org/~/media/Files/Report%20Files/2015/Improving-Diagnosis/Diagnostic Error_ReportBrief.pdf. Accessed December 12, 2015.

5. Singh H, Giardina TD, Meyer AN, Forjuoh SN, Reis MD, Thomas EJ, et al. Types and origins of diagnostic errors in primary care settings. *JAMA Intern Med* 2013;173:418–425.

6. Brennan TA, Leape LL, Laird NM, et al. Incidence of adverse events and negligence in hospitalized patients: Results of the Harvard Medical Practice Study I. 1991. *Qual Saf Health Care* 2004;13(2):145–151; discussion 151–152. doi:10.1136/qshc.2002.003822.

7. Singh H, Thomas EJ, Wilson L, Kelly PA, Pietz K, Elkeeb D, et al. Errors of diagnosis in pediatric practice: A multisite survey. *Pediatrics* 2010;126:70–79.

8. Bartlett EE. Physicians' cognitive errors and their liability consequences. *J Healthc Risk Manag* 1998;18:62–69.

9. Kostopoulou O, Delaney BC, Munro CW. Diagnostic difficulty and error in primary care—A systematic review. *Fam Pract* 2008;25:400–413.

10. Graber M, Gordon R, Franklin N. Reducing diagnostic errors in medicine: What's the goal? *Acad Med* 2002;77:981–992.

11. Mishra D, Gupta P, Singh T. Teaching for reducing diagnostic errors. *Indian Pediatr* 2017;54(1):37–45.

12. Rush JL, Helms SE, Mostow EN. The CARE approach to reducing diagnostic errors. *Int J Dermatol* 2017;56(6):669–673. doi:10.1111/ijd.13532.

13. Bryan CS. *Osler: Inspirations from a Great Physician*. New York: Oxford University Press, 1997.

14. The Joint Commission. Joint commission introduces new, customized tool to improve hand-off communications. 2012. [WWW document] Available at: www.jointcommission.org/assets/1/6/tst_hoc_persp_08_12.pdf.

15. Shannon SE. Ebola, team communication, and shame: But shame on whom? *Am J Bioeth* 2015;15:20–25.

16. Ogdie AR, Reilly JB, Pang WG, et al. Seen through their eyes: Residents' reflections on the cognitive and contextual components of diagnostic errors in medicine. *Acad Med* 2012;87:1361–1367.

17. Nendaz M, Perrier A. Diagnostic errors and flaws in clinical reasoning: Mechanisms and prevention in practice. *Swiss Med Wkly* 2012;142:1–9.

Clinical Vignette 2: Experience Is the Teacher of All Things or Is It?

Harleen Kaur
University of Missouri

Clinical vignette discusses the medical error due to availability heuristic and discusses different types of diagnostic errors.

THE CASE

On a fine Monday morning of the month of December, Dr. Steve, a primary care physician, had a busy clinic with 15 appointments and four walk-ins scheduled for the day. Four out of five patients scheduled till lunch time came with the symptoms of fever, headache, myalgia, running nose, and cough. All were tested for influenza A, influenza B, and streptococcal pharyngitis by taking appropriate mucus sample from the nasal swab and throat swab. All the four patients were positive for influenza A. The afternoon got busy with the walk-ins scheduled, and Dr. Steve had another patient, Ms. Julie, a 56-year-old female with past medical history of diabetes mellitus, hypertension, and chronic kidney disease, who presented to the clinic with similar complaints as mentioned above of fever, myalgia, running nose, headache, and cough for the last 2 days. Keeping in mind all the morning cases turning out positive for influenza virus, Dr. Steve diagnosed her with influenza A infection without performing the diagnostic workup for Flu A and Flu B and rapid strep test for streptococcal pharyngitis and prescribed her a course of Tamiflu 75 mg. Ms. Julie presented to the clinic again in 5 days with worsening of symptoms. She complained of high-grade fever, myalgia, running nose, sore throat, and severe cough. On exam, Ms. Julie appeared really sick, and oral findings were positive for tonsillar exudates and anterior cervical lymphadenopathy. Dr. Steve ordered a rapid antigen detection test for streptococcal pharyngitis, which was positive. He then diagnosed the patient with streptococcal pharyngitis and prescribed amoxicillin clavulanate 500 mg twice a day for 10 days and followed up after 10 days if the symptoms did not get better.

COMMENTS

This clinical scenario explains *availability bias* and *heuristic approach* in a busy clinic, resulting in diagnostic error by taking shortcuts in history, conducting clinical examination, performing incomplete diagnostic workup, and considering the most common diagnosis as the final diagnosis. If the complete diagnostic workup was done on the first doctor's appointment for this patient, then the cause of her upper respiratory tract symptoms would have been clearer and reached a confirmative diagnosis. Also, despite being a patient with chronic kidney disease, she had taken a course of Tamiflu which can have potential harm on the kidney, which was also missed by the physician because of the possible busy schedule.

DISCUSSION

Cognitive errors and heuristic approach play a critical role in clinical decision-making and can result in ineffective approach toward patient care. While heuristic approach (shortcuts) can be beneficial for clinicians in busy hospital settings to reach the diagnosis of the most common complaints, however, overlooking the complete picture of the clinical scenario can result in misdiagnosis or underdiagnosis. Cognitive errors, mainly the availability bias, arise from unconscious heuristic approach by considering the most common diagnosis as the final diagnosis. According to the *dual process theory*, discussed in the earlier chapter, type 1 (nonanalytical reasoning/intuitive) contributes to the development of availability bias and premature closure of the case.

TYPES OF DIAGNOSTIC ERRORS

Table 1 discusses in brief the most common cognitive error seen in clinical setting along with a typical example to illustrate each case better.[1,2]

HOW TO ADDRESS THIS CONCERN

Reducing the diagnostic error can help to reduce the flaws in the medical system and provide improved quality of patient care. However, not much data are available to illicit the strategies to cut down the diagnostic error. Figure 1 provides with some tips to improve the reflective thinking and diagnostic accuracy by omitting the cognitive bias at each step of clinical assessment. As explained

Table 1   Tabulation of Most Common Cognitive Bias Used in Clinical Setting along with the Most Appropriate Clinical Example

Cognitive Bias	Explanation	Clinical Example
Availability heuristic	Considering the most common diagnosis as the final diagnosis	In the month of November, the physician diagnosed four cases with flu in the clinic and considered the fifth case also to be that of flu, without ruling out streptococcal with rapid strep test
Anchoring heuristic	To recommend the initial diagnosis as the final diagnosis without considering the differential diagnosis	Considering the diagnosis of fibromyalgia in a 22-year-old female with aches and pain, and fatigue without detailed diagnostic workup and ruling out other differentials
Framing effect	The initial clinical picture dominates the entire presentation such that further clinical reasoning is affected	A chronic alcoholic with uncontrolled diabetes is given a diagnosis of diabetic neuropathy (for tingling and numbness in both lower extremity) without considering the differential of alcoholic neuropathy
Blind obedience	Giving undue importance to test results or opinion by specialist	A 32-year-old female with a recent history of contact dermatitis got a diagnosis of systemic lupus erythematosus after a positive blood workup for lupus even

(Continued)

Table 1 (*Continued*) Tabulation of Most Common Cognitive Bias Used in Clinical Setting along with the Most Appropriate Clinical Example

Cognitive Bias	Explanation	Clinical Example
		though she had no clinical symptoms suggestive of lupus
Premature closure	Accepting a diagnosis prematurely without considering all the differential diagnosis	Considering a diagnosis of panic attack in a 22-year-old patient with history of palpitation, without ruling out arrhythmia/cardiac cause
Representative	Ruling out a diagnosis because it is not a typical clinical presentation of the case	A physician could not diagnose Miller Fisher variant as Guillain–Barré syndrome because it did not present as typical ascending sensorimotor signs/symptoms
Commission bias	Tendency to perform unnecessary maneuvers, diagnostic test away from the original protocol due to overconfidence, or pressure from seniors	Performing an electroencephalogram in a patient with passing out episodes secondary to hypotension
Omission bias	Hesitant to perform the concerned tests or maneuvers with the fear of being wrong or causing harm	Hesitant to order chest tube placement for suspected pneumothorax, because of concerns of being wrong about the diagnosis

(*Continued*)

Table 1 (*Continued*)   Tabulation of Most Common Cognitive Bias Used in Clinical Setting along with the Most Appropriate Clinical Example

Cognitive Bias	Explanation	Clinical Example
Zebra retreat	Increased possibility of a rare diagnosis but the physician is hesitant to pursue it	Considering hyperemesis gravidarum as the cause of nausea in second-trimester pregnancy when hepatitis should be ruled out
Unpacking principal	Failure to deliver all the relevant information regarding patient during transfer of care	When the first case of Ebola virus was suspected in the United States, failure of transfer of relevant travel history from emergency room nurses to the other provider

in the earlier chapter, we would still emphasize on the *dual process theory* according to which the use of System II (*analytical thinking*) conscious thinking over the System I (*nonanalytical thinking*) unconscious thinking can help to improve the clinical reasoning and reduce the diagnostic errors in clinical setting.[3] *Educational strategies* used in teaching hospital/medical school can help to improve the diagnostic approach right from the beginning in this career. The traditional approach of medical education aimed at basic science theoretical knowledge, and clinical approach and application of that knowledge which is now changed to *problem-based learning* where teaching is facilitated in context to the clinical problem.[4] Gaber et al. introduced the framework of educational interventions to improve the diagnostic error, by *improving the expertise* and *conscious reflective review*.[5,6] The graph in Figure 2 explains the diagnostician progresses from the use of deductive reasoning at basic level to using heuristic at the intermediate level to expert clinical advice with increasing accuracy and reliability at expert level. *Enhancing expertise* involves the ability to have a *satisfactory skill set* which has adequate knowledge base along with the ability to access the disease presentation and reach the clinical diagnosis. It also aims to improve their clinical decision-making skills by long-term efforts in educational training and problem-based learning of the clinical scenario. The *conscious reflective review* aims to reduce the diagnostic error by making the students and residents aware of their subconscious thought process in diagnostic approach and emphasize on reflective thinking to improve the diagnostic process.

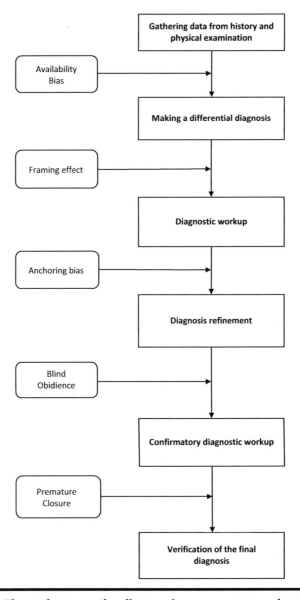

Figure 1   Tips to improve the diagnostic accuracy at each step of clinical assessment.

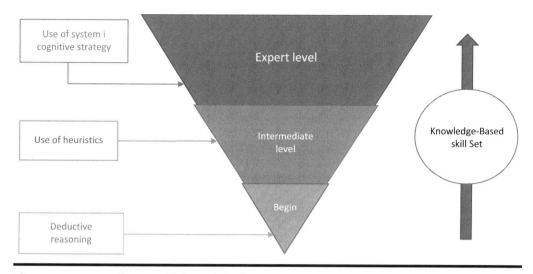

Figure 2   Inverted pyramidal model of diagnostic proficiency.

Lastly, we would like to emphasize on the recommendation laid down by the National Academy of Medicine to improve the diagnostic process and reduce the cognitive bias[7]:

1. Discuss about the future aspects of disease progression and any diagnostic uncertainty related to the state of the disease.
2. Always consider a *second opinion* in cases of dilemma. A team of doctors or expert opinion will definitely give a better advice on the differential diagnosis of the disease.
3. Consider a diagnostic checklist which should include the most common diagnosis and most uncommon diagnosis with increased mortality and morbidity.

REFERENCES

1. Stiegler MP, Neelankavil JP, Canales C, Dhillon A. Cognitive errors detected in anaesthesiology: A literature review and pilot study. *Br J Anaesth.* 2012;108(2):229–235. doi:10.1093/bja/aer387. Epub 2011 Dec 8.
2. Govindarajan R. The implication of diagnostic errors. *Continuum (Minneap Minn).* 2017;23(5, Peripheral Nerve and Motor Neuron Disorders):1458–1466.
3. Nendaz M, Perrier A. Diagnostic errors and flaws in clinical reasoning: Mechanisms and prevention in practice. *Swiss Med Wkly.* 2012;142:1–9.

4. Diemers AD, van de Wiel MW, Scherpbier AJ, Baarveld F, Dolmans DH. Diagnostic reasoning and underlying knowledge of students with preclinical patient contacts in PBL. *Med Educ.* 2015;49:1229–1238.

5. Graber ML. Educational strategies to reduce diagnostic error: Can you teach this stuff? *Adv Health Sci Educ.* 2009;14:63–69.

6. Graber ML, Kissam S, Payne VL, Meyer AN, Sorensen A, Lenfestey N, et al. Cognitive interventions to reduce diagnostic error: A narrative review. *BMJ Qual Saf.* 2012;21:e535–e557.

7. The National Academy of Sciences. Quality chasm series: Improving diagnosis in health care. nationalacademies.org/hmd/~/media/Files/Report%20Files/2015/Improving-Diagnosis/DiagnosticError_ReportBrief.pdf. Published September 2015. Accessed Mar 13, 2017.

Clinical Vignette 3: The Man with the Black Coat

Harleen Kaur
University of Missouri

Clinical vignette discusses the medical error due to framing effects and ways to mitigate it.

THE CASE

Ms. Amanda, a 56-year-old female with a 30-pack-year history of smoking and chronic diabetes, presents to the physician clinic in a private hospital with pain in both the lower extremity mainly involving her legs and underside of the feet. She describes the pain to be cramping pain, on a pain scale of 5 or 6 on 10, mainly starting below her knees and moving to her feet. The pain is associated with tingling and numbness and is worsened by walking and relieved by rest. Sometimes, she says that the pain starts in her lower back region and moves downward. Her most recent HbA_1c was 7.1%. The physician ordered a lower back magnetic resonance imaging (MRI) which was suggestive of disk bulge in L3–L4 levels. The physician made a diagnosis of lumbar spinal stenosis with superimposed diabetic neuropathy. He advised rest and prescribed some pain medication and gabapentin 100 mg three times a day for neuropathy. In the follow-up months, the patients started to complain of worsening pain in her legs that made her wheelchair bound. The physician also tried the epidural steroid injections, but the patient did not have any relief from that as well. Six months passed by, without any improvement, Ms. Amanda transferred her care to a physician in the University Teaching Hospital. When the team of physician, resident, and medical student arrived, thorough history was studied and clinical examination was conducted. On examination, prominent clubbing was noted on all the nail beds of upper extremity. The lower extremity felt cold to touch, and there was decreased pinprick sensation and vibration on the underside of the feet and at the level of the ankles. Ms. Amanda told the team, "Nobody checked my legs earlier." The physician team reassured her, advised her to quit smoking, and ordered a panel of blood test, ankle brachial index (ABI), and Doppler ultrasound of her legs. The ABI was 0.2 (normal >0.9), and Doppler ultrasound showed reduced laminar blood flow in both the lower extremity, with monophasic wave forms at the level of iliac artery, thereby showing more than 50% reduction in the lumen size. A diagnosis of peripheral vascular diseases was made, and bilateral iliac artery stents were placed to relieve the occlusion. In the further course, the patient had consistent improvement in her symptoms and followed up in the vascular clinic thereafter.

COMMENTS

This clinical scenario explains *framing effect*, where the ability to make the diagnosis is biased by the way it is framed. The cause of patient's pain in the legs was attributing from a vascular cause rather than a neurologic cause, but the physician relied on the initial frame of information given her history of chronic diabetes and initial MRI report and considered it to be a neurologic cause of the pain. However, given her history of chronic smoking with superimposed diabetes, a consideration of vascular cause should have been kept in the differential diagnosis and ruled out by the appropriate diagnostic test.

DISCUSSION

What Is Framing Effect?

The concept of framing effect was introduced for the first time by Tversky and Kahneman in 1981, where they described framing effect when the ability to make a decision was biased by the way the whole picture of the information was framed.[1] They introduced the concept of *prospect theory*, in light of which the important data are presented in either positive or negative frames and treated according to the highest value worth of this perception. The decision-makers tend to be risk averse when the information is presented positively and tend to be risk seeking when the same information is presented in a negative way. In short, the decision-makers respond differently to different scenarios of the same problem. Framing effect can influence the medical decision-making capacity, depending on the way it is presented. Armstrong et al. highlighted that framing could be induced when the treatment options are based on probability of survival and mortality.[2]

Framing effect was also noted to be beneficial in preventive behavioral approach (use of vaccination, quit smoking, and adopting healthy lifestyle) as it was more influenced by the gain frame approach (e.g., benefits from the vaccination) than the loss frame approach (e.g., risk of side effects).

TYPOLOGY OF FRAMING EFFECTS

Levin et al. widely explained the different category of framing effects with their possible effect on medical decision-making (Table 1).[3]

1. Risky choice framing effect

It is the standard framing effect, which was introduced first by Tversky and Kahneman. According to this type, the final outcome largely depends upon the different ways in which the information is presented (gain frame or loss frame). Figure 1 explains the description of risky choice framing effect. A common example of this is seen in addictive behavior and motivation to quit drugs. Researchers have found out that a positive frame should be used when the intention to quit and the dependence on nicotine are low, whereas a negative frame should be used when the intention to quit and the dependence on nicotine are high.[4]

Table 1 Summary of Different Types of Framing Effects

Frame Type	Effect of the Frame	How to Measure This Affect
Risky choice (options according to the different level of risk)	Risk preference	Comparing all choices for risky options
Attribute (preference to object/event)	Object/event evaluation	Approach to rating the single object/event
Goal (ultimate aim of the act)	Impact of persuasion	Comparing the adoption of the behavior

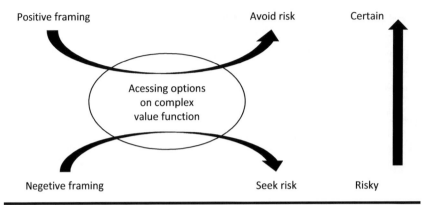

Figure 1   Risky choice framing effect.

2. Attribute framing effect

According to this, some characters of the information are given more importance than others, which ultimately manipulate the final outcome. A known example of this case is that patients prefer a certain treatment option (medical or surgical) when the outcomes are explained on the basis of survival rate compared to the mortality rate.[5] Figure 2 illustrates the attribute framing effect.

3. Goal framing effect

In this type, information is presented in a way to achieve a desired goal. In a positive frame, the information will be presented in a positive frame or in a negative frame, the information will focus on things to avoid, and in both framing, the goal framing effect aims to achieve the same act. Figure 3 explains the goal framing effect. Further to explain

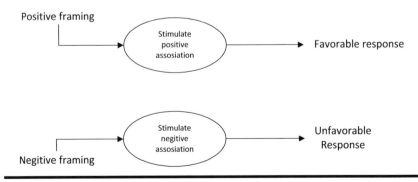

Figure 2   Attribute framing effect.

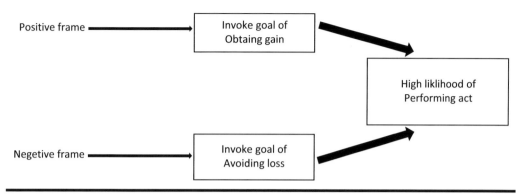

Figure 3   Goal framing effect.

the framing effect, Meyerowitz and Chaiken (1987) cited a common example, when women were explained about the risk/negative consequences of not engaging in breast self-examination to detect breast cancer, and they were more influenced to be involved in it than when explaining the positive consequences.[6] For example, a positive frame looks like, "Research emphasizes that breast examination can help to find the tumor at early more treatable stage," whereas a negative frame would sound like, "Researchers emphasized that women who do not engage in breast examination have decreased chances of finding a tumor at early more treatable stage." Hence, in either case, the frame of presentation changes, but the goal does not change.

How to Address This Concern

The framing effect can impact the medical decision-making capacity of the clinicians. In clinical practice, the physician should aim to see the complete picture of the clinical scenario and then reach the diagnosis. The attribute framing effect and the goal framing effect may hinder with the clinical information processing. The framing effect can be the biggest mislead in the diagnostic process and thereby affect the patient healthcare.

The best way to approach this issue is to again focus on a detailed history and physical examination along with comprehensive diagnostic approach to rule out all the possible differential diagnosis. Further, the stepwise approach to the right diagnostic workup is explained in Figure 4.

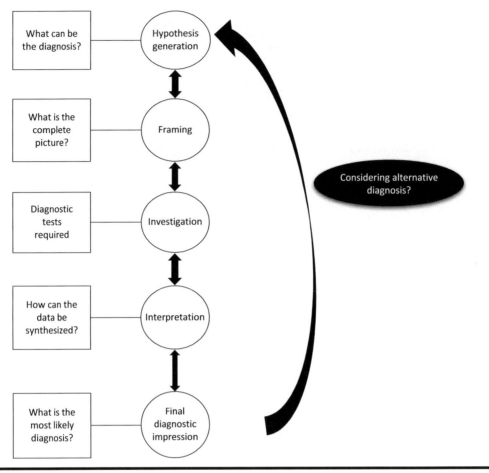

Figure 4 Comprehensive workup of the diagnostic workup.

REFERENCES

1. Tversky, A., & Kahneman, D. (1981). The framing of decisions and the psychology of choice. *Science*, 211, 453–458.
2. Armstrong, K., Schwartz, J.S., Fitzgerald, G., Putt, M., & Ubel, P.A. (2002). Effect of framing as gain versus loss on understanding and hypothetical treatment choices: Survival and mortality curves. *Medical Decision Making*, 22, 76–83.
3. Levin, I.P., Schneider, S.L., Gaeth, G.J. (1998). All frames are not created equal: A typology and critical analysis of framing effects. *Organizational Behavior and Human Decision Process*, 76(2), 149–188.
4. Marjolein Moorman, M., & Putte, B. (2008). The influence of message framing, intention to quit smoking, and nicotine dependence on the persuasiveness of smoking cessation messages. *Addictive Behaviors*, 33, 1267–1275.

5. Wilson, D.K., Kaplan, R.M., & Schneiderman, L.J. (1987). Framing of decisions and selections of alternatives in health care. *Social Behaviour*, 2, 51–59.
6. Meyerowitz, B.E., & Chaiken, S. (1987). The effect of message framing on breast self-examination attitudes, intentions, and behavior. *Journal of Personality and Social Psychology*, 52, 500–510.

Clinical Vignette 4: Don't Question Me!

Harleen Kaur
University of Missouri

Clinical vignette discusses the diagnostic errors due to overreliance on experts. In addition, we will discuss the role of software programs that help in developing your own differential diagnosis and its impact on practice of medicine.

THE CASE

Mr. Rees is a 48-year-old painter by profession who presents to the emergency room (ER) due to fall on an outstretched hand. He complains of pain in the wrist joint involving the right hand going up to the thumb. He further adds that the pain is dull in nature and is 5/10 on a pain scale (pain scale of 0–10, with 0 being the lowest and 10 being the highest). The ER physician examined the patient and ordered an X-ray of the right hand. The patient had mild tenderness on palpation below the thumb and at the wrist joint. He also called orthopedics for consult. Dr. Clarks, a 54-year-old orthopedic physician, came to the ER for the consult, examined the patient, and had a look at the X-ray. Dr. Clarks further said, "Mr. Rees, your X-ray looks perfectly fine, you can go home and take some rest." Dr. Clarks prescribed some pain medication and advised a splint if required. The ER physician tried to discuss the case with Dr. Clarks, regarding the type of fall and the possible differential diagnosis which can be missed on X-ray, but Dr. Clarks replied, "I am too busy right now, I have looked at the X-Ray, there is nothing to worry about." The ER physician discharged the patient. Subsequently, Mr. Rees did not have any improvement in the symptoms, and on the sixth day of the fall, he went to his primary care physician. The primary care physician examined him and send him for an X-ray and further said, "If nothing shows up on the X-Ray we might also get an MRI of the hand to rule out any possible missed fracture." The X-ray did not show anything, and magnetic resonance imaging (MRI) of the right hand was ordered. The MRI showed fracture in the distal third of the scaphoid bone. The primary care physician explained the patient about the diagnosis and sent him to ER for casting of the right hand.

COMMENTS

This case scenario explains blind obedience which occurs due to overreliance on expert opinion or test results. In our vignette, the ER physician was doubtful of the diagnosis but relied on the opinion given by the orthopedic physician. This resulted in delay in the management of patient care, which could have resulted in possible complications of avascular necrosis of the scaphoid bone. On the other hand, the primary care physician did not send the patient to the specialist directly; he first tried to evaluate the diagnosis with the series of diagnostic workup and then, after the confirmation of the diagnosis, sent him to ER for immediate management.

DISCUSSION

Expert opinion in day-to-day practice is essential to clear doubtful diagnosis and to prevent medical error due to underdiagnosis or missed diagnosis. However, overreliance on the expert opinion or laboratory workup can hinder with clinician's decision-making capacity to reach to a differential diagnosis. "Blind obedience" is a cognitive bias that occurs when the physicians overrely on an expert opinion or laboratory workup to reach a diagnosis. This cognitive bias limits the decision-making capacity of the physician, resulting in unnecessary expenditure and ultimately in delay in the treatment provided to the patient.

This chapter aims to highlight the diagnostic errors due to blind obedience in lieu of which we also discuss about the role of software programs as a modified approach to improved patient care and diagnosis.

BLIND OBEDIENCE AND PATIENT SAFETY

Overreliance on expert opinion can blind the clinical clues essential for decision-making in day-to-day practice and delay the accurate diagnosis. The delay in the diagnosis and treatment can be of potential harm to the patient especially in emergency care or critical care setting, where aggressive patient management is required and deferring the patient for a long time for expert opinion or waiting for laboratory workup can increase the risk of harm to the patient.

In addition, the extra diagnostic workup can also result in overdiagnosis and increase unnecessary healthcare burden for the patient. Table 1 highlights the most probable causes of blind

Table 1 Causes of Blind Obedience

Increased work load
Time pressure
Fear of making a diagnostic error
Physician burnout

obedience. Various factors that contribute toward blind obedience include increased stress of work and time constraints resulting in deferring the patient for expert opinion. Second, in order to avoid the risk of diagnostic error, the physician may prefer to get an expert opinion on their patients. Thirdly, physician burnout can very likely increase the chances of blind obedience and other cognitive bias.

The diagnostic process can also be augmented by the use of electronic differential diagnosis software that help to generate a possible differential diagnosis on the basis of clinic information provided.[1] Along with this, the era of *cognitive computing* has brought up a revolutionized approach to healthcare management.

SOFTWARE PROGRAMS FOR DIFFERENTIAL DIAGNOSIS

Various electronic diagnostic aids have been available since the 1960s to help the clinicians with differential diagnosis. The diagnostic support software applications used widely, such as Quick Medical Reference, Iliad, D_xPLAIN, Isabel, Meditels, and Diagnosis Pro, have a huge impact on the healthcare system. They have shown to improve the clinician knowledge base, physician performance and diagnostic accuracy, and quality of care provided to the patients. Studies have shown that these differential diagnosis generators can improve the diagnostic accuracy rates by 70%–95%.[2] In addition, these software programs have also been helpful to reach the diagnosis in difficult cases requiring expertise.[3]

IBM Watson is newly emerged cognitive computing which aims to revolutionize the patient healthcare. With the latest programming involving the native language process, IBM Watson aims to promote healthcare by improving the differential diagnosis and critical or most crucial diagnosis for the given data information, providing evidence-based clinical information

Table 2   Benefits of IBM Watson Cognitive Computing

Improve the physician performance.
Augment the diagnostic accuracy.
Provide new insights for clinicians and researchers, thereby improving their knowledge base.
Reduce the healthcare cost.
Patients can communicate with their physician at any time, anywhere through text messages through cognitive computing.
Diagnostic suggestions are based on latest guidelines and evidence-based study.

for the patient problem, and improving the clinical insights of the physician for each clinical encounter. In cases of physician fatigue or high work load, they can ease the approach to diagnosis and reduce the risk of missing something in regard to the patient diagnosis. And lastly, it is beneficial to effectively reduce the cost and improve the healthcare outcome in hospital setting. Another notable benefit of cognitive computing is that patients can communicate with the physicians through text messages and give an update about their health issue at any time and from anywhere.[4] IBM Watson is also helpful in providing cancer treatment options to oncologists according to the latest evidence and guidelines.[5]

Hence, to conclude, the cognitive computing with the help of IBM Watson has created a "virtual advisor" for the physician to improve the healthcare outcomes for the patients and the numerous benefits of cognitive computing will not only help to reduce time and cost but also improve efficiency and patient care (Table 2).

REFERENCES

1. Wang EY, Patrick L, Connor DM. Blind obedience and an unnecessary workup for hypoglycemia: A teachable moment. *JAMA Intern Med.* 2018;178(2):279–280. doi:10.1001/jamainternmed.2017.7104.
2. El-Kareh R, Hasan O, Schiff G. Use of health information technology to reduce diagnostic errors. *BMJ Qual Saf.* 2013;22(2):1–12.
3. Ramnarayan P, Roberts GC, Coren M, Nanduri V, Tomlinson A, Taylor PM, et al. Assessment of the potential impact of a reminder system on the reduction of diagnostic errors: A quasi-experimental

study. *BMC Med Inform Decis Mak*. 2006;6:22. Epub 2006/05/02. doi:10.1186/1472-6947-6-22; PubMed Central PMCID: PMCPmc1513379.

4. Ahmed MN, Toor AS, O'Neil K, Friedland D. Cognitive computing and the future of health care cognitive computing and the future of healthcare: The cognitive power of IBM Watson has the potential to transform global personalized medicine. *IEEE Pulse*. 2017;8(3):4–9. doi:10.1109/MPUL.2017.2678098.

5. Doyle-Lindrud S. Watson will see you now: A supercomputer to help clinicians make informed treatment decisions. *Clin J Oncol Nurs*. 2015;19(1):31–32. doi:10.1188/15.CJON.31-32.

Clinical Vignette 5: Trouble with the Curve

Harleen Kaur
University of Missouri

Clinical vignette discusses the medical error due to overconfidence in diagnosis and provides a review of literature on it.

THE CASE

Ms. Jane, a 22-year-old female weighing 86 kg (189.5 lbs), present to the neurology clinics with the history of headache for the past 8 months. She said the headache frequency was two to three times a week, lasting for about half a day to 1 day. The pain was dull and constant started on one side and traveled to the back of the head, with the intensity of 5/10 (pain scale of 0–10 with 10 being worst). The headache was sometimes associated with changes in vision/double vision and nausea, but she did not complain of any aura before the migraines started. She adds that she takes Aleve or Ibuprofen when the pain is really intolerable. Dr. Jones is a 63-year-old neurologist who runs a busy clinic. He saw her, diagnosed her with migraines, and prescribed her Imitrex for abortive therapy and Topamax 25 mg twice a day for migraine prophylaxis. When the intern tried to discuss the differential diagnosis and her medication list highlighting the intake vitamin A tablets for her acne, Dr. Jones said, "This is a clear-cut case of migraines, you will see her improvement in the next visit." After 1 week, Ms. Jane had an emergency room (ER) visit because of severe headache and vomiting. ER physician called neurologist on board and discussed to perform a lumbar puncture. On fundoscopic examination, a circumferential halo was seen on the optic disc with no major vessel obscuration, suggesting low degree papilledema. A high opening pressure of 27 cm of H_2O (10–25 cm H_2O) was noted on performing the lumbar puncture followed by magnetic resonance imaging (MRI) of the brain. The MRI of the brain showed normal brain parenchyma with ventricles. The constitutional symptoms of headache with vomiting and high opening pressure in an obese woman with current consumption of vitamin A tablets lead the team of physicians to conclude the diagnosis of pseudotumor cerebri (idiopathic intracranial hypertension).

COMMENTS

This clinical scenario is an example of overconfident judgment and attitude by the physician. Dr. Jones was so confident on his diagnosis that he did not consider the differential diagnosis in this patient and even did not go over her complete history, did not perform an elaborate physical exam, and did not go through her medication list. Such a kind of behavior often leads to misdiagnosis or underdiagnosis and can severely affect the patient health.

DISCUSSION

Overconfidence in judgment and clinical decision-making can largely affect the patient safety and quality of healthcare delivered to the patients. Physician overconfidence is attributed as one of the cognitive biases that results from the miscalibration of one's own accuracy and clinical reasoning, thereby influencing there medical decision-making capacity. Certain factors which influence the overconfident behavior are ego bias,[1] gender,[2] different cultural background,[3] attribution bias,[4] personality,[5] level of difficulty of the task,[6] feedback evaluation,[7] and level of critical thinking.[8] Studies also express that overconfidence is used as a self-assessment tool, and individuals who are relatively less competent tend to be more overconfident.[9] Friedman et al., in their study, determined the accuracy and confidence level of the medical students, residents, and physicians attending across various case scenarios and concluded that the medical students were least accurate and least confident, the physicians were most accurate and most confident, and the residents were more confident but less accurate regarding their diagnosis.[10]

This chapter aims to highlight the thinking rationale behind overconfident judgments and various types of overconfident behavior we encounter in daily practice and finally what strategies we should adopt in order to improve patient care.

The Process of Intellectual Thinking

When the physician encounters the clinical scenario, they start gathering the information/history from the patient to come up with the diagnosis, and sometimes, this information may be gathered too quickly or incompletely depending on the physician decision-making capacity and reflective thinking. According to the *dual process theory,* System I (nonanalytical thinking), which usually consists of heuristics and a shortcut approach to the problem, is adopted by the physicians in clinical setting as it is rapid, effortless, and intuitive thinking in which the new clinical scenario is correlated with one of the old clinical situations in the memory (*pattern recognition*).[11] As a consequence of this, there is very little reflective thinking into the clinical decision-making capacity. However, System II (analytical thinking) involves more of logic and clinical reason and better approach to the differential diagnosis. Studies have shown that a combined use of both System I and System II is optimal for clinical decision-making.[12] Barrorw et al. introduced the *hypothetico-deductive mode* of diagnostic reasoning, according to which in difficult diagnosis the physician tends to make a diagnostic hypothesis from the initial data gathered quickly from the history and gather more data to evaluate this hypothesis and reach a conclusion.[13] This results in *premature closure* of the case scenario without reaching the confirmative diagnosis. Hamm also explained the decision-making capacity in the cognitive continuum theory, according to which the clinical reasoning is a combination of intuitive thinking and analytical thinking, where intuitive thinking or pattern recognition comes from years of experience in the field and can be helpful in fast-paced clinical setting, and analytical thinking is helpful in reflective thinking in cases of difficult diagnosis and again depending on different clinical scenario the judgment should vary from intuitive thinking to analytical thinking.[14]

COMPONENTS OF OVERCONFIDENCE

Berner et al. explained in their study about the various aspects of overconfident behavior and how it can affect the health environment and patient safety[15]:

1. **Attitudinal aspect of overconfidence**
   "I know what I need to know."
   This aspect includes arrogant behavior with no interest in any decision support or feedback evaluation. Such kind of behavior not only affects patient safety but also creates an unhealthy environment with all other coworkers and ancillary staff. Physicians with arrogant and pervasive behavior are overconfident on their judgment and do not pursue a

knowledge-seeking behavior; hence, even when some information relevant to patient safety pops on their computer screen, they rarely review the decision support. Studies have also shown that there is a lot of noncompliance with the treatment guidelines and clinical recommendations goals in physicians with overconfident judgment.[16]

2. **Cognitive aspect of overconfidence**

   "Not knowing what you don't know."

   Cognitive aspects reflect diagnostic error because of lack of insight for the correct diagnosis. Various cognitive bias and heuristic approach discussed in earlier chapters can attribute to the diagnostic errors. The cognitive aspect of overconfident judgment includes breakdown of clinical reasoning, failure to gather complete information from patient data, and inability to reconsider a differential diagnosis. Also, lack of metacognition and reflective thinking in diagnostic process can attribute to diagnostic error due to cognitive bias.

3. **Complacency aspect of overconfidence**

   "No one is perfect."

   Complacency explains that the physician underestimates the error or thinks that some types of error in medical practices are inevitable. Such physicians do not try to reflect those errors on their practice and clinical knowledge but instead feel that nothing can be done. These types of errors can result in misdiagnosis and hugely impact the patient heath care.

STRATEGIES TO CORRECT OVERCONFIDENCE

Effective strategies to correct errors related to overconfidence are summarized in Table 1.

Table 1 Strategies to Correct Overconfidence[17]

Source	Strategy to Correct
Lack of knowledge and awareness in decision-making	Introduce the concept of decision-making approaches at the undergraduate level, with more focus on use of different decision-making modes in different situations

(Continued)

Table 1 (*Continued*)   Strategies to Correct Overconfidence[17]

Source	Strategy to Correct
Cognitive and affective bias	Detailed explanation of different types of bias at the undergraduate level, also emphasizing the role of metacognition and reflective thinking to reduce the cognitive bias
Feedback limitations	Regular, systematic, and reliable feedback evaluation in all clinical domains should be included in the hospital curriculum
Denial of uncertainty	Involve specific training programs to overcome personal and cultural barrier in cases of admission of uncertainty, and acknowledge that certainty may not be possible all the time
Base rate neglect	The data regarding the incidence and prevalence of common disease should be easily accessible, especially in concerned geographic location
Context binding	Involve in metacognitive decision-making approach
Limitations of transferability	Detailed explanation of various cognitive biases and debiasing approaches applicable in all clinical domains
Lack of critical thinking	Introducing the basic courses of critical thinking at undergraduate level
Biased evidence gathering	Reflective thinking and consider-the-opposite strategy

REFERENCES

1. Detmer DE, Fryback DG, Gassner K. Heuristics and biases in medical decision making. *J Med Educ.* 1978;53:682–683.
2. Lundeberg MA, Fox PW, Punccohar J. Highly confident but wrong: Gender differences and similarities in confidence judgments. *J Educ Psychol.* 1994;86:114–121.
3. Yates JF, Lee JW, Sieck WR, Choi I, Price PC. Probability judgment across cultures. In: Gilovich T, Griffin D, Kahneman D, eds. *Heuristics and Biases: The Psychology of Intuitive Judgment.* New York: Cambridge University Press, 2002:271–291.
4. Deaux K, Farris E. Attributing causes for one's own performance: The effects of sex, norms, and outcome. *J Res Pers.* 1977;11:59–72.
5. Landazabal MG. Psychopathological symptoms, social skills, and personality traits: A study with adolescents Spanish. *J Psychol.* 2006;9:182–192.
6. Fischhoff B, Slovic P. A little learning. . .: Confidence in multicue judgment. In: Nickerson, R., ed. *Attention and Performance.* VIII. Hillsdale, NJ: Erlbaum, 1980.
7. Lichenstein S, Fischoff B. Training for calibration. *Organ Behav Hum Perform.* 1980;26:149–171.
8. van Gelder T, Bissett M, Cumming G. Cultivating expertise in informal reasoning. *Can J Exp Psychol.* 2004;58:142–152.
9. Eva KW, Regehr G. Self-assessment in the health professions: A reformulation and research agenda. *Acad Med.* 2005;80(suppl):S46–S54.
10. Friedman CP, Gatti GG, Franz TM, et al. Do physicians know when their diagnoses are correct? *J Gen Intern Med.* 2005;20:334–339.
11. Nendaz M, Perrier A. Diagnostic errors and flaws in clinical reasoning: Mechanisms and prevention in practice. *Swiss Med Wkly.* 2012;142:1–9.
12. Kulatunga-Moruzi C, Brooks LR, Norman GR. Coordination of analytic and similarity-based processing strategies and expertise in dermatological diagnosis. *Teach Learn Med.* 2001;13:110–116.
13. Barrows HS, Norman GR, Neufeld VR, Feightner JW. The clinical reasoning of randomly selected physicians in general medical practice. *Clin Invest Med.* 1982;5:49–55.
14. Hamm RM. Clinical intuition and clinical analysis: Expertise and the cognitive continuum. In: Elstein A, Dowie J, eds. *Professional Judgment: A Reader in Clinical Decision Making.* Cambridge: Cambridge University Press, 1988:78–105.

15. Berner ES, Graber ML. Overconfidence as a cause of diagnostic error in medicine. *Am J Med.* 2008;121(5 Suppl):S2–S23.
16. Cabana MD, Rand CS, Powe NR, et al. Why don't physicians follow clinical practice guidelines? A framework for improvement. *JAMA.* 1999;282:1458–1465.
17. Croskerry P, Norman, G. Overconfidence in clinical decision making. *Am J Med.* 2008;121(5 Suppl):S24–S29.

Clinical Vignette 6: The New Epidemic

Harleen Kaur
University of Missouri

Clinical vignette discusses overdiagnosis and overtreatment, and reviews the current medicolegal environment and its impact on patient safety.

THE CASE

Ms. Kathy is a 56-year-old, healthy female who presents to the emergency room (ER) after a fall. She says that she fell by slipping on ice in the driveway of her house. She had complaints of neck pain after the fall. The pain was 5/10 on the pain scale, mainly located in the cervical region. The pain did not radiate to the arm. She denies any loss of consciousness after the fall. The ER physician examined the patient and ordered an MRI (magnetic resonance imaging) of the brain and cervical spine (C-spine) level to rule out any injury from the fall. Ms. Kathy is an otherwise healthy female and does not take any medication other than a daily multivitamin. The MRI of the spine did not show any abnormal changes in the cervical spine but did show an incidental 23 mm right thyroid mass. Ms. Kathy denies any thyroid issues or radiation exposure. She denies any family history of thyroid cancer. The ER physician explained the diagnosis to Ms. Kathy and took her consent to further investigate the mass. The ER physician consulted the endocrinologist and ordered laboratory blood work for thyroid hormone level followed by ultrasound-guided fine needle aspiration (FNA) of the thyroid mass. Her laboratory results showed TSH of 1.640 microunit/mL (normal: 0.270–4.200), and free thyroxine level was 1.03 ng/dL (normal range: 0.93–1.70 ng/dL). The results of FNA revealed benign appearing thyroid tissue with finding suggestive of nodular hyperplasia. The endocrinologist discussed the diagnosis with her and asked her to follow up if symptoms arise or if she notices any change in the size of the thyroid gland.

COMMENTS

This case scenario depicts overdiagnosis where the risk of harm outweighs the benefits to the patient. The patient had to undergo the FNA procedure for the incidental finding on the MRI report. According to the history, the patient had no thyroid problems in the past, had no radiation exposure, and did not have any family history of thyroid cancer, and her laboratory thyroid workup came within normal limits. The ER physicians and the endocrinologist ordered FNA to rule out underline cancerous pathology. This clinical scenario depicts overdiagnosis from incidentalomas, unnecessary expenditure on extra diagnostic test, with test results mainly attributing to patient reassurance without any significant change in the healthcare outcomes.

DISCUSSION

Medical overuse is the new epidemic and is considered as the most common issue in the healthcare system.[1] Medical overuse is defined as medical care in which the harm potentially outweighs the benefits.[1,2] It may result in overdiagnosis or overtreatment. Overdiagnosis results when individuals got diagnosed with a condition that is unrelated to the present complaints and is less likely to increase the mortality and morbidity threat.[1] Likewise, overtreatment is the therapeutic treatment options offered for the overdiagnosed condition that results in unavoidable expenditure without any significant benefits.[3]

Overdiagnosis can result in unnecessary diagnostic and screening test, use of invasive or therapeutic procedures which may cause harm more that the benefit and lastly use of expensive modality and diagnostic workup increases the healthcare burden. It is estimated that 30% of the healthcare cost is spent on ineffective and unnecessary measures without any significant change in the patient healthcare outcomes.[4,5] In the United States, roughly 200 billion dollars are spent each year on irrelevant diagnostic and treatment modality.[6]

Aim of this chapter is to highlight factors resulting in overdiagnosis and overtreatment, and the inherent challenges associated with medical overuse compromising patient safety and efficient healthcare delivery.

CAUSES OF OVERDIAGNOSIS

Various factors that contribute to overdiagnosis and overtreatment are charted as follows[7]:

1	**Patients** In the Google world, the patient population is more informed and more concerned, as a result of which they request higher diagnostic and therapeutic procedures despite of reassurances.
2	**Technology** Improved technology and increased diagnostic accuracy result in detecting incidental findings, which have lesser impact on patient health outcomes.
3	**Media** The media dramatically exposes the latest medication and diagnostic workup through commercials on televisions, radio, news stations, and magazines which impact the mindset of the general population and convinces them to approach their healthcare provider for the same.
4	**Law** The fear of being sued due to missed diagnosis may result in physician's overdiagnosis and overtreatment.
5	**Healthcare professionals** As a part of defensive mechanism, the physician tends to overemphasize on the diagnosis and incidental finding seen on the diagnostic workup.
6	**Disease** In the era of diagnosis creep, the definitions of the disease entities are expanding, along with unpredictable early stages of the disease, resulting in overdiagnosis and overtreatment.

TERMINOLOGY ASSOCIATED WITH OVERDIAGNOSIS

The term "overdiagnosis" can be expressed in different meanings. Hoffman B, in his review, elaborated the synonyms that can be interpreted as overdiagnosis or overtreatment.[7]

Terminology	*Related Interpretation*
Over-detection	Overdiagnosis
Clinically irrelevant condition	Incidentalomas
Iatrogenic disease	Misdiagnosis
Lanthnic disease	Diagnostic creep
Finding conditions that are not relevant	Hidden false positive
Identify benign abnormalities	False (negative/positive) test results

OVERDIAGNOSIS

The term "overdiagnosis" is used in the medical profession since the 1970s.[8] Black and Welch defined overdiagnosis as "diagnosing a person without specific symptoms of a disease that may (ultimately) never cause symptoms or death during the patient's lifetime."[9,10] However, these definitions are tricky as it is difficult as a clinician to predict if the disease or symptoms will cause mortality in future or not. To simplify the concept of overdiagnosis, we weigh the risk of harm over the benefit provided to the patients by the medical services.

Mafi et al. performed a retrospective cohort study from 1999 to 2010 in the United States on 9,362 patients, data derived from National Ambulatory Medical Care Survey and National Hospital Ambulatory Medical Care Survey to access the services provided to patients with symptoms of headache without any history of trauma or high-risk symptoms, and concluded that the number of patients who were offered advanced imaging modality such as CT or MRI was 6.7% in 1999–2000 and increased to 13.9% in 2009–2010. Similarly, the number of specialty referrals had also increased from 6.9% to 13.2%, and counselling about lifestyle modification had decreased from 23.5% to 18.5% in 2010. This study highlights the overuse of advanced imaging techniques such as CT and MRI and increased referrals in ambulatory settings and emergency department for the common problems such as headache. The clinicians should be familiar with a reasonable diagnostic approach for the common disease nosology and avoid overuse of testing.

Ordering the diagnostic tests to reassure the patients results in false-positive diagnostic error and overdiagnosis. In addition, the patient has to go through unnecessary diagnostic tests which also increase the healthcare cost and expenditure. A systematic review performed in 2011 found 14 clinical trials that evaluated patient reassurance after performing diagnostic testing. The testing did not have any effect on the symptoms, disease progression, worry, or anxiety. Hence, performing diagnostic testing on the symptoms or illness with very low probability of significant disease mechanism, just for patient reassurance, may result in high rate of false-positive diagnostic error and overdiagnosis.[11]

OVERTREATMENT

Overtreatment results in the overuse of medication or unnecessary therapeutic procedures which may be of potential harm to the patient. Srigley et al. performed a study to determine the onset of *Clostridium difficile* in a hospital setting. They concluded that out of 126 cases, 74% of patients who got *C. difficile* infection had one course of inappropriate antibiotic use or prolonged use of empiric antibiotic and prolonged duration of antibiotic therapy. Also the overuse of proton pump inhibitors was seen in 68% of patients in hospital settings which is further known to increase the risk of *C. difficile* infection.[12] This study implies that the overuse of antibiotic or proton pump inhibitor may result in potential infection by antibiotic-resistant bacteria such as *C. difficile* infection which can increase the mortality risk in hospitalized patients. Hence, overtreatment may bring potential harm to the patient than the benefit itself. The physicians should aim to focus on the treatment option and therapeutic procedures based on the latest clinical guidelines and publications in order to avoid the risk associated with medical overuse.

DEFENSIVE MEDICINE

Defensive medicine is practiced by clinicians throughout the United States due to possible fear of malpractice litigation. In addition, defensive medicine is also causing healthcare overuse and increasing the healthcare cost. It is estimated that defensive medicine has increased the cost of healthcare burden in the United States by roughly 124 billion dollars annually.[13] The Massachusetts Medical Society surveyed 3,650 physicians regarding the use of defensive medicine, to which 82% physicians responded using defensive medicine, with overuse of plain X-rays by 22%, CT scans by 28%, specialty referrals by 28%, and hospital admissions by 13%.[14] It is also estimated that roughly 5%–25% of the imaging modality cost is attributed from defensive medicine.[15]

Due to increase in healthcare cost and overuse of diagnostic modality, several states practice the "Tort Reforms." The Tort reforms limit the cost associated with medical malpractice lawsuits and the physician's liability in order to reduce the cost and overuse of diagnostic modality. Li et al. in their study concluded that states that enacted permanent tort reforms (which make it harder to sue the physicians) than temporary tort reforms had shown significant decrease in the overuse of radiographic imaging modality by the physicians. They also noted that states with permanent tort reforms had shown a 7%–8% reduction in radiographic diagnostic modality, which implies 2.4–2.7 million lesser diagnostic tests each year.[16]

CONCLUSION

The concept of overdiagnosis can be challenging to address; however, a unified diagnostic approach to patient healthcare management can be useful to cut down the extra cost, overtreatment, and diagnostic and therapeutic procedures. More awareness should be made at the hospital level about the risk with overdiagnosis particularly associated with screening test, radiographic diagnostic modality, documentation of incidentalomas with the aim to focus the resources and time on the treatment, and prevention of genuine illness affecting the patient morbidity and mortality.

REFERENCES

1. Welch HG, Schwartz L, Woloshin S. *Overdiagnosed: Making People Sick in the Pursuit of Health*. Boston, MA: Beacon Press, 2011.
2. Morgan DJ, Brownlee S, Leppin AL, et al. Setting a research agenda for medical overuse. *BMJ*. 2015;351:h4534.
3. Hoffman A, Pearson SD. 'Marginal medicine': Targeting comparative effectiveness research to reduce waste. *Health Aff (Millwood)*. 2009;28(4):w710–w718.
4. Bloche MG. Beyond the "R word"? Medicine's new frugality. *N Engl J Med*. 2012;366(21):1951–1953. doi:10.1056/NEJMp1203521.
5. Fisher ES, Wennberg DE, Stukel TA, Gottlieb DJ, Lucas FL, Pinder EL. The implications of regional variations in medicare spending. Part 2: Health outcomes and satisfaction with care. *Ann Intern Med*. 2003;138(4):288–298.
6. Berwick DM, Hackbarth AD. Eliminating waste in US health care. *JAMA*. 2012;307(14):1513–1516. doi:10.1001/jama.2012.362.
7. Hofmann B. Diagnosing overdiagnosis: Conceptual challenges and suggested solutions. *Eur J Epidemiol*. 2014;29(9):599–604. doi:10.1007/s10654-014-9920-5. Epub 2014 June 1.
8. Grobin W. Diabetes in the aged: Underdiagnosis and overtreatment. *Can Med Assoc J*. 1970;103(9):915–923.
9. Black WC. Overdiagnosis: An underrecognized cause of confusion and harm in cancer screening. *J Natl Cancer Inst*. 2000;92(16):1280–1282.

10. Welch HG, Black WC. Overdiagnosis in cancer. *J Natl Cancer Inst.* 2010;102(9):605–613. doi:10.1093/jnci/djq099.
11. Rolfe A, Burton C. Reassurance after diagnostic testing with a low pretest probability of serious disease: Systematic review and meta-analysis. *JAMA Intern Med.* 2013;173(6):407–416.
12. Srigley JA, Brooks A, Sung M, Yamamura D, Haider S, Mertz D. Inappropriate use of antibiotics and Clostridium difficile infection. *Am J Infect Control.* 2013;41(11):1116–1118.
13. McQuillan LJ, Abramyan H, Archie A. *Jackpot Justice: The True Cost of America's Tort System.* San Francisco, CA: Pacific Research Institute, 2007.
14. Massachusetts Medical Society. Investigation of defensive medicine in Massachusetts. Nov 2008.
15. Hendee WR, Becker GJ, Borgstede JP, et al. Addressing overutilization in medical imaging. *Radiology.* 2010;257:240–245. doi:10.1148/radiol.10100063. Epub 2010 Aug 24.
16. Li S, Dor A, Deyo D, Hughes DR. The impact of state tort reforms on imaging utilization. *J Am Coll Radiol.* 2017;14(2):149–156. doi:10.1016/j.jacr.2016.10.002. Epub 2016 Dec 20.

Chapter 5

Understanding Human/ Provider Errors

This chapter exposes the challenges faced in the hospital setting due to physician burnout and disruptive physician behavior. Physicians are the pivot of the healthcare team, and such a behavior or lack of up-to-date knowledge on current management protocols can heavily impact the healthcare system. In addition, physician behavior affects the working of the ancillary staff as a whole team in a healthcare setting. This chapter highlights the consequences of physician behavior of physicians, patients, and hospital team and the ways to improve for better patient care and safety.

Clinical Vignette 1: Does Age Bring Wisdom?

Harleen Kaur
University of Missouri

Clinical vignette discusses the medical error due to physician incompetence as he had not kept up with the current literature and never got recertified. In addition, we will discuss the importance of board certification, continued medical education (CME), and the current controversy surrounding it. We will also discuss the post-SGR (Substantial Growth Rate) world and evolving importance of patient safety and quality in the regulatory world.

THE CASE

Ms. Carol, a 51-year-old right-handed female weighing 165 lbs, is examined by Dr. Hawkins for the management of generalized tonic clonic seizure for the past 18 years with no relevant past history of psychiatric or medical concern. Since then, she is on a stable dose of regular release Depakote (valproate) 600 mg twice a day for the management of seizure. She says, "The drug has worked wonder for me," and has not had any episodes since then. She follows up with Dr. Hawkins every 6 months in his outpatient clinic. She also adds, "Dr. Hawkins is really busy." When asked about any follow-up laboratory test, she said, "They checked my labs when they first put me on this drug but stopped checking them since a while ago." Dr. Hawkins is a 73-year-old neurologist specialized in epilepsy roughly 40 years ago. He runs a solo practice which is not affiliated with any hospital.

Recently, Ms. Carol saw her primary care physician (PCP) for anorexia, malaise, nausea, and reduced appetite. Her PCP ordered an abdomen ultrasound and laboratory test including complete blood count (CBC) and liver function test. The CBC showed low platelet count of 95,000/μL and high AST (Aspartate Amino transferase) of 196 IU/L and ALT (Alanine Amino transferase) of 204 IU/L. Ultrasound findings were consistent with steatosis.

COMMENTS

In this vignette, it shows that the patient is most likely suffering from valproate-induced hepatitis. The possible weight gain and low platelet count can also be attributed from the valproate side effect. A more effective management of such a case would have been to wean off the valproate after the seizure was controlled and start on other newer antiepileptic drugs such as oxcarbazepine (with minimal effect on liver) along with levetiracetam (she reports no underlying psychiatric issue) and follow-up with laboratory results every 6 months.

DISCUSSION

The competency of aging physician has been a concern in the U.S. healthcare system for many years. Although an aging physician has explicit fund of knowledge and skills, clinical expertise, and lifetime of experience gained by extensive hard work in this profession, effective delivery of high standard of care toward patient welfare may get impacted by the performance of senior physicians. Moreover, this experience can provide effective diagnostic skills but, on the other hand, may decline their analytical reasoning skills. Most senior physicians depend on the first clinical impression which may impact the diagnosis and result in early closure of the case.[1] Many studies in the past have shown an inverse relation between the seniority of age and practice performance of the physicians[2] with concerns of errors in detailed history taking, comprehensive evaluation of the data, and conclusive results.[3]

Although age is one of the several factors that can affect the clinical acumen of the physicians, the other possible explanation can be the inability to adopt new therapies and advanced standards of care, lack of feedback evaluation from the colleagues, and unwillingness to explore the resources and attend CME program.

In this review, we highlight the proficiency of senior physicians affected by their age and what ways can be adopted to provide quality patient care.

Prevalence

The American Medical Association (AMA) Council reported that the number of physicians over the age of 65 years in 1975 was 50,993; the number increased to 241,641 physicians in 2013.[4] The number has increased to 23% in 2015[4] and 29% in 2016.[5]

Age and Cognition

Situation Cognition Theory

Durning et al. have explained the significant association of age with decline in cognitive performance.[6] The three key elements of

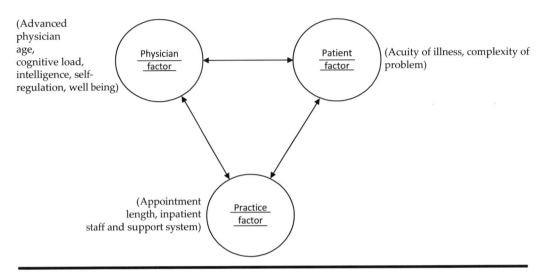

Figure 1 **Situation cognition theory and aging physician. (Courtesy: Durning SJ, Artino AR, Holmboe E, Beckman TJ, van der Vleuten C, Schuwirth L. Aging and cognitive performance: challenges and implications for physicians practicing in the 21st century.** *J Contin Educ Health Prof.* **2010;30(3):153–60.)**

this theory are the patient, the clinician, and the practice settings (Figure 1). The physician factor includes the age of the physician, cognitive load, and clinical acumen; the patient factor includes the complexity of illness in acute or chronic setting, and the practice factor includes appointment length, staff and support system, and patient load. The theory highlights advanced physician age as an important physician factor, affecting the physician thinking in a social setting and thereby impacting the clinical encounter as a whole.

Aging and Information Processing Theory

The two variants of intelligence are the crystallized intelligence and fluid intelligence. The crystallized intelligence is acquired through lifelong professional experiences and clinical acumen, whereas the fluid intelligence involves the analytical and complex problem-solving capacity. Eva et al. explained in their study that normal aging results in significant decline in the fluid intelligence without affecting the crystallized intelligence.[7,8] They further postulate that the errors made by the aging physician are due to the lack of analytical thinking (fluid intelligence) and greater confidence in their knowledge.

Age and Experience

Numerous studies have revealed that it requires at least 10 years of experience in a field to become a skilled professional in that field. Ericcson et al. further explained the concept of *deliberate practice*, which requires consistent effort in the area of expertise, with repeated feedback from peers and capacity to correct the errors and improve the performance.[9] The study emphasizes that there is a significant decline in the cognitive performance with the age of the physician, and hence, the aging physicians should be involved in deliberate practice in order to maintain their cognitive performance.[10] The senior physician has to put in regular and consistent effort in deliberate practice in order to be at par with the younger physicians, which can be accomplished by updating with CME program, recertification courses, and satisfactory peer and patient review ratings.

How to Address This Concern

To address this concern, the AMA Council on Medical Education issued a report in 2015 on "Competency and Aging Physician," addressing the guidelines to access the work performance of the senior physicians and their colleagues.[4] In 2016, the American College of Surgeons (ACS) also released a report on "Statement of Aging Surgeon." The report suggested that the surgeons are less likely to have any deterioration in their cognitive or clinical skills with age. They recommended that doctors aged 65–70 years undergo baseline health assessment and use online tools to evaluate their neurocognitive skills repeatedly.

There is no specific retirement age for the physicians, but three university hospitals in the United States have followed the policy of mandatory physical and cognitive assessment of the senior physicians to access their competency: The University of Virginia Health System, Charlottesville; Driscol Children's Hospital, Corpus Christi; Texas and Stanford Hospital and Clinics, Stanford, California. The University of Virginia allows a mandatory health assessment examination under the Clinician Wellness Program for physicians above the age of 70 years. In March 2014, Stanford University Hospital initiated a peer assessment of the clinicians which involved all the hospital staff members, trainees, faculty, nurses, and coordinators of the department to evaluate the overall performance of the clinicians.[11]

Age is not the only factor to determine the clinical performance of the senior physicians. Various factors can help to improve the competency of the aging physicians. The senior physicians should have the qualities of *adaptability* and *self-directed learning* through trusted websites such as UpToDate or review journal and latest research work on PubMed or WebMD *which* will help to keep them updated with the latest interventions in the field of medicine and dynamic changes in the healthcare system. Further, the physicians should be involved in *CME program* which can effectively improve the physician performance and patient health outcomes.[12] CME highlights the latest clinical practice guidelines, problem-based learning, point of care techniques, and detailed academic update by experts in their field. Also enrolling in local medical society and National Professional Membership Organization can provide with resources and recommendation on current clinical updates in their profession. *Maintenance of Certification* (MOC) is another critical approach to improve the physician competency and high-quality patient care. MOC programs vary according to the specialty and must be taken every 10 years by the physicians. The board recertification is helpful for the physicians to access their clinical acumen and also to keep update with current practices in their specialty.[13] As explained by Durning et al., all these factors will help to improve the physician factor in the situation cognition theory which can effectively impact their clinical performance.[6]

Another important factor affecting the physician performance is the *working environment*. Studies have shown that roughly 20% of the physicians work in *solo practices* in the United States, which limit their interaction with the colleagues of same specialty. Senior physicians working alone are more likely to perform poorly on the MOC program and show significant decline in deliberate practice and cognitive performance.[14] On the other hand, working in healthcare organization has the benefits of peer support, interactive discussions, and advice from mentors which can be an essential tool to improved quality care service.[15]

We further recommend that the healthcare organization include confidential physician assessment evaluation by their peers, supporting hospital staff and patient ratings in order to periodically access the competency of the physician and provide valuable feedback for improvement.

REFERENCES

1. Eva KW, Cunnington JP. The difficulty with experience: Does practice increase susceptibility to premature closure? *J Contin Educ Health Prof.* 2006 Summer;26(3):192–198.

2. Choudhry NK, Fletcher RH, Soumerai SB. Systematic review: The relationship between clinical experience and the quality of health care. *Ann Intern Med.* 2005;142(4):260–273.

3. Caulford PG, Lamb SB, Kaigas TB, Hanna E, Norman GR, Davis DA. Physician incompetence: Specific problems and predictors. *Acad Med.* 1994;69(10 Suppl):S16–S18.

4. American Medical Association. Competency and the Aging Physician. Report 5 of the Council on Medical Education (A-15). Chicago, IL: AMA; 2015.

5. Young A, Chaudhry HJ, Pei X, Arnhart K, Dugan M, Snyder GB. A Census of Actively Licensed Physicians in the United States, 2016. *J Med Regul.* 2017;103(2):7–21. doi:10.30770/2572-1852-103.2.7

6. Durning SJ, Artino AR, Holmboe E, Beckman TJ, van der Vleuten C, Schuwirth L. Aging and cognitive performance: Challenges and implications for physicians practicing in the 21st century. *J Contin Educ Health Prof.* 2010;30(3):153–160.

7. Eva K. The aging physician: Changes in cognitive processing and their impact on medical practice. *Acad Med.* 2002;77(10):S1–S5.

8. Eva KW. Stemming the tide: Cognitive aging theories and their implications for continuing education in the health professions. *J Contin Educ Health Prof.* 2003;23:133–140.

9. Ericsson KA. Deliberate practice and the acquisition and maintenance of expert performance in medicine and related domains. *Acad Med.* 2004;10:S70–S81.

10. Krampe RT, Charness N. *Aging and expertise.* In Ericsson KA, Charness N, Feltovich PJ, Hoffman RR, eds. *The Cambridge Handbook of Expertise and Expert Performance.* New York: Cambridge University Press; 2006: 723–743.

11. SHC-LPCH. Late career practitioner policy March 2014 Stanford. Published 2014. Accessed July 9, 2015.

12. Cervero RM, Gaines JK. The impact of CME on physician performance and patient health outcomes: An updated synthesis of systematic reviews. *J Contin Educ Health Prof.* 2015 Spring;35(2):131–138.

13. Lipner RS, Brossman BG. Characteristics of internal medicine physicians and their practices that have differential impacts on their maintenance of certification. *Acad Med.* 2015;90(1):82–87.

14. American College of Physicians. *The Advanced Medical Home: A Patient-Centered, Physician Guided Model of Health Care.* Philadelphia, PA: American College of Physicians; 2006.

15. Holmboe ES, Wang Y, Meehan TP, Tate JP, Ho SY, Starkey KS, Lipner RS. Association between maintenance of certification examination scores and quality of care for medicare beneficiaries. *Arch Intern Med.* 2008;168(13):1396–1403.

Clinical Vignette 2: The Zero-Sum Game

Harleen Kaur
University of Missouri

Clinical vignette talks about a disruptive healthcare provider and the impact on patient safety. We will also discuss protocols and procedures that should be in place to deal with these situations.

THE CASE

On December 23, 2016, at 6 am, Dr. Richard is rounding on his preoperative and postoperative patients in a busy hospital in New York City. Dr. Richard is a 56-year-old orthopedic surgeon working in the holiday season covering up for other physicians on leave. While he was rounding on his patients, he received a pager and the nurse mentioned that there is call for a patient admitted in the emergency room (ER) with fracture of femur from a motor vehicle accident. Dr. Richard did not say a word and threw his pager at the nurse, although the pager did not hit the nurse or anybody else on rounds. He did not finish the rounds and went to ER to evaluate the new patients and said "I will round on them in the evening, Is there any urgent issue to address." After seeing the behavior of the physician, the nurses did not say anything to him.

COMMENTS

The vignette explains a sheer act of disruptive behavior by the physician. In this vignette, the surgeon showed a disruptive behavior by throwing the pager away, after he heard about the new patient admitted in the ER. Such kind of behavior interferes with the comraderies amongst the physicians and other coworkers. Moreover, in this vignette, the physician did not finish the morning rounds which can also delay the treatment concerns and compromise the healthcare of the patients admitted in inpatient.

DISCUSSION

Physician disruptive behavior in the healthcare system is a matter of potential concern as it can impact the workplace environment and impair the quality of patient care. In 1994, Dr. William Rock addressing this issue said, "In the past, when one of our colleagues displayed an outburst of temper, screamed at a nurse or secretary, used vulgarity or profanity in an abusive tone, displayed unprofessional conduct, verbal harassment, or any of a number of sexual misbehaviors, there was often a tolerance for the offense. There was even greater indulgence if the offender was an older male, high earner, high-ranking executive, or one who enjoyed a respected reputation in the professional community."[1]

But in present century, disruptive behavior cannot be tolerated and can be one of the toughest tasks to manage in the hospital administration. The Council on Ethical and Judicial Affairs-American Medical Association explains disruptive behavior as any verbal or physical conduct that may have a potential negative affect on patient care.[2] Likewise, the Joint Commission on Accreditation of Hospital Organization (JCAHO) described any disruptive behavior to be an act that intimidates others such that the quality and safety of patient care is compromised.[3]

Disruptive behavior can be categorized as insider perpetrated violence, lateral (horizontal) violence, bullying, incivility, relational aggression, and harassment.[4,5] The act of misconduct can be in the form of verbal abuse, irritability, intrusiveness, refusal to perform the assigned task, aggressiveness, or hyperactivity.

This review aims to highlight the concerns of physician disruptive behavior in hospital care settings and its effect in undermining the quality of patient care with focus on prevention and management of this act of misconduct.

FREQUENCY

Quantitative survey suggests the *prevalence* (number of disruptive behavior reported) of physicians with disruptive behavior is less than 10%,[6,7] and the *ubiquity* (proportion of physicians involved in disruptive behavior) is noted to be 6%–18% according to the disciplinary records.[8] Studies have highlighted that disruptive behavior is likely to be more common in surgeons than in other physicians.[9,10] A survey performed by Rosenstein et al., from 2004 to 2007, concluded that disruptive events are seen primarily in general surgery (28%), followed by neurosurgery (20%), cardiovascular (13%), orthopedics (10%), and anesthesia (7%). They also highlighted that disruptive events are seen most often in medical units (35%), intensive care units (26%), operating room (23%), surgical units (20%), and emergency department (7%).[11] Ninety-one percent of perioperative nurses reported physician verbal abuse in an Ohio State report in 2001.[12] Disruptive physician behavior is not only reported by the nurses and ancillary staff but also complained by the junior doctors. A questionnaire survey performed by Quine affirmed that 37% of junior doctors were bullied in their workplace by senior physicians.[13]

SCOPE OF DISRUPTIVE BEHAVIOR

Leape et al. have explained the wide array of disruptive behavior in clinical settings which can have potential impact on the medical students and nursing staff (Table 1). It can be a threat to the safety and well-being of the patients.[14]

Table 1   Different Aspects of Disruptive Physician Behavior

Behavior Category	Description	Examples
Disruptive behavior	Rude conduct evident in behavior and communication	• Angry outburst • Verbal threats • Swearing • Bullying • Throwing objects
Demeaning treatment	Attitudes of demoralizing and exploiting others	• Shaming • Humiliation/torture • Ignoring behavior
Passive-aggressive behavior	Negativistic and skeptical attitude	• Bossy authority • Negative comments about colleagues • Delay responding to calls and messages • Make others look bad
Passive disrespect	Uncooperative behavior that are not malevolent	• Always late for the meetings/rounds • Resistant to follow safety practices • Sluggish responses to request
Dismissive treatment	Behavior that makes patients or staff feel unimportant and uninformed	• Condescending comments • Refusal to work in a team • Snobbish behavior

Source: Courtesy of the Institute for Safe Medication Practices.

CAUSES OF DISRUPTIVE BEHAVIOR

Walrath et al. have categorized the causes of disruptive physician behavior as *intrapersonal, interpersonal,* and *organizational.*[9]

Intrapersonal

Physicians with characteristic personality traits such as passive aggression, narcissism, perfectionism, and type A personality are more prone to the development of disruptive behavior in clinical settings.[15,16] They do not show courtesy, always blame others, and question their competency in the work environment. These physicians avoid effective communication and are always demanding and justify themselves, "I am the one who cares" and "follow as I say."

Psychological states such as underlying depression, fatigue, stress, long working hours, addiction, or burnout may also result in disruptive behavior in the workplace.[9]

Interpersonal

Camaraderie among the physicians with other clinicians, nurses, and ancillary staff is very important to instill a healthy work environment and better patient care. Physician disruptive behavior can impact the interpersonal relations with other colleagues. The authority to have a control on everything and miscommunication of patient information will affect not only the work environment but also the patient care. Psychological aggression in the form of intimidating behavior or passive aggression may affect the working environment of nurses and junior doctors unable to perform their work well.[9]

Organizational

Hospital work environment can be an important trigger for the disruptive behavior. Shortage of physicians/surgeons, nurses, long working hours, exhaustion, few breaks, and long operative list may increase the workload by increasing the stress in the work area. Workplace incivility can affect the teamwork and hinder with quality patient care.

IMPACT ON PATIENT CARE

Patient care can be deeply impacted by disruptive physician behavior in many ways. First, *lack of communication*[17] can result in incomplete transfer of clinical information which may further delay the patient treatment.[18] The nurses and other colleagues may start avoiding physician with aggressive behavior which can result in noncordial relation in the work environment and lack of development of trust in teamwork. A recent study performed in neonatal intensive care unit suggested that rude misconduct showed by the clinicians leads to communication barrier and affects their procedural skills.[19] Another study recently highlighted that surgeons and anesthetics also develop a fear of being criticized, so they relay deceptive information or tend to withhold information.[20] Second, *impaired clinical decision-making* can affect the quality of patient care. Physicians with disruptive behavior show a rude misconduct towards the other clinicians and nursing staff which result in ineffective transfer of clinical order and hinder with patient care. Third, disruptive physician behavior can negatively impact the *technical performance in the operating room.* A lot of clinicians think that disruptive behavior can decrease the focus of the physicians and not only affects their performance in procedural skills but also negatively affects the teamwork.[21]

In 2014, JCAHO released a statistical analysis of 8,645 events reviewed from 2004 to 2014. The most common root causes highlighted by them were human factors, leadership failure, communication failure, and assessment failures (Figure 1). With respect to this rising concern, the Joint Commission, in 2015, introduced a new "Patient Safety System" chapter in the "Comprehensive Accreditation Manual for Hospitals."[22]

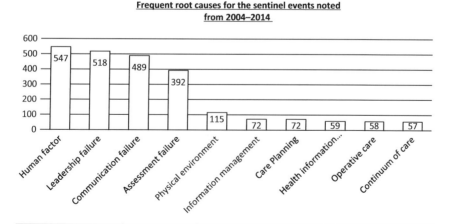

Figure 1   Summary of root cause analyses performed by JCAHO in 2014.

IMPACT ON HEALTHCARE SYSTEM

Studies have shown that disruptive physician behavior *changes the perception of the medical students* towards their medical field of interest. For example, some surgeons do not let the medical students scrub in the operating room or show a rude misconduct to questions asked during surgery. This may cause the medical students to lose their interest in the field or even see these clinicians as negative role models.[23] Also physicians with disruptive behavior tend to *bully the intern year residents* and question their competency, resulting in harassment and work-related stress amongst them.[24] Disruptive behavior also affects the general well-being of the physicians and may result in frequent burnout,[25] lack of teamwork opportunity with other clinician, low self-esteem,[26] and depression. Further, the *economic state* of the hospital is greatly affected by such a behavior. Rawson et al. estimated that in a 400-bed hospital in America, the cost of disruptive behavior including medical error exceeds $1 billion.[27] Not only does it pose to be an economic burden but can also make the institution liable for *legal risk* and litigation which can affect the reputation of the institution.[25]

PREVENTION AND MANAGEMENT

Alexander et al. have explained in their review about the strategies that should be adopted for effective management of disruptive behavior in clinical settings[28]:

1. Maintain effective standard for conduct

    Every hospital should include a *code of conduct*,[29] *workplace ethics*, and oaths, and specify every type of behavior that is considered as a misconduct as a part of their work contract in order to maintain the professional standards of the hospital. It should be mandatory for every clinician to abide by the code of conduct at the workplace, and failure to do so may result in strict legal action against them.[28] Such kind of reinforcement can help to maintain the professional decorum of the hospital.

2. Professional wellness program

    Clinicians' wellness program can be an important tool to access the disruptive behavior of the physicians.[30] Institution should screen the clinicians for disruptive behavior and educate them about the various resources provided by the institution such as peer support, mentorship program for new clinicians, collegial intervention,[28] interprofessional education, and communication and interpersonal skills training that can help them to develop effective code of conduct in the hospital settings.[31] Also it is important to manage the workload including the night shifts and the call schedules of the physicians to effectively manage the work-related stress.

3. Addressing the issue of disruptive physician

Every institute should have the *feedback evaluation* of all the physicians from other clinicians, residents, students, nurses, and ancillary staff. However, if a case of disruptive behavior is reported, it should be handled confidentially with great compassion and respect. The clinician should be acknowledged about his duties and respected for his contribution to the institution. He should be made aware of the various resources offered by the institution including the mentorship program by his senior colleagues that can help with this. Also, the physician should be made aware of the future feedback evaluation to prevent reoccurrence of such episodes. The clinicians should be made aware that recurrent episodes of disruptive behavior can be documented for future note and may *hinder with privileges offered* by the hospital.[27]

SUMMARY

Disruptive behavior can be significant problem in the hospital settings. Although only a small number of physicians are involved, it can pose a huge economic burden and potentially impact the working of the whole team including junior doctors, medical students, and nurses. Such a behavior not only affects the quality of patient care and patient satisfaction but also hampers the reputation of the hospital. Regular feedback evaluation, strict work contract norms, collegial intervention, and equal respect towards all physicians can help combat with this issue.

REFERENCES

1. Rock W. The disruptive physician. *Group Practice J.* 1994, pp. 38, 40, 74.
2. Council on Ethical and Judicial Affairs-American Medical Association. CEJA Opinion—(E-9.045) Physicians with Disruptive Behavior. Available from: www.ama-assn.org/resources/images/omss/cejae-9.045.pdf (accessed November 2016).

3. Joint Commission Resources. Defusing Disruptive Behavior: A Workbook for Health Care Leaders. Oakbrook Terrace, IL; 2007. Available from: www.jointcommissioninternational.org/assets/1/14/DDB07_Sample_Pages2.pdf (accessed November 2016).

4. Mikkelsen EG, Einarsen S. Relationships between exposure to bullying at work and psychological and psychosomatic health complaints: The role of state negative affectivity and generalised self-efficacy. *Scand J Psych.* 2002;43(5):397–405.

5. Hutchinson M, Vickers M, Wilkes L, Jackson D. A typology of bullying behaviours: The experiences of Australian nurses. *J Clin Nurs.* 2010;19:2319–2328.

6. Rosenstein A.H, Russell H, Lauve R. Disruptive physician behavior contributes to nursing shortage. Study links bad behavior by doctors to nurses leaving the profession. *Physician Exec.* 2002;28:8–11.

7. Leape LL, Fromson JA. Problem doctors: Is there a system-level solution? *Ann Intern Med.* 2006;144:107–115.

8. Goettler CE, Butler TS, Shackleford P, Rotondo MF. Physician behavior: Not ready for "Never" land. *Am Surg.* 2011;77:1600–1605.

9. Walrath JM, Dang D, Nyberg D. Hospital RNs' experiences with disruptive behavior: A qualitative study. *J Nurs Care Qual.* 2010;25:105–116. doi:10.1097/NCQ.0b013e3181c7b58e.

10. Gardezi F, Lingard L, Espin S, Whyte S, Orser B, Baker GR. Silence, power and communication in the operating room. *J Adv Nurs.* 2009;65:1390–1399.

11. Rosenstein AH, O'Daniel M. A survey of the impact of disruptive behaviors and communication defects on patient safety. *Jt Comm J Qual Patient Saf.* 2008;34:464–471.

12. Cook JK, Green M, Topp RV. Exploring the impact of physician verbal abuse on perioperative nurses. *AORN J.* 2001; 74:317–320, 322–327, 329–331.

13. Quine L. Workplace bullying in junior doctors: Questionnaire survey. *BMJ.* 2002;324:878–879. doi:10.1136/bmj.324.7342.878.

14. Leape LL, Shore MF, Dienstag JL, et al. Perspective: A culture of respect, part 1: The nature and causes of disrespectful behavior by physicians. *Acad Med.* 2012;87(7):845–852.

15. Whittemore AD. The competent surgeon: Individual accountability in the era of "systems" failure. *Ann Surg.* 2009;250:357–362.

16. Van Norman GA. Abusive and disruptive behavior in the surgical team. *AMA J Ethics.* 2015;17:215–220. doi:10.1001/journalofethics. 2015.17.3.ecas3-1503.

17. Villafranca A, Hamlin C, Enns S, Jacobsohn, E. Disruptive behaviour in the perioperative setting: A contemporary review. *Can J Anaesth.* 2017;64(2):128–140.

18. Rosenstein AH, O'Daniel M. Disruptive behavior and clinical outcomes: Perceptions of nurses and physicians. *Am J Nurs.* 2005;105:54–65. doi:10.1097/00000446-200501000-00025.

19. Riskin A, Erez A, Foulk TA, et al. The impact of rudeness on medical team performance: A randomized trial. *Pediatrics.* 2015;136:487–495. doi:10.1542/peds.2015-1385.

20. Nurok M, Lee YY, Ma Y, Kirwan A, Wynia M, Segal S. Are surgeons and anesthesiologists lying to each other or gaming the system? A national random sample survey about "truth-telling practices" in the perioperative setting. *Patient Saf Surg.* 2015; 9:34.

21. Piquette D, Reeves S, LeBlanc VR. Stressful intensive care unit medical crises: How individual responses impact on team performance. *Crit Care Med.* 2009;37:1251–1255.

22. The Joint Commission. Sentinel Event Statistics Released for 2014–2015; Available from www.jointcommission.org/assets/1/23/jcon-line_April_29_15.pdf.

23. Heru A, Gagne G, Strong D. Medical student mistreatment results in symptoms of posttraumatic stress. *Acad Psychiatry.* 2009;33:302–306.

24. Leisy HB, Ahmad M. Altering workplace attitudes for resident education (A.W.A.R.E.): Discovering solutions for medical resident bullying through literature review. *BMC Med Educ.* 2016;27:127.

25. Laschinger HK, Grau AL, Finegan J, Wilk P. New graduate nurses' experiences of bullying and burnout in hospital settings. *J Adv Nurs.* 2010;66:2732–2742.

26. Pfifferling, JH. The disruptive physician. A quality of professional life factor. *Physician Exec.* 1999;25:56–61.

27. Rawson JV, Thompson N, Sostre G, Deitte L. The cost of disruptive and unprofessional behaviors in health care. *Acad Radiol.* 2013;20:1074–1076.

28. Villafranca A, Hamlin C, Enns S, Jacobsohn E. Disruptive behaviour in the perioperative setting: A contemporary review. *Can J Anaesth.* 2017;64(2):128–140.

29. Paskert J. Collegial intervention and the disruptive physician. *Physician Exec.* 2014;40(50–2):54.

30. Sandy EA, 2nd, Beigi RH, Cohel C, Nash KC. An interview tool to predict disruptive physician behavior. *Physician Leadersh J.* 2014;1:36–39.

31. Kaplan K, Mestel P, Feldman DL. Creating a culture of mutual respect. *AORN J.* 2010;91:495–510.

Clinical Vignette 3: Do We Owe our Patients our Lives?

Harleen Kaur
University of Missouri

Clinical vignette discusses the medical error that happened due to burnt-out physician. In addition, we will discuss the prevalence of the physician burnout, its causes, and the ways to mitigate them.

THE CASE

Dr. Rhodes is a 46-year-old primary care physician who runs a busy practice in New York City. His daily practice runs from 13 to 15 patients per day, and recently, he told his front desk nurse Kathy, "Hey Kathy, book my patients for Saturdays as well." Dr. Rhodes has a busy family life and has to manage expenses by himself for his two sons (aged 6 and 9) extracurricular activities along with managing his own medical school financial loans. Recently, when he came to the office in the morning, he told his nurse, "I nearly missed a car accident today!! Thank God." When Kathy inquired the reason, he said, "Ahh, I am not having a good night sleep for a couple of days, I feel exhausted!" One fine afternoon, his nurse came to his office to enquire about a patient and said, "Dr. Rhodes, this patient Ms. Brown is a 59-year-old female who came yesterday with history of recent onset migraines, you prescribed her Imitrex (Sumatriptan), she has a past medical history of stroke and cardiovascular diseases, I don't think this is the right choice for her." Dr. Rhodes felt embarrassed and told her that he missed to see patients past medical history in the chart and asked the nurse to call the patient to stop this medication and he will prescribe a new medication for her migraines.

COMMENTS

This clinical scenario explains the case of physician burnout from increased workloads with financial and emotional concerns which affects not only the physician health but also the patient safety. In this vignette, serious consequences could have occurred if the nurse would have not looked at the chart and discussed the case with Dr. Rhodes.

Dr. Rhodes has financial concerns with lack of family support and increased responsibility towards his children which is resulting in emotional exhaustion and mental fatigue which may be the contributing factor for near-miss car accident and symptoms of burnout.

DISCUSSION

Burnout was first described by Freudenberger[1] and later developed by Maslach and colleague.[2] Physician burnout is a continuum of stress resulting from low sense of accomplishment, emotional exhaustion, and impersonal attitude towards patient care, leading to mental health issues such as depression and even grave consequences of committing suicide.[2] This epidemic of burnout is affecting the healthcare system of the United States with one-third of the physicians reporting at least one symptom of burnout.[3] The 2015 Medscape Physician Lifestyle Survey reported that 46% of physicians suffered from burnout compared to 2013 when it was 39.8%.[4] The *incidence* of burnout among the medical student[5] is 40% and 76% among the residents.[6] In 2017, the *New England Journal of Medicine* published the suicide case of fourth-year medical student of Icahn School of Medicine as a consequences of burnout, thereby highlighting the importance to address this neglected issue.[7] The *prevalence rate* of burnout varies in different specialties[3] and is briefed in Table 1 (Figure 1). Physician burnout not only affects the physician health but also compromises patient health and safety issues.

This chapter aims to focus on the origin of burnout and its consequences and the most probable ways to cope up with it.

Table 1   Prevalence Rates of Burnout in Various Specialties

Specialty of Medicine	Prevalence of Burnout (%)
Emergency medicine	60–70
Primary care practice	50–60
General surgery	40–50
Dermatology	30–40
Pediatrics	30–40

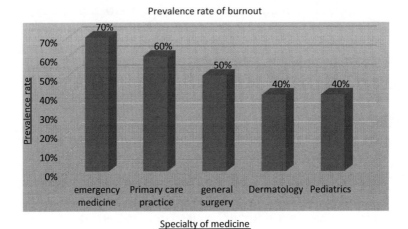

Figure 1   Prevalence rates of burnout in different specialties. (The graph refers to the upper range of values corresponding to Table 1).

CONCEPT OF BURNOUT

Christina Maslach and her colleagues conceptualized burnout on the basis of three main parameters discussed as follows[1]:

1. **Emotional exhaustion**

    Extended responsibility at work can result in extreme physical and mental exhaustion, causing depletion of emotional energy and mental fatigue. Emotional exhaustion can result in difficulty in concentrating at work, thereby limiting the ability of the physician to give their best performance.

2. **Lack of efficiency**

    Reduced efficiency at work may result in a feeling of low sense of accomplishment and discouragement on one's own potentials. This sense of demoralization may result in the inability to complete the tasks on time and give their best performance. The physicians may develop a fear that they may be more prone to making mistakes if they don't work effectively.

3. **Depersonalization**

    Increased workload and mental fatigue may result in physicians developing an indifferent attitude towards the patient's emotions and concerns. This can compromise the physician–patient relations and affect the patient healthcare as well.

CONTRIBUTORS TO BURNOUT

WORK RELATED

Increased workload in the form of long working hours, increased work intensity, increased night call duties, and lack of support from colleagues can be the prominent contributing factors to burnout.[3] Other factor that contributes to burnout is long hours spent on the computer for excessive documentation of patient data and electronic communication between the physician, nurse, and the patient making him the so-called *computerized physician*. Studies have shown that computerized physician results in 29% more risk of burnout.[8] All these factors can potentiate emotional exhaustion and mental fatigue resulting in increased risk of burnout.

PERSONAL FACTORS

Individual factors such as age, gender, relationship status, educational loan/debt, occupation of the partner, number of children, and financial status can increase the risk of burnout symptoms.[9,10] Studies have shown physicians *less* than 55 years of *age* are at double the risk of burnout as compared to physicians more than 55 years of age. *Women* are considered to have 20%–60% increased odds of burnout symptoms as compared to male physicians.[11] Physicians who have *children less than 21 years of age* are at 54% increased risk of burnout as compared to those who have children more than 21 years of age. Lastly, physicians whose *spouse/partner is in nonphysician healthcare* profession are at 23% increased risk of burnout symptoms.[12,13]

CONSEQUENCES OF BURNOUT

Physicians are the paramount of the healthcare system. Physician well-being is of prime importance for the functioning of the entire healthcare system and effective *patient healthcare* and safety. Increased *medical error* and malpractice issue can compromise the patient healthcare and safety.[17] Depersonalization and lack of empathy may jeopardize the physician–patient relations as well. Burnout can imperil *physician health* resulting in mental health issues such as *depression*[14] and anxiety, and even doubles the risk of *suicide*[15] (Figure 2). The risk of suicide in male physicians is 40% higher than that of the general male population, and the risk of suicide in female physicians is 130% higher than that of the general female population.[16] There are increased rates of *alcohol*

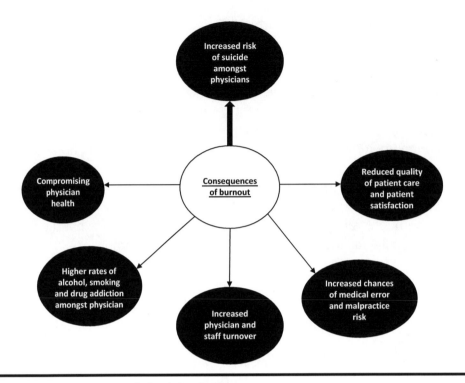

Figure 2   Consequences of physician burnout.

dependence/abuse,[17] smoking, and drug abuse reported in burnout physicians. Certain studies have also reported increased association of *motor vehicle accidents* and near-miss events with physician burnout.[18]

Physician burnout can result in higher *financial burden* for the *healthcare organizations. Reduced workplace productivity* may result in *increased referrals and greater resource utilization.*[19,20] *Job quits* can also occur as a consequence of burnout. It is estimated that the cost to replace a physician in the United States roughly ranges from hundreds to thousands to over one million dollars.[21] Burnout-related increased *medical errors, malpractice claims,* and *early retirement* also pose extra expenditure on the healthcare organization.[22]

HOW TO COPE UP WITH BURNOUT?

To address the concern of physician burnout, strategic approaches have to be made at the personal level and healthcare organization level (Table 2). Addressing these limitations, West et al. concluded that a proportionate reduction in burnout symptoms of emotional

Table 2   Ways to Mitigate Burnout

Personal Factors	Family Factors	Healthcare Organization Factors
Positive thinking and coping	Adaptability	Teamwork
Resilience and stress management	Communication	Cohesion
Exercise and physical fitness	Closeness and support	Camaraderie with colleagues and ancillary staff
Practical attitude/ realism towards work-related goals	Emotional ties	Well-distributed workload and duty hours
Altruism	Socializing and family events	

exhaustion by 14%, depersonalization by 4%, and other symptoms of burnout by 10% can be seen.[23] *Physician-directed strategies* should endorse resilience with attitude of positive thinking and mindfulness with realistic approach to work-related goals. Also, physical fitness, exercise, and meditation can help to maintain a sound mind for a sound body. In addition, emotional ties and support from the family members and engaging in social events and family get-together can be helpful to overcome the emotional exhaustion and mental fatigue.[24] *Health organization-directed strategies* should focus on limitations of the organization in terms of physicians and ancillary staff, and should aim to provide well-planned work schedule focusing on the working hours and on-call duty hours equally for every physician. The organization should perform a *regular burnout assessment* for all physicians as a part of their performance protocol.[25] There are various burnout assessment tools available—some of which can also be assessed online. The *Maslach Burnout Inventory* (MBI) is the standard assessment scale available for burnout.[2] It consists of 22 items scored from 0 to 6, redistributed as 6 items for emotional exhaustion domain (score range 0–54), 5 items for depersonalization domain (score range 0–30), and 8 items for personal accomplishment domain (score range 0–48). A score on emotion exhaustion of 27 or more, depersonalization of 10 or more, and personal accomplishments

Table 3 Maslach Burnout Inventory Scores Suggestive of Burnout

Emotional exhaustion	>27
Depersonalization	>10
Personal accomplishments	<33

of 33 or less is considered as high level of burnout (Table 3). Other assessment tools are also available such as the *Copenhagen Burnout Inventory*[26] and *Oldenburg Burnout Inventory*,[27] but the Maslach Burnout Inventory is considered as the gold standard.

REFERENCES

1. Freudenberger HJ. Staff burnout. *J Soc Issues* 1974; 30: 159–165.
2. Maslach C, Jackson S, Leiter M. *Maslach Burnout Inventory Manual*. Palo Alto, CA: Consulting Psychologists Press, 1996.
3. Shanafelt TD, Boone S, Tan L, Dyrbye LN, Sotile W, Satele D, et al. Burnout and satisfaction with work-life balance among US physicians relative to the general US population. *Arch Intern Med* 2012; 172(18): 1377–1385.
4. Medscape Physician Lifestyle Survey 2015. www.medscape.com/features/slideshow/lifestyle/2015/public/overview#2.
5. Dyrbye LN, Thomas MR, Massie S, et al. Burnout and suicidal ideation among U.S. medical students. *Ann Intern Med* 2008; 149: 334–341.
6. Williams D, Tricomi G, Gupta J, Janise A. Efficacy of burnout interventions in the medical education pipeline. *Acad Psych* 2015; 39:47–54.
7. Muller D. Kathryn. *N Engl J Med* 2017; 376: 1101–1103.
8. Shanafelt TD, Dyrbye LN, Sinsky C, et al. Relationship between clerical burden and characteristics of the electronic environment with physician burnout and professional satisfaction. *Mayo Clin Proc* 2016; 91: 836–848.
9. West CP, Shanafelt TD, Kolars JC. Quality of life, burnout, educational debt, and medical knowledge among internal medicine residents. *JAMA* 2011; 306: 952–960.
10. Shanafelt TD, Hasan O, Dyrbye LN, et al. Changes in burnout and satisfaction with work-life balance in physicians and the general US working population between 2011 and 2014. *Mayo Clin Proc* 2015; 90: 1600–1603.
11. Lanballe EM, Innstrand ST, Aasland OG, Falkum E. The predictive value of individual factors, work-related factors, and work-home interaction on burnout in female and male physicians; a longitudinal study. *Stress Health* 2011; 27: 73–87.

12. Tyssen R, Vaglum P, Gronvold NT, Ekeberg O. Factors in medical school that predict postgraduate mental health problems in need of treatment. A nationwide and longitudinal study. *Med Educ* 2001; 35: 110–120.

13. Dyrbye LN, Thomas MR, Huntington JL, et al. Personal life events and medical student well-being: A multicenter study. *Acad Med* 2006; 81: 374–384.

14. Bianchi R, Schonfeld IS, Laurent E. Burnout-depression overlap: A review. *Clin Psychol Rev* 2015; 36: 28–41

15. van der Heijden F, Dillingh G, Bakker A, Prins, J. Suicidal thoughts among medical residents with burnout. *Arch Suicide Res* 2008; 12: 344–346.

16. Center C, Davis M, Detre T, et al. Confronting depression and suicide in physicians: A consensus statement. *JAMA* 2003; 289: 3161–3166.

17. Oreskovich MR, Kaups KL, Balch CM, et al. Prevalence of alcohol use disorders among American surgeons. *Arch Surg* 2012; 147: 168–174.

18. West CP, Tan AD, Shanafelt TD. Association of resident fatigue and distress with occupational blood and body fluid exposures and motor vehicle incidents. *Mayo Clin Proc* 2012; 87: 1138–1144.

19. Bachman KH, Freeborn DK. HMO physicians' use of referrals. *Soc Sci Med* 1999; 48: 547–557.

20. Kushnir T, Greenberg D, Madjar N, Hadari I, Yermiahu Y, Bachner YG. Is burnout associated with referral rates among primary care physicians in community clinics? *Fam Pract* 2014; 31: 44–50.

21. Fibuch E, Ahmed A. Physician turnover: A costly problem. *Physician Leadersh J* 2015; 2: 22–25.

22. Shanafelt TD, Balch CM, Bechamps G, et al. Burnout and medical errors among American surgeons. *Ann Surg* 2010; 251: 995–1000.

23. West CP, Dyrbye LN, Erwin PJ, Shanafelt TD. Interventions to prevent and reduce physician burnout: A systematic review and meta-analysis. *Lancet* 2016; 388: 2272–2281.

24. Shanafelt TD, Dyrbye LN, West CP. Addressing physician burnout: The way forward. *JAMA* 2017; 317: 901–902.

25. Shanafelt TD, Gorringe G, Menaker R, et al. Impact of organizational leadership on physician burnout and satisfaction. *Mayo Clin Proc* 2015; 90: 432–440.

26. Kristensen TS, Borritz M, Villadsen E, Christensen KB. The copenhagen burnout inventory: A new tool for the assessment of burnout. *Work Stress* 2005; 19: 192–207.

27. Halbesleben JR, Demerouti E. The construct validity of an alternative measure of burnout: Investigating the English translation of the Oldenburg burnout inventory. *Work Stress* 2005; 19: 208–220.

Chapter 6

Tools and Strategies for Quality Improvement and Patient Safety: A Primer for Healthcare Providers

Anudeep Yelam and Raghav Govindarajan
University of Missouri

Quality improvements (QIs) have been implemented for many decades in manufacturing and other industries to decrease the defects and errors. In healthcare, they can be very useful in identifying the errors, ineffectiveness, and inefficiencies in routine practices, and can also be used to address them.

There are many tools and strategies to improve the quality and patient safety. We will highlight few of the most important ones in this chapter.

Definitions

Root cause analysis (RCA): It is an analysis tool that can be used in healthcare for methodical investigation and comprehensive review of an event, enabling appropriate identification of opportunities for improvement.[1]

Plan–do–study–act (PDSA): It is an iterative, four-stage problem-solving model used for improving a process or carrying out change.[2]

Fishbone diagram: A cause-and-effect diagram, also known as an Ishikawa or "fishbone" diagram, is a graphic tool used to explore and display the possible causes of a certain effect.[3]

Lean Six Sigma: It focuses on eliminating defects. In healthcare, it reduces the defects that can result in medical errors.[4]

Root Cause Analysis (RCA)

RCA is a structured approach employed for identifying the causes of close calls and adverse events. It is used to develop preventive measures.[5] The primary aim of RCA is to answer the following three main questions[6,7]:

1. What happened?
2. Why did it happen?
3. What can be done to avoid it from happening again?

Several methods are employed in identifying the root causes and contributing factors including flow diagramming, cause-and-effect diagramming, triggering questions, the five rules of causation, and the action hierarchy.[6]

The paramount goal of RCA is to protect patients by identifying and changing factors within the healthcare system that can be potentially harmful.[8] For performing an effective RCA, a nine-step sequential protocol must be conducted. Table 6.1 describes the stepwise algorithm for conducting an effective RCA.[8]

The Case

A 70-year-old man with a history of diabetes mellitus, hypertension, and myasthenia gravis (MG) of a year of diagnosis with positive serum antibody titers for acetylcholine, treated with pyridostigmine (50 mg every 4 h) and prednisone (5 mg once a day), called an outpatient physician clinic that he is short of breath and would like to know what to do. The nurse left a message to the physician who checked it a few hours later. Immediately after seeing the message, the physician called the patient and came to know that he was taken to the emergency room (ER) and was intubated.

Table 6.1   Stepwise Algorithm for Conducting an Effective RCA

Steps
Step 1: Identify Adverse Event • Honest and open reporting of the adverse events • Committee review of clinical documentation to understand basics of what event happened? When? Who was involved? How and why did it happen? • Identify appropriate RCA investigations
Step 2: Organize a Team • Team should consist of four to six members of clinicians, supervisors, and QI experts with fundamental knowledge on specific area of interest. • Ensure that despite members having different levels of authority, everyone should be treated as equals. • Members should not be directly involved with the case in question. • Appoint an unbiased team leader/facilitator.
Step 3: Develop an Initial Flow Diagram • Use a flowchart to describe the processes leading to the event. • Organize the information to reach a mutual understanding of the problem.
Step 4: Develop an Event Story Map • Use of triggering questions to guide further investigation. • Conduct thorough interviews with all parties involved in event. • Thorough review of clinical documentation surrounding the event.
Step 5: Develop a Cause-and-Effect Diagram • Identify a single problem statement. • Identify actions and conditions that caused the problem statement. • These categories should address communication problems, policies, rules, procedures, and human errors leading to the event.
Step 6: Identify Root Cause Contributing Factors (RCCF) • Describe how a cause led to an effect and increased the likelihood of adverse event. • Apply five rules of causation for crafting RCCF statements.
Step 7: Develop Corrective Actions • Identify barriers and risk reduction strategies to prevent root cause from recurring. • Multiple actions may be required. • Implement a trial test of corrective action.
Step 8: Measure Outcomes • Develop outcome measurements to ensure appropriate implementation of actions. • Track quantifiable data to document effectiveness of actions over time. • Evaluate and fine-tune improvement efforts if needed.
Step 9: Communicate Results • Communicate results of RCA to all staff involved in event and more broadly if applicable.

Comments

The patient in the above scenario seems to have had an episode of myasthenic exacerbation, otherwise known as baseline worsening of symptoms which lead to respiratory failure, a myasthenic crisis.

It is important to recognize myasthenic crisis, as prompt and accurate diagnosis can have better patient outcomes. Despite the availability of clinical bedside assessments, such as single breath count test (SBCT) and neck flexor strength test, there is a general lack of awareness in the value of tools used for assessing MG exacerbations. Therefore, in order to provide more accurate recognition of MG exacerbations, introducing the SBCT as a rudimentary telephonic quantitative diagnostic tool for trained nurses is highly desirable. An RCA for the above problem is described in Figure 6.1.

Plan–Do–Study–Act

PDSA is a QI tool. It provides a structure to test a change that has been implemented. PDSA cycle can be used in a continuous manner for ongoing improvement (Figure 6.2).

The Institute for Healthcare Improvement laid out the following reasons for the use of PDSA to test changes[10]:

- To make sure that the change will result in improvement
- To decide which of the many proposed changes will lead to improvement
- To understand and evaluate how much of the improvement can be achieved from the change
- To ensure the proposed changes would work
- To minimize resistance upon implementation of change

Fishbone (Ishikawa) Diagram

Fishbone (Ishikawa or cause-and-effect) diagram is an analysis tool which provides a systemic way of looking at effects and causes with the goal of identifying and grouping the causes which generate a quality problem.[11]

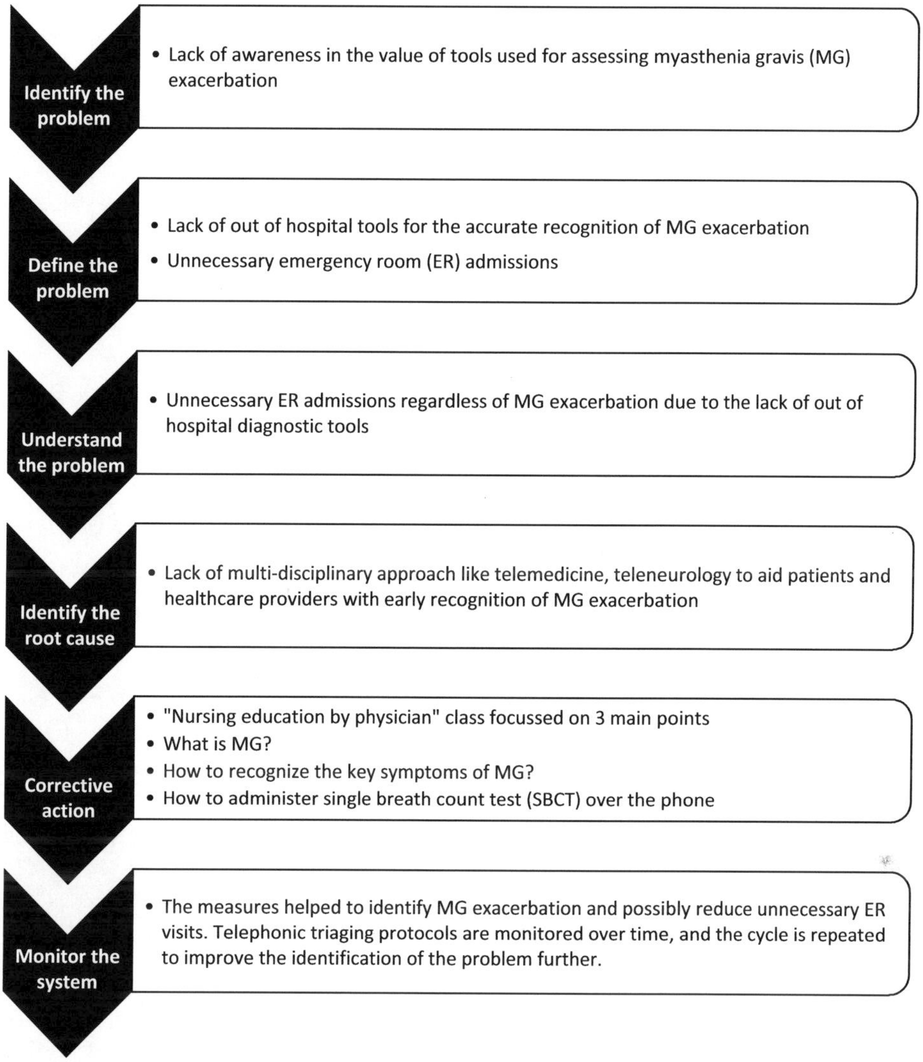

Identify the problem
- Lack of awareness in the value of tools used for assessing myasthenia gravis (MG) exacerbation

Define the problem
- Lack of out of hospital tools for the accurate recognition of MG exacerbation
- Unnecessary emergency room (ER) admissions

Understand the problem
- Unnecessary ER admissions regardless of MG exacerbation due to the lack of out of hospital diagnostic tools

Identify the root cause
- Lack of multi-disciplinary approach like telemedicine, teleneurology to aid patients and healthcare providers with early recognition of MG exacerbation

Corrective action
- "Nursing education by physician" class focussed on 3 main points
- What is MG?
- How to recognize the key symptoms of MG?
- How to administer single breath count test (SBCT) over the phone

Monitor the system
- The measures helped to identify MG exacerbation and possibly reduce unnecessary ER visits. Telephonic triaging protocols are monitored over time, and the cycle is repeated to improve the identification of the problem further.

Figure 6.1   An example of RCA.[9]

The diagram looks like skeleton of a fish and is simple, through bevel line segments which lean on horizontal axis, which suggest the multiple causes for distribution and sub-causes which are producing them.[11]

Procedure for Making a Fishbone Diagram

Agree on a problem statement and write it on the chart. Categorize the major components of the problem and enter them under the

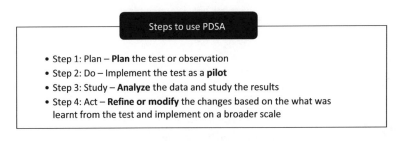

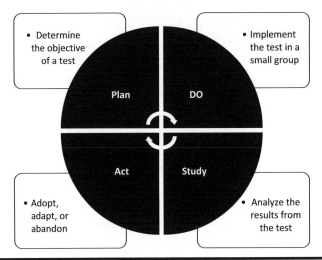

Figure 6.2   PDSA cycle.

generic headings as branches to the main problem, which are shown as follows[12]:

■ Methods
■ Machines (equipment)
■ People (manpower)
■ Materials
■ Measurement
■ Environment

Encourage every person in the organization to write each cause and sub-cause of the problem and to voice their own opinion. An example of the fishbone diagram is shown in Figure 6.3.[13]

Fishbone diagram analyzes the multitude of causes and their sequence, with their representation and hierarchy elements for risk treatment. It can

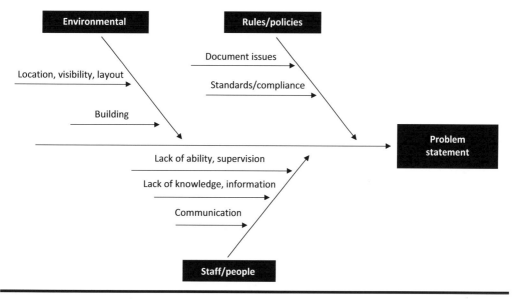

Figure 6.3   An example of the fishbone diagram.

be successfully applied to correctly evaluate the probabilities, weights, and impact of the causes.[11]

Lean Six Sigma

Lean Six Sigma is a business improvement methodology, which aims at maximizing the shareholders' value by improving quality, speed, customer satisfaction, and costs. It achieves these parameters by merging tools and principles from both Lean and Six Sigma.[14]

In healthcare service, it can be used to improve quality of care, efficiency, and financial performance of a healthcare organization. The benefits listed in Table 6.2 were seen on the application of Lean Six Sigma service.[14]

Tools to improve the value flow are listed as follows[15]:

- Quality function deployment
- 5S (sort, set in order, shine, standardized cleanup, and sustain)
- Constraint management
- Level loading
- Pull systems
- Flexible process
- Lot size reduction

Table 6.2   Benefits of Lean Six Sigma in Healthcare Sector[14]

	Problem	*Outcome*	*Benefit*
1	Increase radiology throughout and decrease cost per radiology in a hospital	Significant improvement in radiology throughout and reduction in cost per radiology procedure	A 33% increase in radiology throughout
2	Poor patient safety due to high medication and laboratory errors	Reduced medication and laboratory errors	A 22% reduction in cost per radiology procedure $12 million in savings
3	Overcrowded emergency department	Reduced time to transfer a patient from the ER to an inpatient hospital bed	Improved patient safety significantly $600,000/year in profit

The most common critical failure factors (CFF) in Lean Six Sigma deployment are shown below[16]:

- Lack of top management attitude, commitment, and involvement
- Lack of training and education
- Poor project selection and prioritization
- Lack of resources (financial, technical, human, etc.)
- Weak link between the continuous improvement projects and the strategic objectives of the organization
- Resistance of culture change
- Poor communication
- Lack of leadership skills and visionary and supportive leadership
- Lack of awareness of the benefits of Lean/Six Sigma
- Lack of employee engagement and participation/lack of team autonomy

Many programs and policies fail in the healthcare sector due to resistance to culture change and lack of communication. Although a great deal of data is available in the healthcare sector, the majority of them are not ready for analysis, wasted time, mean poor analysis of data, and high costs. It is difficult to measure patient satisfaction in busy and noisy climate surroundings of hospitals.[16]

We conclude this chapter by discussing the real PDSA example from my (R.G) practice.

The Problem

There was dissatisfaction with consistent low patient satisfaction scores and low staff morale with high staff turnover (2013, 2014, and 2015) in electromyography (EMG) laboratory in the Department of Neurology at the University of Missouri, Columbia.

Comments

This has prompted for changes in the department. We employed PDSA as a tool with the view of improving patient satisfaction scores that can alterably improve patient–physician communication and can likely impact in completing the test for the better diagnostic yield.

We discuss the steps followed in creating the PDSA cycle as follows:

---

1. Plan

Coordinated meetings were conducted quarterly with the intent of improving patient satisfaction scores by boosting employee morale in the EMG laboratory in the Department of Neurology at the University of Missouri, Columbia. These meetings were aimed to establish more positive patient–physician communication by utilizing mentoring, education, and engagement (MEE). The meetings focused on developing core competencies, devising training plans, and implementing strategies

2. DO

The MEE strategies were implemented in September 2015 to improve employee satisfaction with staff morale being the primer for more positive patient–physician communication. Overall patient satisfaction scores were assessed to test for improvement in patient–physician communication.

3. Study

Patient satisfaction for September–December 2015: 74.3%
Patient satisfaction for January–April 2016: 78.8%
Patient satisfaction for May–August 2016: 90.1%

4. Act

Patient satisfaction improved by 15.8% in the EMG laboratory after 1 year of quarterly meetings that utilized MEE strategies aimed at improving employee satisfaction. The success of this PDSA cycles indicates its use for identifying and improving indirect correlates to patient satisfaction.

Steps in preparing and testing a change using PDSA are shown in the following figure:

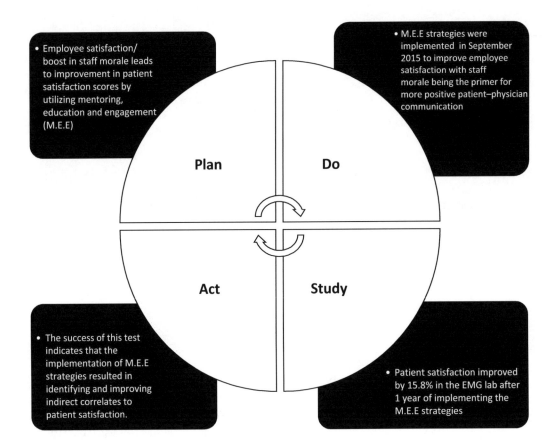

- Employee satisfaction/ boost in staff morale leads to improvement in patient satisfaction scores by utilizing mentoring, education and engagement (M.E.E)

- M.E.E strategies were implemented in September 2015 to improve employee satisfaction with staff morale being the primer for more positive patient–physician communication

Plan   **Do**

Act   **Study**

- The success of this test indicates that the implementation of M.E.E strategies resulted in identifying and improving indirect correlates to patient satisfaction.

- Patient satisfaction improved by 15.8% in the EMG lab after 1 year of implementing the M.E.E strategies

Example of PDSA cycle for testing a change is shown in Figure 6.2.

References

1. Ewen BM, Bucher G. Root cause analysis: Responding to a sentinel event. *Home Healthcare Now* 2013;31(8): 435–443.
2. Definition for PDSA. Available at: https://innovations.ahrq.gov/qualitytools/plan-do-study-act-pdsa-cycle. Accessed on 25 July, 2018.
3. Fishbone diagram definition. Available at: www.ihi.org/resources/Pages/Tools/CauseandEffectDiagram.aspx. Accessed on 26 July, 2018.
4. Lean Six Sigma definition. Available at: http://asq.org/healthcaresixsigma/lean-six-sigma.html. Accessed on 26 July, 2018.
5. Spath P. *Error Reduction in Health Care: A Systems Approach to Improving Patient Safety.* Washington, DC: AHA Press; 1999.
6. National Patient Safety Foundation. RCA improving root cause analysis and actions to prevent harm. Available at: www.ashp.org/DocLibrary/BestPractices/NPSF-Root-Cause-Analyses.pdf. Accessed 12 December, 2015.

7. Guidance for performing root cause analysis. Available at: www.cms.gov/ medicare/provider-enrollment-and-certification/qapi/downloads/guidanceforrca. pdf. Accessed 25 May, 2016.
8. Charles R, Hood B, Derosier JM, et al. How to perform a root cause analysis for workup and future prevention of medical errors: A review. *Patient Safety in Surgery* 2016;10: 20. doi:10.1186/s13037-016-0107-8.
9. Alqadri S, Govindarajan R. Telephonic single breath count test administered by nurses in diagnosing myasthenia exacerbation (P3. 119). *Neurology* 2017;88(16 Supplement): P3.119.
10. PDSA def. Available at: www.health.state.mn.us/divs/opi/qi/toolbox/pdsa.html. Accessed on 26 July, 2018.
11. Ilie G, Ciocoiu CN. Application of fishbone diagram to determine the risk of an event with multiple causes. *Management Research and Practice* 2010;2(1): 1–20.
12. Fishbone (Ishikawa) diagram. Available at: http://asq.org/learn-about-quality/ cause-analysis-tools/overview/fishbone.html. Accessed on 25 July, 2018.
13. How to use the fishbone tool for root cause analysis. Available at: www. cms.gov/medicare/provider-enrollment-and-certification/qapi/downloads/ fishbonerevised.pdf. Accessed on 25 July, 2018.
14. Laureani A, Antony J. Standards for Lean Six Sigma certification. *International Journal of Productivity and Performance Management* 2011;61(1): 110–120.
15. Pyzdek T. The Six Sigma handbook. Revised and expanded. A complete guide for green belts, black belts, and managers at all levels. 2003. doi:10.1036/0071415963.
16. Albliwi S, Antony J, Abdul Halim Lim S, van der Wiele T. Critical failure factors of Lean Six Sigma: A systematic literature review. *International Journal of Quality & Reliability Management* 2014;31(9): 1012–1030.

Index

For Product Safety Concerns and Information please contact our EU
representative GPSR@taylorandfrancis.com Taylor & Francis Verlag GmbH,
Kaufingerstraße 24, 80331 München, Germany

Printed and bound by CPI Group (UK) Ltd, Croydon, CR0 4YY
01/05/2025
01859211-0001